When it comes to the global orphan crisis the church faces a challenge that is filled with great complexity and urgency. From international adoption to in-country orphan care solutions, there is plenty of debate over ethics, solutions, and the way forward. *In Defense of the Fatherless* is a timely and needed addition to this conversation. It is honest, frank, thoroughly biblical, and offers thoughtful solutions to move forward in caring for orphans and widows. In an age where the church can be tempted to quick fixes and simple solutions *In Defense of the Fatherless* helps the reader understand the complexity of the orphan and widow crisis and the urgency of providing families for children. This book will challenge, convict and fuel a conversation that is much needed today for the church to move forward in its calling to care deeply for the widow and the orphan. The authors join the chorus in calling for a revolution in the Christian adoption and orphan care movement while reminding the reader that most of the world's orphans are living in vulnerable families. If we want to change the world for orphans we must care deeply for the whole family. Further, I applaud them for reminding the reader throughout that the calling to make a difference in the orphan and widow crisis reflects the very heart of the gospel and our Savior. The church is the answer to this crisis and we cannot do this alone. I am thankful that Sara and Amanda have provided a much-needed resource for the church to take the next step forward in the movement with greater effectiveness, wisdom, and love.

You may not agree with everything written in this book but I believe it offers an important and needed framework that has great potential to bring people from different sides of the conversation to the same table. I believe as we do this greater collaboration can happen, change will take place where needed, and more creative efforts will be imagined for the sake of the orphan and widow.

Jason Kovacs
Co-Founder of Together for Adoption and Director of Ministry Development
for The ABBA Fund, Austin, Texas

Over recent years, there has been a welcome focus on the global issue of orphans and not only our responsibility for them, but the opportunity to model the gospel in our care for them. This book commends such concern, but challenges us to go much further. The Bible almost always talks about 'orphans and widows', and the authors argue that both must be the focus of our attention. International adoption, they argue, isn't always the answer, and in some situations may even compound the problem. This book should be on the 2015 reading list for all those in church leadership. It will certainly challenge, maybe annoy, definitely instruct, even surprise and probably provoke. But when the issue is as significant as this, nothing less is neither adequate nor helpful.

Steve Timmis
Executive Director of the Acts 29 Network & Pastor, The Crowded House
Sheffield, England

Adoption is close to the heart of God. This book presents a realistic and responsible look at how and why Christians should respond to international adoption. It is heart-warming to see how Christians have responded to God's call for justice.

Nola Leach
CEO, CARE, London

In *Defense of the Fatherless* authors Brinton and Bennett reveal some of the sobering and rather painful realities in overseas adoptions—highlighting the particular problems of some Christian agencies. There are well-intentioned but very damaging mistakes that churches and Christians must avoid and work against for the good of the orphans, their families, and the glory of God. Brinton and Bennett point to a better way through following God's command to care for the poor. I highly recommend this book for all who are considering or are somehow involved with international adoption.

Bill Bertsche
Executive Pastor, The Moody Church, Chicago, Illinois

More than anyone I know Sara Brinton has lived out the message of this book. Here you will find a wealth of wisdom and a clear challenge from God. Watch out. Your life may never be the same.

Phil Moore
Author of *Gagging Jesus* and the 'Straight to the Heart' commentary series
Leader of Everyday Church, London

Sometimes you read a book that offends you because it forces you to rethink your worldview on a key topic. If you read *In Defense of the Fatherless* with a willingness to struggle and admit past mistakes, as well as a desire to learn, you just might find a new way forward on what it means to care for the fatherless on a deeper, more holistic level.

Chris Marlow
Founder & CEO, Help One Now
chrismarlow.me
Raleigh, North Carolina

For years I thought adoption was just for couples who were infertile. Then I met some who adopted for compassionate reasons. But it wasn't until I met Amanda and her husband and watched them walk through their heartbreaking attempt to adopt African children that I became aware of the incredible challenges associated with adoptions, specifically international adoptions. This book has given me a further understanding of the need, and even more importantly, the changed perspective of adoption that is so important for Christians today. Any couple thinking of adopting, any church wanting to be involved in solving this problem should read this book. The problem is more complex than you think; the answer is firmly rooted in the simplicity of the gospel.

Mary Whelchel
Director of Women's Ministries, The Moody Church
Chicago, Illinois

As an adoptive mom, I believe that *In Defense of the Fatherless* presents an important and thought-provoking paradigm shift how we can view orphan care, orphan prevention, and family preservation through a more holistic lens. *In Defense of the Fatherless* is the book every adoption and family preservation advocate has been waiting to read.

Jessica Honegger
Founder and CEO of Noonday Collection
Austin, Texas

In Defense of the Fatherless brings a balanced and unique approach to orphan care and makes us all ask the questions: are we, as the church, caring for orphans and vulnerable children well? And how can we do better?

Megan Parker
Co-Founder, Abide Family Center, Jinja, Uganda

This book offers careful research, sound theology, and practical resources regarding care for orphans, vulnerable children, and widows. It provides an important perspective on short-term mission trips and investigates some harmful international adoption procedures and practices. You'll be informed and inspired to care wisely for orphans and vulnerable families and celebrate amazing organizations empowering mothers to raise and provide for their children.

Lindsey and Justin Holcomb
Co-authors of *Rid of My Disgrace* and *Is It My Fault?*
Orlando, Florida

In DEFENSE *of the* FATHERLESS

Redeeming International Adoption & Orphan Care

SARA BRINTON & AMANDA BENNETT

CHRISTIAN
FOCUS

Unless otherwise indicated, Scripture quotations are from *The Holy Bible, English Standard Version*, copyright © 2001 by Crossway Bibles, a division of Good News Publishers. Used by permission. All rights reserved. ESV Text Edition: 2007.

Scripture quotations marked NIV are taken from the HOLY BIBLE, NEW INTERNATIONAL VERSION®. NIV®. Copyright©1973, 1978, 1984 by International Bible Society. Used by permission of Zondervan. All rights reserved.

Sara Brinton is a writer and entrepreneur with a passion for reforming international adoption and orphan care. She leads marketing for Noonday Collection, a business that uses fashion to create opportunity in developing countries. Sara and her husband, Mark, live in Austin, Texas with their four children, including daughter Gabrielle who was adopted from Uganda.

Amanda Bennett is a lawyer passionate about obtaining justice for vulnerable families and children. Amanda uses her experience of having to walk away from a fraudulent international adoption to provide advice to adoptive families in similar situations. Amanda has a JD from Northwestern University School of Law in Chicago, Illinois and now lives in Kigali, Rwanda with her husband and son. She serves on the board of directors for Reeds of Hope, a non-profit serving vulnerable families and children in DRC.

Copyright © Sara Brinton and Amanda Bennett 2015

paperback ISBN 978-1-78191-551-6
epub ISBN 978-1-78191-556-1
Mobi ISBN 978-1-78191-557-8

10 9 8 7 6 5 4 3 2 1

Published in 2015
by
Christian Focus Publications,
Geanies House, Fearn, Ross-shire,
IV20 1TW, Scotland, Great Britain.

www.christianfocus.com

Cover design by
Daniel van Straaten

Printed by
Bell and Bain, Glasgow

CONTENTS

Introduction 7

1. The Orphan Crisis 19

2. Growing up in an Orphanage 41

3. To Visit Orphans 63

4. International Adoption: At what cost? 85

5. Seeking God's Heart for the Fatherless 117

6. The Father's Hands 129

7. Families not Institutions 145

8. Make a Lasting Difference 173

9. Redeeming International Adoption 201

10. First Families First 227

11. Defending the Fatherless 255

12. Good News for Broken Families 281

Introduction

Sara's Story

The idea for this book began as many conversations with friends about adoption. As a mother of a daughter adopted from Uganda, I end up talking about adoption almost every day. I see this as an opportunity to share God's heart for orphans and the Gospel: we adopted because we are adopted. I also see it as a great responsibility.

This book is the conversation I would love to have with a friend who is learning about the orphan crisis, considering adoption, or starting an orphan care ministry. It is the conversation I wish someone would have had with me several years ago. I have learned so much about adoption and orphan care over the last few years – much of it the hard way.

We began praying about adoption five years ago. At the time, I was pregnant with our youngest son. My pregnancy was complicated, and we knew he would be our last biological child. One of my nurses at the hospital where I spent several weeks of my pregnancy was a good friend. She and her husband were in the process of adopting a baby boy from Ethiopia.

Their story inspired our whole family. We watched them wait and then rejoiced when they brought their son home. Our family began to pray, learn and dream about adoption. We waited until our son was eighteen months old to start the process.

In that season of waiting and learning, we began to ask questions about how to adopt a child who truly needed a new family. Like many parents considering adoption, we wanted to find a trustworthy agency to help us navigate the complicated process.

We watched news reports and read articles describing corruption in adoption. The stories were often critical of Christian families and adoption agencies. At first I categorized these as attacks – maybe even spiritual warfare. Agreeing with the growing movement of Christians who described adoption and orphan care as war, I reasoned *Satan hates adoption. The last thing he would want is for an orphan to be adopted into a Christian family.*

As a Christian, I wanted to be able to trust a Christian adoption agency to do what was best for orphans and families. Yet as we continued to learn, I could not silence my conscience. I realized that adoption was full of ethical questions. Ethics is about deciding what is right and what is wrong, often in complicated situations. I wanted to believe that adoption was always right, that it was absolutely good. But I began to see that adoption necessarily involves loss. Adoption always involves painful decisions.

I will never forget the moment my daughter, Gabrielle, was placed on my chest. My husband and I were sitting in an African orphanage. She was six months old, but still the size of a newborn. I kissed the top of her head, feeling the softness of her curly black hair. As her tiny, brown fingers wrapped around mine, I thought she was the most beautiful person I had ever seen. My emotions in that moment were the same as when each of my biological sons was placed in my arms the first time. In that moment, I became Gabrielle's mother.

At the same time, however, there was another mother who had sat in that room. A few months before I first held Gabrielle in my arms, my daughter's first mother experienced the most painful loss. She was unable to care for her precious daughter, who shared her warm smile and soulful eyes. With both love and desperation, she made the painful decision to leave her daughter in an orphanage and then to place her for adoption. I can scarcely imagine the depth of her sorrow.

As I reflect on this moment, I see how important it is that we protect vulnerable orphans and families. There are times children are separated from their families due to death, disease, abuse, or neglect. Most of the time, however, children are separated from their families due to poverty. Families in desperate situations make the decision to place a child in an orphanage or for adoption because they feel they have no other choice. Moments like these require great care to protect vulnerable children and families from exploitation. Sadly some people who are involved in caring for vulnerable orphans and families are seeking selfish gain.

As I went through the adoption process, my eyes were opened to the truth of what was happening in many international adoptions. In many countries popular for international adoption today – including Ethiopia, Uganda and Democratic Republic of Congo – corruption is widespread. There are not sufficient safeguards in place to stop corrupt adoption agencies, orphanages and officials from taking advantage of vulnerable children and families.

Amanda's Story

I never got to hold the children we adopted. I now trust that I was never meant to hold them physically. Like many people who decide to adopt, my husband and I had been unable to have children biologically (I've since given birth to a son). After years of infertility, doctors' appointments, medicines and surgeries, we took the leap into adoption.

As Christians, we believed adoption was about more than just a beautiful way to grow our family. We believed it to be a calling and a mission for our family. Trusting the Lord's leading, we picked a Christian adoption agency and chose to adopt hard-to-place children: an older sibling group. Having previously spent time in East Africa, we decided to be a pilot family for a program in the Democratic Republic of Congo.

One in five children in the DRC will die before the age of five.[1] DRC is a beautiful, vast country that has been devastated by colonialism, war, slavery, poverty, and corruption. We believed there was great need for families to adopt the country's orphans.

---

1   World Bank, Child Mortality Data, 2013. Available from http://data.worldbank.org/indicator/ SH.DYN.MORT. 24 Mar. 2014.

When our adoption agency failed to provide us with good evidence that the children we had adopted were legal orphans, we hopped on a plane to find out for ourselves. We landed in Kinshasa full of hope, still optimistic that we would be bringing our adopted children home. Within two days of being on the ground, however, we found all the answers we had been seeking. The children were not orphans in any sense of the word. They had a mother, father and extended family who loved and wanted them. They were made to look like orphans on paper for the purpose of international adoption.

Broken-hearted, I returned to America determined to sound the alarm to other families that not all in international adoption is as it seems. Like Sara, my heart was broken for orphans. Now my heart is equally broken for vulnerable families who become victims of injustice through corrupt systems of international adoption and orphan care. Sadly, these systems are often created and funded by well-intentioned Christians. I believe the Church can do better and wants to do better.

Who are we to write this book?

Writing about adoption and orphan care is a heart-wrenching experience. Who wants to volunteer to write about how Christians with good intentions are involved in exploiting orphans and trafficking children? *Not us.* There have been countless times as we have been writing this book that we have questioned *Why us? Who are we to write this book?*

Let us make this clear at the outset: We did not set out to become experts on international adoption and orphan care. We are not scholars or academic experts in international relief and development. We are not pastors who attended seminary. In many ways, we are unqualified to speak on these subjects.

But like most of our readers, we are moms. Sara is an adoptive parent. Amanda has been through an entire adoption process. We have friends who have adopted and are adopting. We are Christians involved in orphan care ministry at our churches and in our community. We don't write as authorities on international adoption. We write as fellow pilgrims walking with you on a path set out for us by the Father of the fatherless. It is only by the grace of God that we can write the truth with confidence and conviction. The Bible calls Christians to 'bring justice to the fatherless,'

(Isa. 1:17). A relentless pursuit of God's heart for the widow and the orphan forms the heart of this book.

Break my heart for what breaks yours

For much of the twentieth century, Evangelical Christians viewed the gospel as a sort of contract with God. The good news proclaimed by this older generation was that through Jesus' death on the cross, your sin could be forgiven and you could enter into a personal relationship with God. This narrow understanding of the gospel influenced how Christians lived. The focus of Christian missions became the proclamation of the gospel, not the meeting of physical needs. Although Christians throughout the history of the church have cared for orphans and widows, in the last century many abdicated their God-given responsibility to the least of these. Caring for the fatherless and the poor was increasingly left to government institutions.

While this understanding of the gospel is accurate – and we are saved from sin only through Jesus' death on the cross – it is not complete. When Jesus began His ministry, He quoted the prophet Isaiah: 'The Spirit of the Lord is upon me, because he has anointed me to proclaim good news to the poor,' (Luke 4:18). According to Jesus, the good news is that He is the King and His kingdom is coming. The gospel is good news to the poor because in the coming kingdom of God, there will be an end to poverty and injustice – and the orphan crisis. According to author Brian Fikkert:

> The mission of Jesus was and is to preach the good news of the kingdom of God, to say to one and all, 'I am the King of kings and Lord of lords, and I am using My power to fix everything that sin has ruined.'[2]

God has a heart for the poor and the vulnerable. It is impossible not to see this throughout the Bible. God's people are called to reflect God's heart. The purpose of the Church on earth is to make visible the invisible: to make God's character and His kingdom visible on earth. While the kingdom of God will not be complete until Jesus returns as the glorious King, the kingdom is already here among God's people. As God's people, we are called to fight injustice and to meet the physical needs of the poor – not in order to gain God's

---

2   Corbett, Steve, and Brian Fikkert. *When Helping Hurts*. 1st ed. Chicago, IL: Moody Publishers, 2009. Kindle Edition.

favor, but because we have received His grace. We are called to be people who offer justice and mercy to a broken world in response to and as a demonstration of the gospel.

A new generation of Christians sees the gospel as more than a contract with God. No longer do we see missions as something people go and do halfway around the world. Increasingly Christians and churches are calling themselves missional. By this we mean that we are on mission with Jesus. As Jason Kovacs writes:

> This mission includes not only the declaration of this good news but also the demonstration of it in our world. Mission is both declaring the words and works of Jesus and doing in the world what he has commanded us to do.[3]

While being missional often means a renewed focus on reaching our neighbors, we no longer define neighbors as just people who live next door. Our generation is globally aware and globally connected. Tim Keller defines neighbor as anyone who we see in need.[4] As a generation that has grown up with CNN, Google™ and Facebook™, the needs of the world's poor are in front of us daily. We have been challenged by books such as Gary Haugan's *Good News about Injustice* and Richard Stearns' *The Hole in Our Gospel* to consider how God calls Christians to respond to injustice and poverty. Our generation has had unprecedented access to international travel – and millions of us have gone on short-term mission trips to the developing world. We cannot say we are unaware of suffering around the world.

Break our Hearts

> I see a generation rising up to take the place…Heal my heart and make it clean. Open up my eyes to the things unseen. Show me how to love like You have loved me. Break my heart for what breaks Yours, everything I am for Your Kingdom's cause as I walk from earth into eternity.
>
> 'Hosanna' by Hillsong United[5]

---

3   Cruver, Dan, John Piper, Scotty Smith, Richard D. Phillips, Jason Kovacs. *Reclaiming Adoption*. 1st ed. Adelphi, Maryland: Cruciform Press, 2011. Kindle Edition.

4   Keller, Timothy J. *Generous Justice*. 1st ed. New York, N.Y.: Dutton, Penguin Group USA, 2010. Print.

5   *Hosanna*. Brooke Ligertwood, 2006 Hillsong Music Publishing. Sydney, Australia.

A little more than ten years ago, I (Sara) graduated from Seattle Pacific University with a degree in International Relations and Global and Urban Ministry. I will never forget the challenge given to our graduating class:

> Open the Bible and the newspaper, side by side. And pray this dangerous prayer: *God, break my heart for what breaks yours.*

The media is full of stories of brokenness: war, famine, corruption, injustice. Sometimes it is hard to understand how a loving God could allow so much suffering in the world. But as Christians, we believe that God's heart is grieved for the suffering of people and the brokenness of creation. When our hearts cry out that this is not how things should be, we are reflecting God's heart.

These words challenge us to open our eyes to see the brokenness in the world around us. They compel us to seek God's heart and ask how we, as God's people, should respond.

Writing this book has brought me face to face with the things that break the heart of God.

God calls Himself a 'Father of the fatherless' – and I believe His heart is broken over the millions of orphans and vulnerable children in the world today. Hundreds of millions of children in the world today live in extreme poverty. Twenty-six thousand children die every day as a result of poverty. Poverty makes children vulnerable to hunger, disease, illiteracy, discrimination, violence, and trafficking. None is more vulnerable than the child who is separated from the love, care and protection of a family.

Over the last ten years, God's people have awoken to God's heart for the fatherless. There is a growing movement within the Evangelical Christian church to care for orphans. While the movement started in America, it is now spreading around the world. Thousands of Christian families are adopting not because of infertility but in response to God's call. Likewise, thousands of churches are developing orphan care ministries. The focus of these ministries is often building or supporting orphanages or visiting orphans on short-term mission trips. If there are millions of orphans in the world, encouraging Christians to adopt and get involved in orphan care must be good.

But good intentions are not enough – and sometimes our best efforts end up hurting the people we want to help.

International adoption is controversial. Over the last decade, as the Christian adoption and orphan care movement has exploded, the number of children adopted from overseas has declined. In 2004, Americans adopted nearly 23,000 children from overseas. In 2013, this number dropped to just over 7,000. This is the lowest level since 1992.[6] This trend has been mirrored globally, as the total number of internationally adopted children fell from 45,000 in 2004 to fewer than 30,000 in 2010.[7] If you ask experts why there has been such a dramatic decrease in international adoptions, you will get wildly different answers.

Journalists and academics claim economic development, the widespread availability of contraception and changing attitudes toward single motherhood mean fewer children are in need of international adoption.[8] Many experts who have investigated international adoption point to corruption in countries such as Guatemala, Vietnam and Ethiopia for causing the decrease. In recent years, dozens of articles, books and documentaries have documented widespread corruption in international adoption. Critics of international adoption argue for more regulation to protect vulnerable families and children from exploitation in the adoption process.

Conversely, many in the adoption and orphan care movement tell a very different story. They claim there is a global orphan crisis with millions of children in need of international adoption. They argue that restrictive and arbitrary policies prevent good families from adopting children who are growing up in orphanages or on the streets. Many within the movement minimize evidence of corruption in adoption. Christian adoption advocates blame red tape for making adoption too difficult and expensive. Adoption advocates see the decline in international adoptions as a crisis and lobby for policies that would make adoption easier and faster.

The truth is both sides of the controversy are right. Red tape is making international adoption difficult and preventing thousands of orphans from being adopted by good families. At the same time, corruption in international adoption exploits vulnerable families. In many countries that are popular for international adoption, there

---

6   Bureau of Consular Affairs, U.S. Department of State, *FY 2013 Annual Report on Intercountry Adoption*, March 2014. Available from http://adoption.state.gov/content/pdf/fy2013_annual_report.pdf. 24 March 2014. See also Crary, David. 'Foreign Adoptions By Americans Decline Sharply'. ABC News 2014. Web. 24 Mar. 2014.

7   Selman, Peter. *Global Trends In Intercountry Adoption: 2001 - 2011*. 1st ed. National Council for Adoption, 2012. Web. 18 May 2012.

8   United Nations Department of Economic and Social Affairs. *Child Adoption: Trends and Policies*. New York: United Nations, 2014. Web. 18 May 2012.

is significant evidence of corruption in the process of international adoption and the approach to orphan care.

Will we look the other way?

> You may choose to look the other way but you can never say again that you did not know.
>
> William Wilberforce[9]

Christians are called to defend widows and orphans. Like God who identifies with the vulnerable, we are called to identify with the powerless, to take up their cause. As Christians, we are called to fight against corrupt adoption practices that exploit vulnerable families. But some Christians are involved in concealing, justifying and participating in corruption in international adoption. Likewise some Christians are supporting and visiting orphanages that harm the children we're called to help.

At the heart of this issue, we believe Christians are afraid to look at the truth. We do not want to talk about corruption in adoption and orphan care because we fear for what will happen to the orphans who are left behind if more countries close to international adoption. Many Christians are unwilling to ask hard questions about their own adoptions. Christians hesitate to accuse others of corrupt practices for fear of being called divisive. Families who do speak out about the corruption they see or experience are often criticized. In the face of this fear, Christians are looking the other way or hoping that corruption is rare. We believe it is time for change.

In writing this book, we have opened our Bibles and spread out literally thousands of pages of research. We have opened our eyes to the truth in the Bible and the evidence in the research – and prayed that God would break our hearts for the things that break His. Initially, we set out to answer one crucial question: how should Christians respond to corruption in international adoption and orphan care?

As we traveled around the world and interviewed dozens of adoptive families and adoption experts, we discovered other important questions: Are there really 151 million orphans who are living without the love and protection of a family? Can adoption end the orphan crisis? Why are there 8 million children living in orphanages? Is there an overwhelming need for Christians to build

---

9   'William Wilberforce Quotes.' Goodreads.com. n.p. n.d. Web. 1 Jun. 2014.

and support orphanages? Are mission trips to visit orphanages helpful to vulnerable children? How can we support poor families to prevent children from being orphaned? How can we get to the root cause of the orphan crisis?

If you are reading this book, we imagine you are already thinking about some of these questions. We hope this book will challenge you to ask new questions. We pray this book will open your eyes and that together we can stand up to defend widows and orphans. As we begin this journey together, we want to tell you a little about the structure of this book.

In the first chapter, we will examine the truth about the global orphan crisis. We will also consider the assumptions of the growing Christian adoption and orphan care movement.

In chapters two through four, we will consider the three main ways Christians have responded to the orphan crisis: supporting orphanages, visiting orphans on short-term mission trips, and encouraging adoption. We learn that responses to the crisis, while well-intentioned, are sometimes misguided and harmful to vulnerable families and children.

In chapters five and six, we will dig into the Bible to seek God's heart for widows and orphans. We will discover how God calls His people to respond to His heart by protecting and providing for widows and orphans.

In chapters seven through nine, we will discover principles for reforming international adoption and orphan care. These chapters include stories from families, organizations and churches around the world who are living out James 1:27 without building orphanages.

Finally, in chapters ten through twelve, we will learn effective ways to protect and provide for orphans by addressing the root causes of the orphan crisis. Through these final chapters, we will discover the unique role churches can play in getting to the very root of the orphan crisis.

This book is designed to ask questions and to challenge assumptions. It may be helpful to read this book with your husband or wife, a close friend or a small group. Each chapter ends with questions for reflection and discussion that are designed to help you wrestle with the truth and seek God's heart. Use these questions to start a conversation in your local church – or join in the conversation online at defenseofthefatherless.com.

We hope you'll take this journey with us. There may be times as you read this book that you want to throw it across the room. Researching and writing this book broke our hearts and challenged our assumptions. So throw the book across the room if you need to, but please pick it back up. Join us in wrestling with the truth and in fighting for justice. Our prayer for you as you read this book is that your heart would be broken and your assumptions challenged, but that you would ultimately be inspired and encouraged. There is much we can do as the people of God.

The Orphan Crisis

Orphans are easier to ignore before you know their names. They are easier to ignore before you see their faces. It is easier to pretend that they're not real before you hold them in your arms. But once you do, everything changes.

DAVID PLATT, *RADICAL*[1]

Sara's Story: When Everything Changes

I will never forget the first time I saw her face. I was sitting in the car, waiting to pick up my son from preschool. The director of our adoption agency had just called to tell us about a baby girl who needed a family. She emailed the photo, and I looked at it on my phone as I sat in the parking lot. Ayana was fifteen months old and HIV positive. She was born to a young woman who had been raped and who was now dying of AIDS. I wanted to fly half way around the world and to wrap my arms around the mother and daughter, to promise her that Ayana would be safe and loved.

Before we heard about Ayana, my husband and I had never considered adopting a child who was HIV positive. We knew very little about HIV and were scared about what it would mean to have a child living with HIV in our home. At first, we said no. But as we learned the truth about HIV and prayed for Ayana, our hearts

---

1   Platt, David. *Radical*. 1st ed. Colorado Springs, Colo.: Multnomah Books, 2010. Print.

changed. After two months, we said yes. I called the adoption agency to let them know we wanted to adopt Ayana.

The next day, I got a phone call that forever changed my life. Ayana was dead. She had burned her hand playing too close to the cooking fire. The burn had become infected. Her little body, weak with malnutrition and untreated HIV, could not fight the infection. The orphanage had taken her to the hospital, but it was too late. She was gone.

In that moment, my heart broke. In my head, I knew about the impact of HIV in Africa. I knew the statistics about AIDS orphans. I had a degree in international relations and had spent years working in relief and development. But in that moment, the once incomprehensible statistic had a face, a name, a story. I was overwhelmed with grief and then anger at the evil and injustice in Ayana's little life. In time, these feelings grew into a passion to make a difference in the lives of orphans – one child at a time.

A few months later, a young American woman living in Uganda named Kristin[2] heard about a little girl who was begging on the streets. Kristen went to visit Zahra. What she saw alongside a busy road in Kampala would change the course of both their lives.

> What made me stop for her was that she was so sick, to the point of dying. At 5 years old, she weighed less than 20 pounds and her eyes were hollow. She was filthy, and she sat in her own urine. Her legs wouldn't move and her left arm was paralyzed. She was totally helpless.

When Kristen tried to pick up Zahra, the tiny girl fought her arms and sobbed fearfully. Zahra had spent her days on the side of the road, holding out her hand to beg for money. Kristen remembers the hard truth underneath the tiny girl's tears: 'She had been exploited. She knew that if she had money in her hands, she would be fed a small meal. If she didn't make anything that day begging, she would starve.'

Kristen knew the situation was too terrible to walk away: 'I had a gnawing sense that God wanted me to do more for this little one.' When Kristen returned to visit Zahra for a second time, the girl looked worse. Kristen took immediate action to become Zahra's foster mom, figuring that the child could live with her temporarily until she figured out a safe, long-term plan.

The next few days were some of the hardest of Kristen's life: 'as soon as I picked Zahra up, I noticed she had a high fever and

---

2   Names have been changed to protect the privacy of the child and adoptive family.

was shaking violently. Her entire body was damp and she looked terrible. I was terrified that she might not even make it through the first night.' Kristen got on a motorcycle and took Zahra to the nearest clinic. She was started on intensive IV treatment for malaria and dehydration. That night Zahra had a seizure and her body went from scorching hot to dangerously cold.

'I prayed like I've never prayed before,' Kristen remembers. 'After a few days with Zahra where we both fought for her life, I knew there was something special about her. I have always wanted to adopt, but didn't think this was something I would do before getting married. Within a few weeks of having her in my care, I knew that God was calling me to be her mom. I knew that He had been preparing me for Zahra all along.'

I met Kristin and Zahra a few weeks later over lunch in Uganda. Our family had brought a bag of clothes and shoes for the girl who was still tiny but now growing quickly. Kristen decided to adopt Zahra despite an uncertain future. Kristen was scared of what caring for a child with special needs as a single mother might look like, but she resolved to submit herself completely to God. As Kristen wrote on her blog the week she decided to adopt Zahra:

> This week I am choosing love. Crazy, beautiful love. I know that this is a good choice. Love is always a good choice. I think that this choice will allow me to be a small part of God's redemptive plan. That it will open me up more and more to His will and that my heart will gradually soften and melt so that my love can be more easily shared. That it will drastically change the rest of my life.

What unfolded over the next year is nothing short of a miracle. In less than six months, Kristen completed the adoption process and was able to bring Zahra home. Kristen said yes to God's call to adopt Zahra as a single mom – but before the adoption was complete, God had a plan to provide Zahra with a mommy and a daddy. As she walked through the difficult adoption process, Kristen reconnected with an old friend, Thomas. They fell in love. After visiting Kristen and Zahra in Uganda, Thomas asked Kristen to be his wife. They were married just a few months after Kristen and Zahra returned home from Uganda.

In Uganda, doctors believed that Zahra would never walk or talk. Since coming home, she has been diagnosed with cerebral palsy, epilepsy and hearing loss. But Zahra is strong and learning to do things the doctors said were impossible. Zahra can walk, run, jump, swim, and dance. She can talk, sing, write her name, and count to forty. She attends school and receives the medical care she needs. As Kristen and Thomas reflect on the last year, they believe 'the biggest impact on Zahra's life has been the power of love and acceptance: knowing and believing that she is worth it. She is a unique and special little girl and we are honored that God chose us to be her family.'

It only takes one to change the life of one.

This is a book about millions of children who are fatherless. Like Ayana and Zahra, every one of these children has a face, a name, a story. The stories of Ayana and Zahra illustrate an important truth: children who have been orphaned, abandoned or separated from their families are among the most vulnerable people in the world. Without protection and provision, orphans and vulnerable children often have no future. Like Ayana, thousands of these children die every day of hunger and preventable disease. Yet like Zahra, each of these children has the potential to thrive with the love of a family.

Before you become overwhelmed by the magnitude of the problem, remember it only takes one family to change the life of one orphan. Of all the numbers I will write about in this book, *one* is the most important. What you do with what you learn in this book can make all the difference in the world to one child – or one family.

The Christian Adoption and Orphan Care Movement

About ten years ago I went on a mission trip to Guatemala. At the time, my husband and I were hoping to start a family, but struggling with infertility. When I began to feel queasy after eating food in a rural village in Guatemala, I hoped the feeling was morning sickness – not food poisoning. On the flight home, there were half a dozen American and European couples bringing home newly adopted babies. A seed was planted: if we could not have children of our own, we could adopt. At the time, most people who considered adoption did so in response to infertility.

Over the last ten years, however, the evangelical church has awoken to God's heart for the fatherless. Christians have opened their eyes to see the millions of children around the world who have lost one or both parents to AIDS, violence or poverty. A growing number of churches are responding with great compassion to launch orphan care ministries. Likewise, an increasing number of families are pursuing adoption not because of infertility, but in response to God's call.

Thousands of Christians have discovered God's heart for orphans. Influential evangelical pastors, including John Piper, Rick Warren and David Platt, have challenged their congregations – along with millions of evangelical Christians across the United States – to consider what the Bible teaches about orphans and adoption.

In 2006, a few dozen Christians interested in adoption and orphan care gathered in Little Rock, Arkansas to plan and pray 'about how God would have them care for orphaned and vulnerable children.'[3] This was the first Orphan Summit and the birth of the Christian Alliance for Orphans.

Since 2006, the Orphan Summit has been an annual event. In 2012, the Summit was attended by more than 2,000 people.[4] The Summit is the largest of dozens of adoption and orphan care conferences held across the United States, including Together for Adoption and Created for Care.

The adoption and orphan care movement is not confined to America. Over the last eight years, the Christian Alliance for Orphans has grown to become 'an international movement of concerned Christians and churches.'[5] Orphan Sunday began as a movement of churches in Zambia, where pastors called their congregations to care for the orphans in their communities. Orphan Sunday spread to the United States in 2003. In 2009, the Christian Alliance for Orphans took up the cause, promoting Orphan Sunday across the nation and around the world. Orphan Sunday provides an opportunity for churches to spotlight God's heart for orphans and how ordinary people can get involved in adoption, foster care and global orphan care. In 2011, more than half a million Americans were involved in Orphan Sunday. By 2013, Orphan Sunday was celebrated in dozens of countries around the world, including Australia, Brazil, Philippines, Rwanda, Ukraine, and the United Kingdom.[6]

---

3   Carr, Johnny, and Laura Captari. *Orphan Justice*. 1st ed. Nashville, TN: B & H Publish Group, 2013. Print.

4   Medefind, Jedd. 'ECFA Article On The Christian Orphan Care Movement'. *Christian Alliance for Orphans*. 2012. Web. 13 Jul. 2012.

5   Carr, Johnny, and Laura Captari. *Orphan Justice*. 1st ed. Nashville, TN: B & H Publish Group, 2013. Print.

6   Orphansunday.org. 'Orphan Sunday Map'. *Christian Alliance for Orphans*. 2014. Web. 12 Feb. 2014.

Five years ago, our family began considering adoption. We brought dinner to friends who had just adopted a child from Ethiopia and asked for wisdom. They gave us a copy of Russell Moore's *Adopted for Life*. This book opened our eyes to the truth that Christians are adopted by God – and left us with a deep conviction that we were called to adopt. At the same time, I began reading the blogs of dozens of adoptive families. The awakening of the Christian adoption and orphan care movement has coincided with the growth of social media. Blogs have had a powerful voice in inspiring thousands of families to consider God's heart for orphans.

As a result of these influences – and what I believe is a movement of God – thousands of Christian families are stepping up to care for orphans. While the Christian adoption and orphan care movement is diverse, its supporters share several important beliefs. First, God cares passionately about orphans. Second, Christians are adopted by God and this is central to understanding the Gospel. Third, Christians are called to be involved in adoption and orphan care in response to and as a demonstration of the Gospel.

Some within the movement argue that adoption itself is evangelical in nature:

> The ultimate purpose of human adoption by Christians, therefore, is not to give orphans parents, as important as that is. It is to place them in a Christian home that they might be positioned to receive the gospel, so that within that family, the world might witness a representation of God taking in and genuinely loving the helpless, the hopeless, and the despised.[7]

Christian families and churches are responding to what we believe to be a vast and overwhelming crisis. We have been told there are 151 million orphans: children who are alone in the world, without the love and protection of a family.[8] When we hear the statistics, we imagine a world full of vulnerable children who are growing up in orphanages or on the streets.[9]

---

7   Cruver, Dan, John Piper, Scotty Smith, Richard D. Phillips, Jason Kovacs. *Reclaiming Adoption*. 1st ed. Adelphi, Maryland: Cruciform Press, 2011. Kindle Edition.

8   This is the estimate of the number of orphans, including single and double orphans, as of April 2013. This is the statistic we use throughout the book. Childinfo. 'Orphan Estimates'. 2014. Web. 3 Feb. 2014.

9   Throughout this book, we have made the decision to use the words 'orphan' and 'fatherless' interchangeably. The Hebrew word *yathom* is used throughout the Old Testament to describe an orphan or a fatherless child. The Greek work *orphanos* in James 1:27 has the same meaning. While we understand terms orphan and fatherless can be perceived as hurtful, no harm is intended. We use these terms to reach a certain audience where the terms orphan and fatherless are understood to mean children who have experienced the death of their parents or separation from their families by being institutionalized or living on the streets.

As Christians, we believe God designed children to grow up in families. We assume that without adoption, these children will grow up without families. And so we compare the number of Christians in the world – nearly 4 billion – with the number of orphans – 151 million – and conclude that adoption is *the* answer.

If this assumption was true and if the orphan crisis was as simple as 151 million children waiting in orphanages or on the streets for new families, then adoption would be the best answer.

But we recognize the solution to the orphan crisis is not this simple. We assume the orphan crisis has overwhelmed the capacity of many communities. Domestic adoption is still rare in many developing countries. Many countries are closed to international adoption. Adoption is not an option for every child who has been orphaned or abandoned. So in response, we pour resources into building orphanages. We visit orphans on short-term mission trips and provide for their needs through monthly sponsorship. We accept that these are the primary ways to care for orphans who cannot be adopted.

Often when we are told about the orphan crisis, we're overwhelmed with statistics and challenged to do something. We believe that doing almost anything is better than doing nothing.

But are these assumptions true? Are there truly 151 million children in the world today who are growing up without the love of a family? Is international adoption the only hope for these orphans to have a family? In circumstances where adoption is not possible, shouldn't Christians build, support and visit orphanages?

How we answer these questions is important. If we misunderstand the nature of the orphan crisis, our response, however well-intentioned, might harm the people we want to help. The Bible calls Christians to defend and care for the fatherless. But effective obedience to this Biblical command requires asking deeper questions. Good intentions are not enough. In our enthusiasm to do something, our response to the orphan crisis runs the real risk of exploiting vulnerable families and children.

In James 1:27, we're told 'religion that is pure and undefiled before God, the Father, is this: to visit orphans and widows in their affliction.'[10] The word visit in the Greek is *episkeptomai*, which is also used to describe a doctor visiting a sick patient. The Greek

---

10   *The Bible, English Standard Version.* Wheaton: Crossway, 2014. Print. Unless otherwise specified, all Bible verses quoted or referenced in this book are from the English Standard Version.

word for affliction is *thlipsis*, which means both physical need and anything that burdens the spirit. A good doctor diagnoses a patient's problem while also caring for his physical needs and providing comfort.

If we are to follow the words of James 1:27, we must be like a good doctor visiting a patient. It is good to meet the physical and emotional needs of orphans and widows, but we must not stop there. The orphan crisis is a symptom of a far deeper problem. Like a good doctor, we cannot be content with just treating the symptoms. We must seek to diagnose and heal the brokenness at the root of the orphan crisis. In this chapter, we will examine statistics about the fatherless in the world today, but we will not stop there. We will go deeper, exploring the reasons why children and families are vulnerable.

Who are the fatherless in the Bible?

> This is what the Lord Almighty says: 'Administer true justice; show mercy and compassion to one another. Do not oppress the widow or the fatherless, the foreigner or the poor.' (Zech. 7:9-10, NIV)

From beginning to end, the Bible is a story about God, who calls Himself a Father, adopting a fatherless people. God's people are called to protect and provide for the fatherless in response to what we have received and as a reflection of the Father's heart.

God's compassion is not limited to the fatherless. Throughout the Bible, we see God's heart for the vulnerable, including orphans, widows, immigrants, and the poor. In ancient Jewish culture, these four groups of people would have been at risk of starvation and exploitation. God likewise called His people to protect and care for orphans, widows, immigrants, and the poor.

When the Bible speaks of the fatherless, it refers to children who would have been highly vulnerable in ancient Jewish culture. God designed children to grow up in families and with loving, protective fathers. The fatherless in the Bible represent all children who lack the protection and provision of a father. In a similar way, widows would have been vulnerable to exploitation. Men as husbands and fathers are called to protect and provide for women and children. Especially in a patriarchal society, widows and orphans were particularly vulnerable because they lacked the very person God intended to care for them.

Who are the fatherless in the world today? Just as the people of Israel were called to protect and provide for orphans, widows, immigrants, and the poor, God's people today are called to care for the vulnerable in our communities and around the world. This includes refugees, migrant workers, and the homeless, as well as some single parents and elderly people.[11] It includes the victims of trafficking, forced labor and sexual slavery. It includes people living in countries devastated by war, political oppression and violence. It also includes orphans and widows.

The Orphan and Widow Crisis

It is interesting that the Bible seldom separates orphans and widows. From Deuteronomy to James, God calls His followers to defend and care for orphans and widows together. There is an assumption that widowed mothers are caring for fatherless children – and that these families are vulnerable.

Yet as we Christians have opened our hearts to orphans, we have largely separated orphans and widows. We picture orphans as children on the other side of the world, living alone on the streets or in crowded orphanages. At the same time, we picture widows as the elderly grandmothers down the street. We have largely ignored that fact that the vast majority of the world's orphans live with their widowed mothers or fathers. Our hearts are broken over the world's orphans – but we've missed the world's widows. The truth is there is an orphan *and* widow crisis.

As we consider the following statistics, it's important to understand that truly reliable statistics do not exist. To try to define the scope of the orphan crisis, researchers have to make estimates using limited, imperfect tools. Nevertheless, considering statistics about the orphan and widow crisis is helpful because it gives us a panoramic view.

According to UNICEF, children are considered orphans if they have experienced the death of one or both parents.[12] By this definition, there were an estimated 151 million orphans in the developing world including Africa, Asia, Eastern Europe, and Latin America in 2013.[13] This number includes 'children who have lost both parents, but also those who have lost a father but have

---

11   Keller, Timothy J. *Generous Justice*. 1st ed. New York, N.Y.: Dutton, Penguin Group USA, 2010. Print.

12   UNICEF Press Centre. 'Orphans'. N. p. 2008. Web. 22 Mar. 2012.

13   Childinfo. 'Orphan Estimates'. N. p. 2014. Web. 3 Feb. 2014.

a surviving mother or have lost their mother but have a surviving father.'[14] There are approximately 18 million children who are double orphans, having experienced the death of both parents.[15]

The orphan crisis is a problem all around the world, but it is particularly acute in Africa and Asia, where there are 58 and 71 million orphans respectively.[16] There are 25 million orphans in India and 17 million in China.[17]

The orphan crisis is not just a problem in developing countries. Millions of children are impacted all over the world when parents harm or abandon children. Family breakdown and sinful patterns of addiction, abuse and neglect affect children everywhere. This is as true in the United States as it is in Europe, Asia, Africa, or Latin America. There are hundreds of thousands of children in the foster care systems of the United States, United Kingdom and other developed countries. There is a need for Christians to be involved in caring for orphans in our own communities.

Yet the majority of the world's orphans are in countries that are poor. The focus of this book is on empowering Christians to make a lasting difference in the lives of orphans in the developing world.

What about widows? There are 245 million widows in the world today. Of these, 115 million widows live in extreme poverty.[18] While we often think of widows in our communities as elderly women, this is far from the global reality. In the developing world, widows are often young women caring for children, alone in providing food, shelter, education, and protection for their families. In regions where the HIV/AIDS epidemic and war are prevalent, widows are often younger and more vulnerable. Most widows living in extreme poverty live in countries where they face discrimination on account of their gender and marital status.[19]

Recent studies indicate that 'there are *half a billion children* who depend on the care and support of these widows.'[20] The children of widows living in poverty are extremely vulnerable. Children often

14   UNICEF Press Centre. 'Orphans'. N. p. 2008. Web. 22 Mar. 2012.

15   Childinfo. 'Orphan Estimates'. N. p. 2014. Web. 3 Feb. 2014.

16   ibid.

17   Newton, Gary. 'U.S. Government And Partners: Working Together On A Comprehensive, Co-ordinated And Effective Response To Highly Vulnerable Children'. 1st ed. Washington, D.C.: N. p. 2009. Web. 21 Mar. 2012.

18   Ondimba, Sylvia Bongo. 'The World Must Support Its Widows'. *The Guardian* 2011. Web. 22 Mar. 2014.

19   ibid.

20   Haugen, Gary A, and Victor Boutros. *The Locust Effect*. USA: OUP, 2014

are forced to leave school to go to work, and girls are 'at high risk of sexual exploitation.'[21]

As we consider the orphan crisis and how we are called to respond, we need to see that God's heart extends not just to orphans but to all children and families who are vulnerable as a result of poverty and injustice. At the same time, making a distinction between children who lack the love and care of a family and children who live in vulnerable families is extremely important.

These numbers alone would suggest that the orphan crisis is overwhelming – and that there is a huge need for international adoption. When I first heard the statistics of the orphan crisis, I pictured millions of babies and young children growing up in horrible institutions and older children living on the streets literally waiting for families. But the truth is the majority of the world's orphans do not live in orphanages or on the streets – and only a tiny fraction of the world's orphans need international adoption.

How many children are living in orphanages or on the streets? Research suggests there are up to 8 million children living in orphanages.[22] Though the statistic of 100 million children living or working on the streets is commonly cited, this has no basis in fact. According to a UNICEF report, 'the exact number of street children is impossible to quantify, but the figure almost certainly runs into the tens of millions across the world. It is likely that the numbers are increasing.'[23]

But even children who are living in orphanages or on the streets are not necessarily orphans who have experienced the death of a parent. Millions of children have been abandoned or separated from families due to poverty, trafficking, abuse, or neglect. Nevertheless, these children, though not technically orphans, should be considered among the fatherless because they lack the protection and provision of a family. We will dig deeper into the research of children living in orphanages and on the streets in the next chapter.

If you take away one thing from this book, we pray it would be this: most orphans live with their families. More than 90 per cent of the world's orphans live with their surviving mother or father.

21   Ondimba, Sylvia Bongo. 'The World Must Support Its Widows'. *The Guardian* 2011. Web. 22 Mar. 2014.

22   Medefind, Jedd. *Christian Alliance For Orphans White Paper On Understanding Orphan Statistics*. 1st ed. Christian Alliance for Orphans, 2012. Web. 15 Apr. 2012.

23   Thomas de Benítez, Sarah. *State Of The World's Street Children*. 1st ed. London: Consortium for Street Children, 2011. Print.

Millions more are living with grandparents or other extended family members. When considering international adoption as a solution to the orphan crisis, we must distinguish between children who are truly alone, without the love of a family, and those who, despite the death of at least one parent, still have a loving family. Orphans who have families do not need adoption.

If God's compassion is not limited to orphans, should our compassion extend only to orphans who have lost their families and who need adoption? Or as the people of God are we called to protect and provide for all who could be considered vulnerable?

The majority of the world's orphans live in families vulnerable to poverty and injustice – and in need of mercy. The one thing nearly all vulnerable families have in common is poverty. Families living in poverty may not be able to provide children with food, clothing, shelter, school fees, or medical care. These families are at risk of violence, injustice, and discrimination.

When Christians talk about adoption as the answer for the orphan crisis, we are missing the bigger picture. There are millions of children worldwide who have been orphaned, abandoned or separated from their families by abuse or neglect who would benefit from adoption. But most of the world's orphans are living with their widowed mothers. If the Bible calls Christians to care for 'orphans and widows in their distress' (James 1:27), this is a fact we should not overlook.

Digging Deeper into the Orphan and Widow Crisis

If we are going to live out James 1:27, we need to be like a good doctor. While many Christians have responded to the orphan crisis believing doing anything is better than doing nothing, we must *primum non nocere,* or first do no harm. This fundamental principle is taught to doctors in medical school. If a doctor does not accurately diagnose a problem, the treatment may cause more harm than good – doing something may be worse than doing nothing at all. In the same way, if we fail to accurately diagnose the problem, we may cause more harm than good.

So before we go further, we need to step back and seek to understand the complicated issues at the root of the orphan and widow crisis. We need to ask why hundreds of millions of children are orphaned, abandoned and exploited in the world today. We need to learn more about the most significant issues at the root of the global orphan crisis, and ultimately we need to think biblically about these issues. The orphan crisis is part of a bigger picture reflecting brokenness in the world. Injustice and poverty are symptoms of a deeper problem: sin and brokenness as a result of the fall.

HIV and AIDS

The HIV and AIDS epidemic has radically transformed the world in which children live.[24] Globally there are 34 million people living with HIV. The epidemic is most acute in Sub-Saharan Africa, where 23 million people are living with HIV. In the past three decades more than 30 million people have died of AIDS. Though huge advances have been made in the fight against HIV and AIDS, 2.7 million people were newly infected with HIV and 1.8 million people died of complications from AIDS in 2010.[25]

The HIV and AIDS epidemic has had a devastating impact on children and families. There are 2.1 million children living with HIV and many more have died of AIDS. Children who are HIV positive are more likely to be orphaned as a result of the death of a parent. There are 17.5 million AIDS orphans, children who have lost one or both parents to AIDS.

Children and families affected by HIV are often victims of stigma and discrimination. In communities severely impacted by the epidemic, children and families are more likely to live in poverty. Children affected by HIV may be marginalized, denied access to education and health care, or even abandoned. Furthermore, orphans are more likely to be forced to have sex and are far more vulnerable to becoming infected with HIV. [26]

All of these numbers create a sense of urgency. Though the evangelical church largely ignored the AIDS epidemic until recently, Christians are now responding with great compassion. Our eyes are open to see that the epidemic has orphaned millions of children. We assume these AIDS orphans are growing up without the love and care of a family and we want to do something to help. As a result, a growing number of ministries are involved in building

---

24   'Convention On The Rights Of The Child: HIV/AIDS And The Rights Of The Child'. *Committee On The Rights Of The Child, Thirty-Second Session*. United Nations, 2003. 1-2. Print.

25   UN AIDS. *Nearly 50 per cent Of People Who Are Eligible For Antiretroviral Therapy Now Have Access To Lifesaving Treatment*. 2011. Print.

26   'Convention On The Rights Of The Child: HIV/AIDS And The Rights Of The Child'. *Committee On The Rights Of The Child, Thirty-Second Session*. United Nations, 2003. 1-2. Print.

and supporting orphanages to care for children affected by HIV and AIDS. Likewise, a growing number of families feel a burden to adopt children who have lost their parents to AIDS – or who are HIV positive.

But is it accurate to say that AIDS orphans are growing up without families? While 17 million children have experienced the death of one parent to AIDS, upwards of 90 per cent of AIDS orphans continue to live with their families. Most orphans continue to live with their surviving parent. Even as the number of children who have been orphaned by AIDS in Africa is increasing, the number of children who are unable to live with their extended families remains small. In Sub-Saharan Africa where there are more than 12 million AIDS orphans, poverty remains the primary reason why families struggle to care for orphans.[27]

When we understand that most AIDS orphans are living with their families or in their communities, our approach to helping is different. Children and families affected by HIV and AIDS are vulnerable to poverty, illness, stigma, and exploitation. The answer for these vulnerable families is not building orphanages or removing children from their families. Whenever possible, we can support keeping vulnerable families together. Only when AIDS orphans cannot be cared for by their families should international adoption be considered. While orphanages may provide shelter in a time of crisis, long-term institutional care should always be a last resort.

Conflict

Living in North America or Europe, we often take peace and security for granted. War seems like something that is far away, even when we know someone who serves in the military. We shield our children from the harsh reality of conflict around the world. Yet for millions of children who live in countries affected by conflict, there is no hiding from fear and violence.

Children living in war-torn countries are especially vulnerable. Millions of children are suffering as a result of conflict. We live in an increasingly violent world where the very nature of conflict is changing. In the past, women and children were protected, and war was fought primarily by national armies. Over the last fifty

---

27   Richter, L.M., and A. Norman. 'AIDS Orphan Tourism: A Threat To Young Children In Residential Care'. *Vulnerable Children and Youth Studies*. 2010. Print.

years, there has been a shift. The majority of the world's conflicts take place within countries, along splits between religious, cultural and ethnic lines. Families are no longer spared.

Perhaps the most shocking example of violence in recent history is the 1994 genocide in Rwanda, where Hutu extremists massacred their Tutsi neighbors as well as thousands of moderate Hutus who did not join in the violence. Over a period of 100 days, nearly one million people were killed. The brutal violence did not spare women or children. The genocide tore apart hundreds of thousands of families, leaving more than half a million children orphaned.

In the world today, children are the most vulnerable victims of war. Children are slaughtered, starved, raped, maimed, and forced to witness extreme brutality.[28] Children likewise suffer as a result of terrorism.[29] Between 1985 and 1995, an estimated two million children were killed in conflict. Three times as many were seriously injured or permanently disabled, often by landmines.

Increasingly, children are forced to participate in war. Three hundred thousand children under the age of 18 are child soldiers.[30] Furthermore, conflict often forces families to flee their homes. Globally there are more than 10 million refugees and 15 million internally displaced people.[31]

Children living in war-torn countries may be orphaned, abandoned or separated from their families. Desperate parents who are unable to protect or provide for their families may leave children in orphanages, fearing they have no other way to ensure their survival.

How should we care for children who are fatherless as a result of conflict? Without question, orphans and vulnerable children living in war-torn countries need protection and care. There may be situations where building or supporting orphanages provides children with lifesaving care through a crisis. Nevertheless, these orphanages should be seen as temporary and transitional. To the

---

28 'Promotion And Protection Of The Rights Of Children: Impact Of Armed Conflict On Children'. *United Nations General Assembly.* New York: United Nations, 1996. 9-15. Print.

29 'Report Of The Special Representative Of The Secretary-General For Children And Armed Conflict'. *United Nations General Assembly.* New York: United Nations, 2007. 16. Print.

30 www.bbc.co.uk. 'Child Soldiers | Children Of Conflict | BBC World Service'. *BBC World Service.* 2014. Web. 8 Sep. 2014.

31 'UNHCR Global Appeal 2013 Update - Populations Of Concern To UNHCR'. *United Nations High Commissioner for Refugees.* 2013. Web. 8 Sep. 2014.

greatest extent possible, the priority should be reuniting children with their parents and supporting vulnerable families. Many countries that have been popular for international adoption, such as Guatemala and Nepal, have experienced recent war. In the aftermath of war, however, these countries often lack safeguards to support vulnerable families and protect children from trafficking.

Injustice

God promises to bring justice to the fatherless. He likewise calls His followers to defend the fatherless. Widows and orphans are particularly vulnerable to exploitation. When the poor are victims of injustice, they have nowhere to turn. In the world today, millions of vulnerable children and families suffer injustice. Here are several examples of how widows and orphans are victims of injustice.

Illegal property seizure

A widowed mother caring for orphaned children in Africa is at risk of having her property rights violated after the death of her husband. Ruthless people prey on the vulnerable widow, stealing her land and her home. In Uganda, for example, more than one in five widows and orphans are victims of illegal property seizure after the death of a husband or father.[32] For many families, this injustice can be the difference between life and death. Without a home or land, a widowed mother may have no way to provide shelter, food and education to her children.

Physical and sexual abuse

Another form of injustice in the world today is the physical and sexual abuse of women and children. Around the world, 150 million girls and 73 million boys have experienced sexual abuse. More than 300 million children have experienced physical abuse.[33] But many countries fail to protect vulnerable children and women from abuse. Even when cases do go to trial, perpetrators are unlikely to be held accountable. Weak, corrupt legal systems fail to protect vulnerable children from abuse and exploitation.[34]

---

32   International Justice Mission. 'Injustice Today'. N. p. 2014. Web. 22 Mar. 2012.

33   Krug, Etienne G. et al. 'World Report On Violence And Health.' Geneva, Switzerland: *World Health Organization*, 2002. Print.

34   Haugen, Gary A, and Victor Boutros. *The Locust Effect*. 1st ed. Print.

Trafficking and slavery

Every year, more than 1.2 million children are trafficked and forced into various forms of slavery.[35] Nearly 2 million children are exploited through child pornography and prostitution.[36] Another 8.4 million children are forced to work under horrific circumstances. There are nearly 30 million slaves in the world today– this is more than over the course of entire trans-Atlantic slave trade.[37] Trafficking generates more than 32 billion dollars in profit every year for those who sell men, women and children into slavery.[38]

This issue is inextricably linked with the orphan crisis. Children of desperately poor families are often at risk of being coerced or sold into slavery. In Haiti, for example, there are an estimated 300,000 'restaveks' or child slaves – who are often forced to work from dawn to dusk, starved, beaten and abused.[39] Children who grow up in orphanages are particularly vulnerable to being forced into slavery.

In recent years Christians have awoken to both God's heart for orphans and God's heart for justice, but few are talking about the connection between the orphan crisis and injustice. Injustice is often a reason why a child is separated from the love and security of her family. Furthermore, vulnerable children and families are sometimes exploited through the process of international adoption. Defending the fatherless means not simply advocating for the rights of children who need new families to be adopted, it is also about defending the rights of vulnerable families.

Poverty

Extreme poverty is the most significant reason why children are orphaned or separated from their families. Poverty, not the absence of family, is the most common reason children are placed in orphanages.[40]

Globally, 1.2 billion people live on less than $1.25 a day: the international standard of extreme poverty.[41] Approximately 428

35 International Labour Office. *Every Child Counts: New Global Estimates On Child Labour*. Geneva: International Labor Organization, 2002. Print.

36 International Justice Mission. 'Casework: Sex Trafficking'. N.p. 2014. Web. 8 Sep. 2014.

37 Walkfree.org. 'Walk Free Homepage'. N. p. 2013. Web. 22 Mar. 2014.

38 International Justice Mission. 'Injustice Today'. N. p. 2014. Web. 22 Mar. 2012.

39 Restavekfreedom.org. 'Home'. Restavek Freedom Foundation, 2014. Web. 8 Sep. 2014.

40 USG Special Advisor for Orphans and Vulnerable Children, *U.S. Government And Partners: Working Together On A Comprehensive, Coordinated And Effective Response To Highly Vulnerable Children*. Washington D.C.: United States Government, 2009. Print.

41 Worldbank.org. 'Poverty Overview'. *World Bank*, 2014. Web. 8 Sep. 2014.

million children live in extreme poverty and 640 million – or nearly one third of the world's children – lack adequate housing.[42]

Hunger

More than 170 million children live with hunger and chronic malnutrition. In developing countries, poor families spend 50-80 per cent of their income on food. Parents are often forced to decide which child will get to eat on any particular day. Every year, 10.9 million children under the age of five die in developing countries. Of those, 6 million children will die before their first birthday. Malnutrition and hunger are the cause of 60 per cent of these deaths.

Water

There are a billion people in the world – one in nine – who do not have access to clean water. Clean water to drink is the most basic human need. Contaminated drinking water is one of the leading causes of infant and child mortality. When families do not have access to clean drinking water or adequate sanitation facilities, children frequently suffer from diarrhea, which kills between 1.6 and 2.5 million children every year. In developing countries, the burden of gathering water falls particularly hard on young girls, who may not be able to attend school because they spend hours every day hauling water for their family's needs.[43]

Education

A good education is essential for a child to escape poverty. Yet 72 million children in the developing world cannot attend primary school.[44] When families cannot afford school fees, food, clothing or housing, children may be forced to leave school to help the family earn income. The root cause of most child labor is poverty and lack of access to school.

Medical Care

Often families who are poor lack access to desperately needed medical care. This has a particularly serious impact on vulnerable women and children. The reality that poor women lack access to medical care

---

42   'The Millennium Development Goals Report'. New York: United Nations, 2007. Print.

43   ScienceDaily. 'Novel Compound May Treat Acute Diarrhea'. N. p. 2014. Web. 4 Jun. 2012.

44   'The Millennium Development Goals Report'. New York: United Nations, 2007. Print.

during pregnancy and birth contributes significantly to the orphan crisis. According to the World Health Organization, approximately 1,000 women die every day from pregnancy or childbirth-related complications. Nearly all maternal deaths occur in poor countries, mostly in Africa and Asia.[45] Though there are many reasons why children may be separated from their families, the one thing most orphans and vulnerable families have in common is poverty.

Poverty is often at the root of injustice. It is overwhelmingly the poor who are oppressed and exploited. It is the poor who suffer as the victims of common everyday violence. When a family has adequate resources, they are able to survive a crisis. But families who are poor – especially in the developing world – have no safety net.

When a vulnerable family cannot afford to care for their children, they may make the decision to abandon a child to an orphanage. Poor mothers struggling to provide for their families may be forced into prostitution or may have no way to defend their property rights. Fathers who are unable to afford the cost of formula to feed their baby after the death of the child's mother or who need to work may have no choice other than to place children in an orphanage. Children who have been orphaned or abandoned as a result of poverty are vulnerable to abuse and trafficking – including trafficking for the purpose of international adoption. Although many factors contribute to children being separated from families, poverty is almost always at the root. It is poverty that pushes most children into orphanages.

Brokenness and Sin

But what is poverty? Most of us would answer that poverty is a lack of money or things. But poverty in the Bible is much deeper. Poverty from a Biblical perspective is about much more than a lack of financial resources. Poverty is ultimately about broken relationships.

God created men and women in the image of God. We are designed to live in relationship with God, others, ourselves, and creation. We are created to live in a joyful, intimate relationship with God. We are designed to live in loving community with others. As image bearers, we have been given dignity and worth. We are called to steward and care for the world God has created.

---

45   Halftheskymovement.org. 'Issues: Maternal Mortality'. N. p. 2014. Web. 26 Mar. 2014.

After the fall, however, all of these relationships are broken. As a result of sin we are separated from God and from others. Our identity is distorted by pride and shame. Our relationship with creation is broken. This brokenness sometimes results in material poverty.[46]

As Christians we understand children are often separated from their families as a result of sin. Parents sin, and they are sinned against. Sometimes this sin results in a child being orphaned or abandoned by their biological family. A parent's laziness may contribute to a family's poverty. A father's violence or greed may lead him to neglect or abuse his child. Or a mother may be exploited and forced into prostitution, leading to HIV infection and unplanned pregnancy.

Ultimately brokenness and sin are at the root of the global orphan crisis. We live in a world where there are 115 million widows caring for 500 million children living in extreme poverty, a world where 8 million children are growing up in orphanages and 30 million people are being exploited as slaves, a world where every ninety seconds a woman dies in childbirth and every five seconds a child dies because of hunger. All of this is evidence of this brokenness – and evidence that we need the God of justice and mercy to intervene. If we want to see the end of the orphan crisis, we need to follow God's heart to the poverty, injustice and brokenness at the root of the orphan crisis.

A revolution that will sweep the world?

Evangelical Christians have awoken to God's heart for the fatherless. Christians have opened their eyes to see the desperate needs of orphans and are responding with great compassion. A growing number of Christian families are adopting. Likewise, a growing number of churches are passionately engaged in orphan care. Christian leaders are uniting behind a powerful vision: ending the global orphan crisis. The Christian adoption and orphan care movement has been described as a 'revolution that will sweep the world.'[47]

But something is wrong. While Christian families consider adoption and churches launch orphan care ministries, few in the

---

46   Corbett, Steve, and Brian Fikkert. *When Helping Hurts*. 1st ed. Chicago, IL: Moody Publishers, 2009. Kindle Edition.

47   Medefind, Jedd. 'Session 1, Christian Alliance For Orphans Summit 8'. Lake Forest Park, California. 2012. Speech.

movement acknowledge that the global orphan crisis is not as simple as 151 million children who are growing up without the love of a family. Moreover, few in the movement are talking about the root causes of the crisis. As a result, Christians are unintentionally hurting the vulnerable children and families we are called to help. We are also missing a tremendous opportunity.

Although some Christians engaged in caring for orphans understand that most of the world's orphans live in vulnerable families, this is seldom the focus of conferences, sermons, books, or blogs about the global orphan crisis. The truth that most orphans live in vulnerable families is less compelling than the myth that there are 151 million orphans who are alone, without the love of a family.

When we understand the scope of the orphan crisis, we feel compelled to help. But understanding the scope of the crisis is not the same thing as understanding the nature or the cause of the global orphan crisis. The emotional response to the global orphan crisis – the feeling that *we have to do something* – is a good place to start but a harmful place to end.

Without understanding the connection between poverty, injustice and the orphan crisis, many Christians are responding with actions that have unintended consequences. Christians are responding to the global orphan crisis primarily by supporting orphanages, going on mission trips to visit orphans, and encouraging adoption. While all of these approaches may be necessary and at times helpful, they do nothing to address the poverty and injustice at the heart of the crisis. We are treating the symptoms rather than the cause of the orphan crisis.

When Christians believe there is an overwhelming need for international adoption, they feel compelled to adopt not just by a desire for a child, but by a deep conviction that God calls Christians to care for orphans and that these children have no other options. When Christians believe adoption is *the answer* to the global orphan crisis, some are willing to adopt at any cost. Some believe so passionately in adoption that they are willing to justify all sorts of injustice – including coercing poor families, bribing government officials, trafficking children, or closing their eyes to corruption – in order to get a child home.

Adoption is a wonderful blessing for children who need new families. But most of the world's orphans have families to love, protect and care for them. For these children, adoption is not the answer. A similar conviction drives Christians to build, support and visit orphanages – despite all of the evidence that orphanages create orphans and harm children.

The next three chapters will help you to *first do no harm*. We will look at stories and research to understand why orphanages, mission trips and adoption can be harmful to the orphans and vulnerable families we are called to help. In the second half of the book we will look at how we can address the issues at the root of the orphan crisis in order to make a lasting difference.

QUESTIONS FOR DISCUSSION AND REFLECTION

1. How have you seen the Christian Adoption and Orphan Care Movement impact your church?

2. Do you agree that there is an orphan and widow crisis that needs to be addressed by the church?

3. How do you see the role of sin in the orphan and widow crisis?

4. Is doing something in response to this darkness better than nothing?

Growing up in an Orphanage

Sara's Story: Even the best institutions cannot replace families

I lingered at the front door of a good friend's house. My kids were already in my minivan, hers were clamoring for lunch. We were both adoptive mothers. In God's providence, our conversation was about trusting God completely with the lives of the children we hoped to adopt, the children we loved as our own.

Moments later, I sat down in the driver's seat and glanced at my phone. I had been waiting anxiously, expecting an email with an update on our adoption. We were hoping to adopt a shy girl named Grace.[1] We had spent several months with Grace in Uganda waiting for a court date before making the heart-wrenching decision to return to the United States to continue waiting.

I saw a new message from the director of the orphanage. I closed my eyes and remembered the last time I held Grace. She wrapped

---

1   The names of the children and orphanage have been changed for security.

her arms and legs around my body and held on with all her strength as I said goodbye. I told her I loved her and promised I would come back soon. I remembered how in the two months we were together in Uganda she transformed from an orphan to a daughter. For the first time in many years, Grace knew what it felt like to be special to someone – to be treasured by a mother.

My hands trembled as I read the email. My chest pounded, and my eyes burned. The director of the orphanage had decided we could not adopt Grace, the little girl we had come to love as our own.

A few weeks earlier, we had questioned how the missionaries who led the orphanage were handling our adoption case. When we asked serious questions about the process, they became defensive and angry. They said Grace would be just fine where she was, growing up at the orphanage.

We were heartbroken. While we knew we had done the right thing in asking difficult questions to make sure the adoption was ethical, we grieved the loss of a child who was never legally ours. We felt both sadness and anger as we wrestled with the news that Grace would grow up without a family. Our home was full of reminders of Grace: her pictures on the walls, her bed made with brightly colored sheets, her closet full of dresses and shoes.

Like many Christian families, we had started the adoption process full of hope. We understood God's heart for orphans. We believed that we had been adopted into God's family. We wanted to adopt out of obedience to God, love He had poured into our hearts, and desire for more children. But we were left heartbroken, deeply aware of the injustice of it all.

I began to reflect on my experiences in Uganda and to ask questions. I was angry at the broken system that kept Grace living in an orphanage without a family. I was determined to seek God's heart and the truth.

The first time we visited Village of Hope, the orphanage where Grace was living, we thought it was an amazing place. My husband and I were on a trip visiting ministries caring for orphans in Uganda, especially those children affected by HIV and AIDS.

In the first days of our trip, we visited several baby homes in Kampala. At one home, I picked up a small girl wearing clothes soaked with urine. She was filthy and desperate for attention. Most of the staff were busy with their tasks, indifferent to the children's needs.

At another home we fed newborn babies. The infants had only fifteen minutes to finish their bottle before they were put back in their cribs, where they would lay for the next three hours. My husband held a tiny baby boy who was a premature. After two of our biological sons, we understood the special care and attention prematurely-born infants need to learn how to suck from a bottle. The baby boy was weak and not able to get more than a few drops of formula. When his time was up, Mark tenderly laid the boy in his crib, fearing the worst. Without more personalized care, it was likely this child would not survive.

Both of these orphanages were as dark and broken as any place we could imagine. Village of Hope was completely different. The orphanage was situated on acres of rolling hills, surrounded by forests brimming with monkeys and fields full of sugar cane and tea. Village of Hope farmed much of their land, providing healthy food for the children in their care to eat. Their facility included a church, a primary school, a medical clinic and a small guesthouse for visiting short-term mission teams. The houses for the children were built like a small village. Children lived in small groups with fairly consistent caregivers. Compared to children we had seen at other orphanages, the children here seemed healthy.

After spending the day at the orphanage, we thought Village of Hope was a remarkable place. We returned to the United States and applied to adopt a child from Village of Hope. Although Village of Hope had placed many of their youngest and healthiest children for international adoption, they had never placed a child with special needs. We felt called to adopt a preschool age child with special needs and the missionaries matched us with Grace. We later returned to Uganda and spent two months visiting and living in the guesthouse at Village of Hope.

This experience opened my eyes to the truth about growing up in an orphanage. Even the best institutions cannot replace families.

The day I returned to Village of Hope, it felt empty. The website said the village was home to more than 100 orphans; however there were only a few dozen children around. I asked where the children were. One of the missionaries explained that it was a school holiday and many of the children had gone home to see their families. The children who remained at the home were the ones who were truly fatherless. I was shocked. Why were so many children who had homes and families living in an orphanage?

I learned that nearly all of the 'orphans' who lived at Village of Hope had at least one surviving parent. Most children were living in the orphanage because their families were desperately poor, unable to afford the cost of food, school or medical care.

Life at Village of Hope was much more comfortable than life for Ugandan children living in the surrounding villages. The children were given a free, high-quality education. They were given health care. The children ate three meals a day and had access to clean, safe drinking water. They had closets full of clothes, shoes and toys. They slept in beds and lived in houses much larger and nicer than the typical Ugandan family. They even enjoyed many of the extras typical of American or European childhood: watching movies, drinking soda, eating ice cream, and going swimming.

It made sense why families living in desperate poverty would place their children at the orphanage. Village of Hope seemed to offer the children a chance at a brighter future. But the truth was more complicated.

Although the missionaries and staff were caring, there was no way they could provide individual attention and affection to more than 100 children. The little ones struggled with attachment issues. The young adults who grew out of the orphanage struggled to build a life in the community. They lacked skills and social connections to find jobs. Most of the children who had been successful in secondary school could not afford to go to college. Although their physical needs were met, the children grew up disconnected from their culture and separated from their families.

We began to wonder why the orphanage was full of children who were not orphans. Most children had biological families living near the orphanage. Why didn't the missionaries make more of an effort to reunite the children with their families?

Village of Hope spent more than $100 a month to care for each child. This is more than most Ugandan families earn in a month and three times as much as the missionaries pay the caregivers. We wondered if the missionaries had ever offered financial assistance so that children could remain with their families. Was spending $100 a month to care for a child in an orphanage a better response to poverty than spending $100 a month to support a vulnerable family?

Many of the healthy babies and toddlers had been placed for international adoption. Why wasn't the orphanage pursuing domestic adoption as an option for some children? Why weren't they advocating for their older and special needs kids to be adopted internationally?

What would Grace's future look like if she grew up in an orphanage instead of a family?

Growing up in an Orphanage

Grace is not alone. An estimated 8 million children worldwide live in orphanages.[2] Extreme poverty, AIDS, abuse and neglect, conflict and natural disasters leave millions of children separated from their families. The millions of children who live in orphanages and other forms of residential care are among the most vulnerable in the world.[3] These children need protection and care.

In the last ten years, there has been a significant movement as Christians have embraced God's call to care for orphans. We have opened our eyes to the global orphan crisis and are responding by building, supporting and visiting orphanages. Christian families and churches often see this as the easiest and most practical way to care for orphans.

This has been particularly true in Africa. As Christians have embraced their responsibility to care for the millions of children who have lost parents to AIDS in Africa, we have rushed to build orphanages. In Ghana, the number of children's homes increased from 10 in 1996 to 140 in 2009. In Zimbabwe, the number of children in institutional care doubled between 1994 and 2004.[4] In Uganda, more than one million children have experienced the death of at least one parent to the HIV and AIDS epidemic. Since 1996, the number of baby and children's homes in Uganda has grown from 36 to 420 in 2012. Most of these orphanages have been supported by Christian faith-based organizations.

---

2   It is difficult to determine how many children are living in orphanages. Many governments, particularly those in the developing world, do not know how many orphanages exist within their borders, much less the number of children within them. In many countries, local and international organizations operate institutions with little or no government oversight. The term orphanage is not accurate, because most children living in institutions are not orphans. Most children would not be there if their parents had adequate support. In this chapter, I use the words institution, orphanage, baby home and children's home synonymously to refer to residential facilities in which groups of children are cared for by paid staff.

3   Save the Children. *Keeping Children Out Of Harmful Institutions*. London: Save the Children, 2009. Print. (1)

4   ibid.

But is supporting institutional orphan care the right thing to do?

According to the UN Convention on the Rights of the Child, children have a *right* to grow up in a family. As Christians, we agree. We know that God designed children to grow up in families. Families have a critical role in promoting children's care and wellbeing. Parents have a responsibility to protect and provide.

We know millions of children have been orphaned. Millions more children have been abandoned by their parents or separated from their families by poverty, violence, abuse, natural disasters, and conflict. Some of these orphaned and vulnerable children end up living in orphanages or on the streets.

Do children living in orphanages have nowhere else to go? Do orphanages protect children from harm – or are they ultimately harmful to children? When should Christian families and churches support institutional orphan care? Does supporting institutional orphan care have the unintended consequence of destroying families?

To answer these critically important questions, we need to consider a few things. First, we need to understand the reasons why millions of children are growing up in orphanages. Second, we need to consider the impact of institutional care on children. Third, we need to consider whether building and supporting orphanages is really the best response to the orphan crisis.

Why are children in orphanages?

We often picture the children in orphanages as children who have no one, alone and unloved. But most children do not grow up in an orphanage because they are alone in the world. The reasons why children are placed in children's homes are not entirely the same as the reasons children are orphaned. The overwhelming majority of children living in institutions have families. At least four out of five children growing up in an orphanage have a mother or a father and many more have extended family. In some cases, the family may love and want to care for the child.

In most developing countries, there is limited support for poor or marginalized families. In the United States, the government provides social services to families living in poverty, ensuring most children have access to housing, food and medical care. But families living in poverty in the developing world have no safety net. When a poor family faces a crisis, they may have few options. Most parents love their children and want to care for them. Parents in desperate situations may make the heart-breaking decision to place a child in an orphanage believing this is the only way the child can survive.

Likewise, in most developing countries, there is limited government support for family-based care for children who need alternative placements. Children end up in institutions because the government does not support or allow foster care or adoption. Supporting vulnerable families and family-based care requires an investment of time and resources many developing countries are unwilling to make. As a result, life in an institution is the only alternative to life on the street for children who have been separated from their families.

Poverty

Most children are in orphanages not because they are orphans but because their parents cannot afford to care for them. For parents lacking resources and support, putting children in an institution may seem like the best way to provide them with food, clothing, education, and health care. Poor parents are also more likely to leave children in orphanages when they migrate to find work. Single mothers may have no other way to provide for their children after the death of the father and primary breadwinner. Likewise, single fathers may not be able to feed or care for their children after the death of the mother.

Discrimination

Families who face discrimination for being an ethnic minority are more likely to place their children in an orphanage. Likewise, children who face discrimination due to their HIV status, disability or gender are more likely to be abandoned. In India, 90 per cent of the abandoned or orphaned children are girls.[5] The discrimination and social exclusion experienced by many vulnerable families prevent them from finding the support and resources they need to care for and protect their children.

Disability

In many developing countries, there is little support for parents to care for disabled children. Without resources, these parents may

---

5   India Human Rights Commission 2007.

feel no choice other than placing a child in an orphanage. In Eastern Europe, approximately 14 per cent of children in orphanages are disabled.

HIV and AIDS

Worldwide, more than 17 million children have lost one or both parents to AIDS. Although traditionally orphans in Africa were cared for by extended families, the number of AIDS orphans has stressed the traditional system. In Sub-Saharan Africa, 44-72 per cent of orphans are AIDS orphans.[6]

Conflict

Children may be orphaned or separated from their families as a result of war, violence and conflict. War affects every area of a child's development and children affected by armed conflict are among the most vulnerable in the world. There are more than 3 million orphans in Iraq, many of whom have been separated from their parents as a result of violence. Children separated from their families during conflict are at risk of becoming child soldiers. In Northern Uganda, more than 10,000 children have been abducted and forced to become fighters in the Lord's Resistance Army.

Natural Disasters

Children are often separated from their families during or after natural disasters. Although thousands of children may be separated from their parents due to earthquakes, tsunamis or other disasters, most of these children have biological families. These families may be unable to parent because of poverty exacerbated by the disaster.

Broken Families

Many children are in care as a result of brokenness and sin in the family. In the developed world, most children are in care as a result of abuse or neglect. Abuse and neglect of children are prevalent worldwide.

Social Orphans

Some children are placed in care for social reasons, such as drug addiction, mental illness or incarceration of a parent. In Eastern

---

6   Avert.org. 'Children Orphaned By HIV And AIDS | AVERT'. AVERT, 2014. Web. 8 Sep. 2014.

Europe, approximately one in four children in residential care is a social orphan.[7]

Trafficking

In many developing countries, there is another issue that comes into play. Caring for orphans can be a lucrative business. Poor parents may be encouraged to place their children in institutions as a means for unscrupulous organizations to make money on child sponsorship. Likewise vulnerable families may be bribed, coerced or threatened into placing children in an orphanage by people hoping to profit from trafficking or international adoption.

The most significant reason why children are in orphanages is poverty. Families living in poverty often lack the resources to survive the crises described above. When a family has savings, owns property or has insurance, they are prepared to weather a crisis, such as the death of a parent or a natural disaster. Likewise, when a family has access to medical care, they can cope with disability or disease. It is overwhelmingly the poor who suffer injustice and are victims of trafficking and injustice.

What is the impact of institutional care?

If we believe God designed children to grow up in families, it is not surprising that orphanages are harmful to children. The abundance of evidence from studies around the world demonstrates the serious problems associated with children growing up in institutional care.

For more than fifty years, child-development specialists have recognized that institutions consistently fail to meet children's developmental needs. Children's homes may be able to provide a vulnerable child with food, clothing and an education. But children need more than good physical care.

Furthermore, many orphanages in the developing world do not have sufficient resources to provide children with adequate food, clothing, medical care, and education. Often orphanages have life-threateningly poor nutrition, hygiene and health care. In some cases, children are not able to attend school. In many orphanages, children have to share beds or sleep on the floor. They may only have one meal a day. There may be no facilities for children to play.

---

7   Dillon, Sara. 'The Missing Link: A Social Orphan Protocol To The United Nations Convention On The Rights Of The Child'. *Human Rights and Globalization Law Review*, Vol. 1, p.39, 2008. Print.

The children may receive little or no individual attention from staff. Few orphanages have adequate child protection policies. This puts children at risk of physical and sexual abuse.

As Christians in America or Europe, we often think about orphanages in two categories. We imagine dark, lonely institutions where babies lay for hours in their cribs with no one to comfort them. We know this is not how children should grow up. At the same time, we support 'good' orphanages that seem to offer orphaned and vulnerable children a brighter future. While there is a difference and some institutions do a decent job of caring and providing for children, we need to understand that even the best orphanages are not the same as loving families.

Institutional care is associated with many negative consequences for children's development. Here are examples of how growing up in an orphanage impacts children:

Lower IQ: When children receive a lack of human eye contact and visual stimulation, essential processes within the brain are never triggered, causing brain-stunting and low IQ.

Developmental Delays: When children do not have toys or a place to play, they are left with reduced motor skills and language abilities.

Stunted Growth: In many orphanages, children suffer severe nutritional deficiencies and stunted growth as a result of poor nutrition.

Poor Health: Children in orphanages are often sick as a result of overcrowding, poor hygiene and lack of access to medical care. A recent study by Yale University found that children who are separated from their parents at birth and who grow up in orphanages experience genetic changes that affect the immune system and the development of the brain.[8]

Social and Behavioral Problems: New evidence suggests that children under the age of three are particularly vulnerable to developmental damage caused by institutional care. A recent study in Romania followed the growth and development of children living in institutional care compared with children raised at home or in

---

8   ScienceDaily. 'Orphaned Children Exhibit Genetic Changes That Require Nurturing Parents, Study Finds'. N.p., 2014. Web. 8 Sep. 2014.

foster families. The findings of the study are shocking. Compared to children living in a family environment, the institutionalized children had significantly stunted growth, lower IQ and levels of brain activity, and were far more likely to have social and behavioral problems.[9]

The importance of attachment

In the 1940s, researchers began to study the importance of a child developing a relationship with a primary caregiver for normal development. The development of attachment theory shed light on why institutions are harmful to children, especially babies and toddlers. There is a critical period of development in early childhood. A child who lives in an institution for the first three years of his life is at risk of permanent developmental damage as a result of the lack of family-based care. In most orphanages, young children do not experience the continuity of care they need to form a secure, lasting attachment with a caregiver.

Newborn babies are completely dependent on their parents to provide for all their needs. When a baby cries because she is hungry and the mother responds by feeding her, the baby learns to trust the mother. As this cycle is repeated thousands of times in a young child's life, the baby forms a secure attachment to her mother and father. This early attachment is critical.

The child's first attachment to their primary caregiver, usually their mother, is considered a blueprint for all later emotional attachments.[10] From this first relationship, children learn how to love and to be loved. The ability to trust and love is essential to all relationships. The absence of this early bond puts children at a considerable risk for anxiety and depression and makes it much more difficult for children to build future relationships.

It is almost always impossible for baby homes to provide ongoing and meaningful contact between a child and a consistent caregiver. In most orphanages, there is a high ratio of children to staff and the paid caregivers are not able to respond consistently to babies' needs. Furthermore, many orphanages rely on volunteers to help feed, bathe and care for babies and toddlers. This deprives

---

9   Save the Children. *Keeping Children Out Of Harmful Institutions.* London: Save the Children, 2009. Print.

10   Browne, Kevin. *The Risk Of Harm To Young Children In Institutional Care.* London: Save the Children UK, 2009. Print.

young children of the opportunity to form a secure attachment with a caregiver and sets them up for a lifetime of emotional pain.

When my husband and I (Sara) first traveled to Uganda, we spent one day at a babies' home that is known internationally for rescuing abandoned babies. This organization is considered to be the best children's home in Uganda. The facility is clean, organized and well-equipped to provide for children's physical needs.

As volunteers, we spent the day working alongside two women who were assigned to care for twelve babies up to six months of age. In order to care for such a large number of infants, the women followed a rigid schedule. In the morning, the women brought the babies from their cribs outside to lay on a blanket in the shade. They prepared bottles and fed the babies one or two at a time, propping the older babies on pillows. Then they gave the babies baths and dressed them in clean clothes. When this routine was finished two hours later, they put clean sheets on the babies' beds, swaddled them and put them in their cribs, where they would sleep for several hours. Throughout the day and night, the babies were fed and changed on a schedule.

While the babies' physical needs are met and the orphanage is doing some things that were developmentally appropriate – such as swaddling the babies for sleep – the babies are deprived of the opportunity to form a meaningful relationship with a consistent caregiver. Though the home provides some continuity of care for the first three years, this relationship is broken when the child turns three and is placed with older children.

Furthermore, as it would be impossible for two women to meet even the physical needs of twelve babies or toddlers, the organization relies on volunteers for help. Some volunteers spend one day while others stay for a few months. This means that many of the babies are cared for by new and different people almost every day. As these children are unable to form a secure attachment to a primary caregiver, which is critical to development, they are likely to face future problems.

In our time in Uganda, we visited more than a dozen children's homes. At every orphanage, my husband and I were approached by young children desperate for attention and affection. Although such behavior may initially seem to be an expression of friendliness, it is actually a symptom of a significant attachment problem. A young child who has a secure attachment to their parents or other caregiver is more likely to be cautious, even fearful of strangers, rather than seeking to touch them.

Violence, Exploitation and Trafficking

Children who live in institutions are at significant risk of exploitation. They are vulnerable to neglect, violence and abuse, which often go unreported. Children living in institutions are often isolated and powerless to defend themselves. Children who have attachment problems are emotionally vulnerable and at risk of sexual abuse, as their craving for attention makes them obvious targets of exploitation.

Although it is difficult to assess abuse and violence in institutions, various studies around the world suggest abuse is widespread, affecting boys and girls of all ages. Since children growing up in orphanages are isolated and lack consistent caregivers who might notice the signs of abuse, children can be abused without much consequence to the offenders. Children may be violated through systematic rape and other forms of sexual abuse; physical harm such as beatings and torture; and psychological harm including isolation, the denial of affection and humiliating discipline. Children with disabilities are at increased risk of being abused.[11] Studies in Eastern Europe and Asia have found that between one third and two thirds of children living in orphanages were victims of beatings and other types of physical abuse.[12] A survey of children living in institutions in Romania found that one in five girls reported being blackmailed into sexual activity, and one in twenty reported being raped.[13]

Children who are living in institutional care are also at risk of being trafficked for child slavery, prostitution or international adoption.

Consider how vulnerable children are exploited by institutions in Nepal. There was a civil war in Nepal from 1996 to 2006. While the war claimed more than twelve thousand lives, the resulting economic devastation has destroyed hundreds of thousands more. Child traffickers prey on families in rural villages who are struggling to afford school fees. The traffickers promise to place the

---

11   Save the Children. *Keeping Children Out Of Harmful Institutions.* London: Save the Children, 2009. Print.

12   ibid.

13   ibid.

children in orphanages where they will receive a good education. The traffickers demand large sums of money from the families and remove the children from their villages.

While there are some orphanages in Nepal that provide needed care to children in crisis, the majority exploit children for profit. As in other developing countries, 85 per cent of the children living in orphanages in Nepal have at least one surviving parent. There are approximately 800 orphanages in Nepal. More than 80 per cent of these orphanages are located in Kathmandu Valley and other tourist destinations. Corrupt orphanage owners use vulnerable children, especially children with special needs, to extract huge donations from volunteers and tourists. These donations rarely benefit the children, who are victims of abuse and neglect. Some children are enslaved as street beggars and domestic servants.[14] When Nepal was open for international adoption, some children were exploited through international adoption. Child traffickers would falsify the children's documents, declaring them to be orphans and making them available for adoption.[15]

What happens when institutionalized children grow up?

Orphanages are not able to provide children with the sense of identity and social connection found in family and community. Likewise, children are not given the life skills and experiences they need to integrate back into their communities. These challenges make the transition from living in the orphanage to living independently difficult.

Many of the orphanages we visited in Uganda claimed to be developing the next generation of leaders for the country. In contrast, experts in child development argue 'institutional care is creating "lost generations" of young people who are unable to participate fully in society.'[16]

Children who grow up in orphanages struggle with lasting developmental problems and trauma. They typically have lower levels of literacy. Even children who are successful in secondary

---

14   Pattisson, Pete. 'Nepal's Bogus Orphan Trade Fueled By Rise In "Voluntourism".' *The Guardian* 2014. Web. 28 May. 2014.

15   Nextgenerationnepal.com. 'The Challenge'. 2014. Web. 8 Sep. 2014.

16   Save the Children. *Keeping Children Out Of Harmful Institutions*. London: Save the Children, 2009. Print.

school may have no chance to continue their education after leaving care. Where care institutions are cut off from communities, children are unable to develop social networks essential for later in life. After years following a structured routine in which they had little or no choice, young people may lack the judgment to navigate an independent life. Young adults who grew up in institutions are especially vulnerable to exploitation as they are accustomed to following instructions without question. They often lack basic life skills and struggle to find work and to develop relationships.

Research in Russia has shown that one in three children who leave residential care becomes homeless; one in five ends up with a criminal record and one in ten commits suicide.[17] Within one year of leaving the orphanage, often between the ages of 15 and 18, half of the children are involved in crime or prostitution.[18]

Orphanages have been called an outdated export. We have stopped building and supporting children's homes in the United States and the United Kingdom. Awareness of the harm caused by institutional care has led to the growth of alternatives. Foster families care for children in our communities who are separated from their parents until they can be reunited with their biological families or placed in adoptive families.

Is supporting orphanages the best response to the orphan crisis?

The research is overwhelmingly clear: long-term institutional care is harmful to children. While orphanages may provide lifesaving shelter during a crisis, children need the love and security provided by families. If we believe God designed children to grow up in families, this should hardly be surprising. But despite the evidence, the number of institutions and the children living in institutional care continues to grow across much of the developing world.

We've learned that children are living in institutions because of brokenness, injustice – and most significantly – poverty. Children are, by and large, not living in orphanages because they lack a family. But is institutional care an appropriate and effective response to poverty?

Research answering this question has consistently found that putting children in institutional care is expensive, ineffective and harmful. When orphanages are built in communities facing severe

17   ibid.

18   Orphanoutreach.org. 'Reach Out To Orphans'. 2014. Web. 8 Sep. 2014.

economic stress, children are pushed out of poor households to fill the orphanages. If the orphanages were not there, the children would have remained with their families and in their communities. According to missions expert Steve Saint:

> Often charity to help the poor attracts more people into poverty. One example I have noticed takes place when North Americans try to care for the needs of orphans in cultures different from our own. If you build really nice orphanages and provide great food and a great education, lots of children in those places become orphans.[19]

Orphanages are not just bad for children. They are expensive. Institutional care is one of the most costly ways of looking after vulnerable children. Residential care facilities require upkeep: staff must be paid, buildings maintained, food prepared, and services provided. Actual costs vary, but comparisons consistently demonstrate that many children can be supported in family care for the cost of keeping one child in an orphanage.

In Romania, the World Bank calculated that institutional care cost between $201 and $280 per month, per child. Professional foster care would cost $91 per month, per child. Adoption and family reunification would cost, on average, $19 per child.

A cost comparison in east and central Africa by Save the Children UK found that orphanage care was ten times more expensive than community-based care. Another study in Tanzania found that the annual cost for one child in residential care is more than $1,000, about six times the cost of supporting a child in foster care. A study in South Africa found residential care to be up to six times more expensive than providing care for children living in vulnerable families.

Let's put these statistics in perspective. It costs about $100,000 to care for fifty children in an orphanage for a year. This means approximately $2,000 per child. If we tried to care for all of the world's 151 million orphans in institutions it would cost over 300 billion dollars annually. The United States' development budget is only $20 billion a year. Caring for the world's orphaned and vulnerable children in institutions is not sustainable. Furthermore, the resources currently used to support orphanages could go much further if used to fight poverty and support community- and family-based care for children.[20]

---

19 Saint, Steve. 'Projecting Poverty Where It Doesn't Exist.' *Mission Frontiers* 2011. Web. 4 Sep. 2012.
20 'Families, Not Orphanages.' *Better Care Network*, 2010. Print.

If orphanages are harmful to children and very expensive compared to the alternatives, why do governments as well as Christian ministries, churches and families continue to support institutional orphan care?

The Orphan Economy

Many of the organizations and individuals involved in orphan care are opposed to change. Missionaries, caregivers and staff rely on the institutional model for their own livelihood. In the same way, the ministries and organizations running orphanages depend on the orphan economy.[21]

Orphanages provide a vital fundraising model for many non-profit and faith-based organizations. As a result, people within the orphan care industry are opposed to change. Once an orphanage is built it becomes a fixed resource that needs upkeep, even when alternatives to care for vulnerable children are more cost effective. The orphanage becomes like a business that must attract donations in order to survive. Many orphanages depend on income from child sponsorship. Some orphanages keep the children living in horrible conditions to attract generous donations from well-meaning visitors. Others provide children for international adoption in exchange for financial support or donations from adoption agencies or adoptive families.

I (Amanda) recently visited an orphanage in DRC run by Americans for the purpose of international adoption. Nearly all of the children – 55 of 58 – had been referred to American and Canadian families for international adoption. The orphanage and adoption agency required each adoptive family to pay $300 per month as an orphan care fee. As a result, the orphanage was generating approximately $16,000 per month in a place where middle class professionals earn less than $100 a month. Very little of this made it to the children. The facility was run down. The children ate one meal a day and slept on floors. There were no diapers for the babies and toddlers. When some birth families learned about the permanency of international adoption, they returned to take their children home. Reluctant to lose that income, the orphanage staff refused to release the children.

---

21 Orphan Economy is a term first used by Mark Riley to describe how institutions become dependent on donations and lose focus on what is best for children. Riley, Mark. 'Institutionalized Genocide And The Orphan Economy'. Rileys in Uganda 2010. Web. 5 Feb. 2012.

The danger is that institutions lose focus on what is in the best interest of children and are driven by what is best for the institution.[22] When orphanages depend on income from sponsorship of the children living in the institution, they have no incentive to reunite children with their biological families. When orphanages depend on funds from international adoption, they have no incentive to place children for domestic adoption. When orphanages are focused on filling beds, they are less likely to use funds to hire social workers who can investigate and reunite children with their families. These perverse incentives often keep children separated from their families or lead to corruption in international adoption practices.

Governments see a simple solution

After a natural disaster or in response to the AIDS epidemic, orphanages seem like the easiest and most practical way to support orphaned and vulnerable children. Governments looking for simple solutions to what seems like an overwhelming problem see supporting institutions as the most straightforward option. Supporting family-based care takes more time to generate results. Governments struggle to build the infrastructure necessary to support family-based services, such as foster care and domestic adoption. Institutional care provides a relatively easy, visible and contained solution to the problem of orphaned and abandoned children.

In too many countries, the government is unwilling to make a political and financial commitment to invest in the most vulnerable children. If governments were willing to develop programs that would increase the capacity of families to care for and protect their own children, fewer children would be abandoned into institutions. But the poorest children and families have no voice, and many governments are unwilling to invest. Building institutions is a way of sweeping out of sight the poorest and most marginalized children.

The media embraces a human interest story

In the aftermath of the December 2004 tsunami in Aceh, Indonesia, it was widely feared that an exceptionally high number of children had become separated from their families and that many had lost

---

22   Save the Children. *Institutional Care – The Last Resort*. London: Save the Children, 2009. Print.

one or both parents. The media embraced this human interest story, misreporting tens or even hundreds of thousands of 'tsunami orphans.' The Indonesian government, with assistance from international donors, invested in institutional care.

In the years following the tsunami, children's homes received more than $5.43 million in international aid. But the majority of the children affected by the tsunami had not lost their parents. Nearly all – more than 97 per cent - of the 'tsunami orphans' living in institutional care were placed there by their own families. The families, who were no longer able to afford school fees due to poverty exacerbated by the tsunami, placed the children in orphanages in an effort to provide an education. If governments and international donors had been willing to direct assistance to families and communities, the children could have remained with their families.[23]

Charitable giving is driven by results

Even when governments prioritize family-based care, donors may prefer to support institutions that can easily demonstrate results. Many institutions use the concept of a children's village, with small groups of children living together with a fairly consistent caregiver. The houses are clustered together in a landscaped setting and the villages often include a medical clinic, church and primary school. These villages are attractive to overseas donors, yet they still perpetuate many of the negative aspects of institutional care. The children living in these villages are easily recognized as orphans while also being perceived as privileged by the surrounding community. These institutions often separate children from their families and make it difficult for children to transition to adulthood in the community.

Like many countries in Africa, Zimbabwe has been severely affected by HIV and AIDS. As of 2004, approximately 1.2 million children had lost one or both parents to AIDS. The response of ordinary people in Zimbabwe has been remarkable and demonstrates the strength and resilience of communities. In keeping with long-held cultural values, extended families are caring for 98 per cent of the children who have been orphaned by AIDS. Many extended families have taken in AIDS orphans despite their own poverty.

---

23   Save the Children. *Keeping Children Out Of Harmful Institutions*. London: Save the Children, 2009. Print.

In 1994, the government of Zimbabwe developed a national orphan care policy that supported traditional methods of care and discouraged forms of care that removed children from their communities and culture. The policy recommended foster care and adoption for children who could not remain in their communities and discouraged institutional care.

Despite government policy to the contrary, the number of institutions and the rate of children living in institutional care is increasing. The unfolding of the AIDS epidemic and the resulting orphan crisis in Africa has attracted media attention and charitable giving from overseas. Many Christian churches and organizations saw the orphan crisis as an emergency and focused on the construction of orphanages. Of the 25 orphanages established in Zimbabwe between 1994 and 2004, 85 per cent were built by a Christian faith-based organization. This has been a well-intentioned but misguided effort that has largely ignored the tradition of the extended family in Africa caring for orphaned children.

Although the influx of AIDS orphans has placed a significant burden on the traditional system, a more effective strategy would have provided support to communities and families caring for orphans, rather than taking orphaned children away from their communities and families.[24]

Why do Christian churches and families support orphanages?

Like many governments and international organizations, Christian families and churches often see supporting an orphanage as the easiest and most practical way to care for orphans. In the book *Orphanology*, Tony Merida and Rich Morton argue that supporting orphanages is at the heart of how Christians should respond to the orphan crisis: 'orphan ministry means being engaged in institutional orphan care.'[25] Christian families and churches are unaware of the potential harm that can be caused by the inappropriate use of institutional care. We fail to understand the reasons why children are placed in institutions. We do not realize

---

24   UNICEF and Zimbabwe Ministry of Public Service, Labour and Social Welfare. *Children In Residential Care: The Zimbabwean Experience.* UNICEF, 2004. Print.

25   Merida, Tony, and Rick Morton. *Orphanology.* 1st ed. Birmingham, AL: New Hope Publishers, 2011. Print.

that by supporting orphanages, we divert resources away from families, communities and local churches that could provide care to vulnerable and orphaned children.

Sometimes we are looking for a simple, convenient way to get involved in a messy problem. We are doing what is easy rather than what is in the best interest of children. Providing support to families, communities and local churches to encourage and equip them to care for orphans is much more difficult than giving donations and sending short-term mission teams to an orphanage.

We may be blinded by our own materialism: we would rather see smiling children living in a brightly painted orphanage than children living with a foster family in humble surroundings in Africa, Asia or Latin America. We elevate children's obvious physical needs over their deeper emotional and spiritual needs. We believe that it is better to feed, clothe and educate a child than to leave a child with a poor family. We are uncomfortable seeing children growing up in poverty, and so we build orphanages that provide a higher standard of living.

In this chapter, we've learned that growing up in an orphanage is harmful to children and that orphanages separate children from their families and communities. We have learned that most children are placed in orphanages due to poverty and that committing resources to institutions is not a solution to poverty. We have learned that institutions are more expensive and less effective than family and community-based care for children.

As Christians who understand God's heart for the fatherless, we have a responsibility to do orphan care differently. Building and supporting orphanages is a well-intentioned but misguided response to the orphan crisis. As Christians, we know God intends for children to grow up with a mother and a father. We need to shift our priorities from supporting institutions to supporting families.

We have learned that most children are placed in orphanages due to poverty. Instead of caring for children in orphanages, we can empower vulnerable families to prevent their breakdown. We've learned that long-term institutional care is harmful to children. We can use our resources to help orphanages provide good quality care for children in a crisis, while also reuniting children with their families and encouraging local adoption. At the same time we can advocate and invest in foster care as an alternative to institutional care.

Questions for Discussion and Reflection

1. How many children worldwide are living in orphanages? Why are children placed in institutional care?

2. What are the harmful impacts of institutional care? What impact does growing up in an orphanage have on children of different ages?

3. Is building and supporting orphanages an effective response to poverty?

4. Why do Christian families, churches and organizations continue to support orphanages? What do you think about the idea of the 'orphan economy'?

5. Are good intentions enough?

To Visit Orphans

*Religion that is pure and undefiled before God,
the Father, is this: to visit orphans and widows
in their affliction and to keep oneself unstained
from the world.*
(James 1:27)

What is wrong with visiting orphans?

Rebecca first travelled to Ghana, West Africa in 2011 just after graduating from high school. She spent three months volunteering with an organization in the Kumansi area that worked with vulnerable children, many of whom were affected by HIV. Rebecca remembers her experience: 'during my stay I lived with a local host family, ran a sexual assault prevention program, taught at a free summer school, worked in orphanages, sought sponsorship for HIV positive children, filmed, photographed and produced my own documentary, and most of all, fell in love with Africa.'[1]

Over the last three years, Rebecca has travelled back and forth from her home in Chicago to Ghana. In January 2014 she moved 'permanently and indefinitely' to Ghana to establish an education center.

---

1   Kuntz, Rebecca. 'Interview About Orphan Care And Volunteers In Orphanages In Ghana'. 2014. In person

Although Rebecca is quick to acknowledge she is not an expert, she has a unique perspective on the orphanage system in Ghana. When a new orphanage is set up, the Ghanaian or expat founders will get children from the community 'by convincing families that the orphanage can provide better than they can.' Poor families place their children in an orphanage hoping for the best, but often the kids end up exploited:

> The orphanage will have volunteers and tourists come through the orphanage to see how desperately they need funds. The kids are kept in unsanitary and unsafe conditions to appeal for more donations. The visitors don't know the proper questions to ask, the accreditation of the orphanage, the background of the kids, or where the money will be going. They hand over the donation and it goes directly into the pocket of the director.

Rebecca has also encountered situations where pastors will gather children in a community, set up a so-called 'orphanage,' and then appeal to churches abroad for funds. The American or European Christians want to do their part in caring for orphans, and so make generous donations without asking appropriate questions or holding the local leaders accountable.

Ghana is a stable African country where the economy is growing and English is the national language. As a result, Ghana is a popular destination for volunteers and short-term mission trips. Based on her experience, Rebecca estimates that 75 per cent of the volunteers travel to Ghana to work in orphanages, typically for less than a month. Rebecca, who was once a volunteer in an orphanage, describes the system and its impact on children:

> Volunteers typically work at private orphanages and make a large donation in order to work there. The volunteers don't have to get a background check or show a resume or anything, they can walk in. The kids get attached to the volunteers, but the volunteers are gone a few weeks later. It's traumatic.

Rebecca now believes the system is designed to meet the needs of the visitor, not the needs of the children. Short-term missionaries feel like they are making a difference, but they are actually causing harm:

> The volunteers buy candy, toys and sweets for the kids, which messes up their diets and nutrition. It then becomes expected

that every volunteer give the children a sweet. I've visited places where the kid's teeth are literally rotting out because of lollipops and ice cream from volunteers and lack of dental hygiene. These in-and-out trips are causing so much harm. Most of the time, the volunteers never see or understand the harm they are causing. The local leaders and long-term missionaries see the devastation and aftermath of it all.

A Tidal Wave

In recent years, the number of Evangelical Christians going on short-term mission (STM) trips has increased dramatically. By definition, a 'short-term missionary' is someone who spends between one week and two years on a mission trip. In 1998, there were 450,000 Americans who went on STM trips. As of 2003, this number grew to one million. By 2006, more than 2.2 million American short-term missionaries flooded the world. Nearly one in four American adults who claim to be an evangelical Christian has participated in an STM trip.[2]

The growth in Christian STM trips is part of a larger trend of volunteer tourism, often called voluntourism. Growing numbers of tourists want to see the world and make a difference at the same time. Ecotourism and cultural tourism, both closely related to voluntourism, are the fastest growing segments of the global travel industry.[3]

As Americans and Europeans are more globally aware, many tourists are seeking a meaningful, authentic experience. Instead of spending a week or two at a resort, many travelers are interested in discovering and giving back to the communities they visit. There is an overwhelming perception that many communities around the world need the help of short-term missionaries and volunteers. A recent survey of people who participated in voluntourism found that only 1 per cent of people thought volunteers had an overall negative impact on people and that communities would be better off without their help.[4] Voluntourists and short-term missionaries share a genuine desire to help and believe they can make a difference in a short period of time.

---

2   Corbett, Steve, and Brian Fikkert. *When Helping Hurts*. 1st ed. Chicago, IL: Moody Publishers, 2009. Print.

3   McGray, Douglas. 'The Rise In Voluntourism'. *Travel and Leisure* 2014. Web. 16 Feb. 2012.

4   GeckoGo. 'Volunteer Travel Insights'. N.p., 2009. Web. 16 Feb. 2012.

What do people do on mission trips?

Before modern air travel made the farthest corners of the earth accessible to anyone with money and a few days to spare, the decision to become a missionary was life-changing and permanent. Missionaries would have to raise a small fortune to sail to Africa or Asia and would often never return.

Now millions of Christians every year travel all over the world on STM trips. Most volunteers want a life-changing experience but can only take a week or two away from their life at home. More than half of the 2.2 million short-term missionaries went on trips that were less than two weeks long.[5] The average length of a trip is just eight days.[6]

Visitors to developing countries typically arrive with abundant resources, limited time, and a perception that they need to accomplish something tangible. Teams often focus on building projects, providing medical care, doing evangelism, or working with children. When short-term missionaries return, however, they rarely talk about what they accomplished. They share what they learned and how the experience changed their life.

Why do Christians go on mission trips?

Christians believe in missions because Jesus tells us to 'go therefore and make disciples of all nations' (Matt. 28:19). These are Jesus' final words to His disciples after His resurrection, before He ascends into heaven. From Genesis to Revelation, the Bible says we are blessed to be a blessing. We are called to proclaim and incarnate the Gospel. Incarnational ministry means more than telling people about Jesus. According to British missiologist Krish Kandiah, 'when Christ incarnated the Gospel for us, he met the spiritual, physical, social and emotional needs of those he ministered to.'[7]

While few Christians make overseas missions their life's work, many feel called to go on a mission trip to proclaim the gospel and serve the poor. There is a deeply held belief that STM teams can meet profound needs, especially in the developing world. There is also evidence that mission trips are life-changing for participants. Many go on these service adventures seeking spiritual and personal growth.

---

5   Corbett, Steve, and Brian Fikkert. *When Helping Hurts*. 1st ed. Chicago, IL: Moody Publishers, 2009. Print.

6   Salmon, Jacqueline L. 'Churches Retool Mission Trips'. *Washington Post*. 4 Jul. 2008.

7   Kandiah, Krish. 'Mission Priorities, Mark Dever And Lausanne'. KrishK 2010. Web. 15 Sep. 2012.

The Bible passages most commonly referenced as reasons why Christians are called to go on short-term mission trips are Luke 9 and 10. In Luke 9, Jesus sends out the twelve disciples to 'proclaim the kingdom of God and to heal,' (Luke 9:2). Jesus gives the disciples two jobs. First, the disciples are to proclaim the kingdom of God, to share the gospel or good news that Jesus is the King. Second, the disciples are to demonstrate the coming of the kingdom of God by caring for people's physical needs. By healing the sick and feeding the hungry, they reveal that the coming of God's kingdom is good news.

In Luke 10, Jesus sends out seventy-two missionaries into the towns where He is about to go. Jesus says the 'harvest is plentiful but the laborers are few,' (Luke 10:2) and commands them to pray for more laborers. Like the disciples, these missionaries are called to proclaim the gospel and heal the sick. Many believe these passages are examples of the first short-term mission trips and that Christians today should follow the example of Jesus' disciples.

As evangelical Christians have awoken to God's heart for the fatherless, there has been a growing movement to send short-term mission teams specifically to care for orphans. Supporters of this type of mission trip say the Bible is clear: Christians are called 'to visit orphans and widows in their affliction' (James 1:27). Like a doctor visiting a patient, the purpose of visiting orphans is to see their needs and to respond with compassion. Increasingly, churches, ministries and adoption agencies send teams of volunteers to 'be love' and provide care for children living in orphanages.

Many Christians believe sincerely that there are overwhelming needs in the developing world that STM teams can meet. It is true there are profound needs in many parts of the developing world. As American or European Christians, we have resources that we believe can be used to meet these needs. When we understand how much we have been given, we feel a responsibility to give generously or to do something to make a difference.

Awareness of the AIDS epidemic, which has orphaned more than 12 million children in Africa, has fueled a growing interest in orphan care. Many Christians have responded to the AIDS epidemic by building or supporting orphanages. Likewise, many Christians believe that children living in orphanages desperately need the love and care that can be offered by a visiting missionary. Visiting Orphans is a Christian organization that partners with churches and adoption agencies to lead mission trips to orphanages around the world. A blog written by Amanda Lawrence, the former Executive

Director of Visiting Orphans, shared her heart: 'it burdens us as we know how much these children need each one of us.'[8]

Perhaps most significantly, Christians believe the purpose of short-term mission trip is to change the heart, perspective, values, and life of the person who goes.[9] Research has found that the majority of those who participate in a short-term mission believe the trip changed their life in some way. The most common areas of personal growth include: becoming more aware of other people's struggles (25 per cent), learning more about poverty, justice, or the world (16 per cent), increasing compassion (11 per cent), deepening or enriching their faith (9 per cent), broadening their spiritual understanding (9 per cent), and boosting their financial generosity (5 per cent).[10] Others said their short-term mission experience helped them feel more fulfilled, become more grateful, develop new friends, and pray more. Some studies, however, suggest that the 'life-changing' effects of mission trips may be short-lived. As the number of American short-term missionaries has exploded, the number of long-term missionaries, who go abroad from several years to a lifetime, has fallen.[11]

We are not throwing stones

I (Sara) was a brand new Christian when I went on my first mission trip as a sixteen-year-old high school student. My first experience actually studying the Bible and worshiping with other Christians was under the stars in Mexico, where a friend invited me to go on a mission trip for spring break. In Mexico – as I played with poor children and soaked in the words of Paul to the Romans – I became a disciple. I realized that following Jesus would cost me everything.

This week among poor children in Mexico changed my life. I am quite certain, however, that it did not change theirs. Not long after the candy wrappers blew away in the wind, when the new soccer balls and freshly painted walls were covered with mud, these children and their communities were left in the dust.

As we write about this topic, we know many of our readers will be challenged or even offended. If you are like us, your life

8   Lawrence, Amanda. 'Enter Into His Labor'. *Visiting Orphans* 2011. Web. 22 Feb. 2012.
9   Wright, Jamie. 'Sorry, Poor People, It's Not About You'. *Jamie the Very Worst Missionary* 2011. Web. 15 Sep. 2012.
10   Weber, Jeremy. 'Short-Term Missions'. *Wheaton Magazine*. Spring 2013. Web. 4 Sep. 2014.
11   ibid.

has been changed by an experience traveling, serving or living in another culture. I (Sara) have participated in STM trips to Mexico, Guatemala and Argentina. I spent time researching and writing in more than a dozen countries in Europe, Asia and Africa. When our family adopted our daughter Gabrielle, we spent three months in Uganda. I have lived and worked as a social entrepreneur in London. These experiences have informed my view of the world and shape my everyday life.

God spoke to me when I (Amanda) participated in a STM trip to Mexico. Witnessing the sacrifices and lifestyle choices of life-long missionaries and their families showed me a deeper side of Christianity that I had yet to see in my own life. This life looked like what Jesus was talking about when He described what it means to be a Christian. Since then, we've travelled all over East Africa and have lived in Rwanda for over a year, and these experiences have taught me more than years of formal higher education.

Nevertheless, we believe something has gone wrong. Millions of people are soliciting billions of dollars each year to do something not for others, but for themselves. We have good intentions, but we do not understand the impact of our actions. This is especially true for mission trips that send teams to orphanages in the developing world.

While we do not want to fuel controversy, we hope our readers will consider seriously the impact of STM trips on vulnerable children, families and communities. We believe it is possible for short-term missionaries to make a lasting difference, and we will address this in chapter 10. The focus of the rest of this chapter, however, will be on understanding why short-term mission trips to orphanages can be harmful to the orphans we're called to help.

Counting the Cost

Here is the staggering truth: Americans spend upwards of 2.2 billion dollars on short-term missions every year.[12]

Consider a typical mission trip where a group of students travel to Africa to spend two weeks volunteering at an orphanage. The cost per participant is approximately $3,500. The group of 16 teenagers and 4 adults will spend $70,000 on the adventure. On the trip, the students will play sports with the older kids in the orphanage. They will hold

---

12   Livermore, David A. *Serving With Eyes Wide Open*. 1st ed. Grand Rapids, Mich.: Baker Books, 2006. Print.

babies and play games with the young children. They will spend one or two afternoons doing some type of evangelism in the community. They will paint a few walls and build a bathroom. They will spend almost half of their time traveling and visiting tourist sites.

But how far could $70,000 go in a country where millions of people live on less than $2 a day?

The cost of the mission trip likely represents half of the orphanage's annual operating budget. These resources could be used to provide better care for the children by hiring more staff to lower the caregiver to child ratio, or by providing more nutritious food and medical care for the children.

More importantly, these resources could be used to help get children out of orphanages. The $70,000 could provide approximately 100 life-changing microenterprise loans to help poor families start a small business that would allow them to provide for their children. Or it could pay the annual salaries of fifty far more effective indigenous workers, such as social workers to support vulnerable families and therapists to care for children with special needs. When we compare the impact of the mission trip with what impact the same resources could have in a community, it is hard to justify the cost of short-term mission trips as wise stewardship.

Harming local communities and churches

It's not just that our resources could do more good if they were spent on reducing poverty, supporting vulnerable families or planting churches. Often short-term mission trips are harmful to the communities they visit.

Taking work from local people

Visiting missionaries and volunteers almost always do work that could be done – often better and cheaper – by local people. There is no shortage of manual labor in the developing world. When volunteers are willing to pay for the opportunity to paint walls or build houses, they are taking jobs away from local people who need them. Likewise, when short-term missionaries work with children in orphanages or schools, they are taking jobs away from local teachers and caregivers.

The same is true of sending teams to provide medical care in the developing world. While there are crisis situations where specially trained doctors and nurses have an essential role to play, many medical mission trips are costly compared to their impact. The cost to send a team of American doctors, nurses, and therapists overseas could pay the salaries of many underemployed medical professionals in the developing world.

Visiting missionaries can have an important role to play in encouraging and equipping local churches and communities. But much of the time, short-term missionaries do not consider whether someone from the local community could do what they are doing.

Disempowering the local church

Some short-term missionaries do not partner with local, indigenous churches. Teams often go alone or partner with orphanages or ministries led by Americans or Europeans. We underestimate the impact of failing to come alongside the local church.

Indigenous church leaders know the culture and needs of their community far better than visiting missionaries. If you have traveled overseas, you have probably experienced wearing, saying or doing something that did not fit the local culture. But short-term missionaries often underestimate the importance of culture and do little to prepare for the challenges of cross-cultural ministry. Without knowledge of the local culture and language, it is very difficult for visiting missionaries to do effective evangelism.

Furthermore, visiting missionaries can make ministry harder for the local church after they go home. For example, many people go on short-term mission trips to lead vacation Bible schools for children. The visitors bring lots of resources, such as toys, sports equipment and technology, as well as donations of food, clothing and shoes. All of this is intended to help the local community – and to make the VBS fun and exciting. But this has an unintended consequence. After the visiting missionaries go home, the local church is unable to offer the same resources to their communities. The kids are left with 'boring locals' the rest of the year.

When wealthy visitors are anxious to take on projects, local Christians may surrender their responsibility to be the church in their communities. Bringing in teams of volunteers from halfway around the world – whether to hold babies, play soccer with children, or paint walls – is not sustainable or reproducible. The communities we visit often have profound needs, but these needs can be met by the local church. We may have a role to play in encouraging the local church to see that God calls them to care for orphans and meet the needs of their neighbors. But as long as we come in and meet the needs from the outside, we are depriving communities of the opportunity to be who they are called to be.

Providing relief instead of development

Many short-term mission trips provide *relief* when what is needed is *development*. Relief is designed to meet immediate needs during a time of crisis. For example, in the aftermath of an earthquake, people may need emergency food, water, shelter, and medical care. On the other hand, development is designed to empower people to meet their own needs. Most short-term missionaries go to communities where providing relief instead of development will only make things worse.

Relief is easy and development is hard. It is straightforward to start a feeding program that meets the physical needs of hundreds of children facing malnutrition. It is much more complicated to address the poverty at the root of hunger – and to empower families to care for their children. As a result, short-term mission trips often focus on providing relief, such as feeding hungry children, building houses or digging wells.

With abundant resources and limited time, we want to solve problems quickly. Mission trips often focus on short-term projects, not lasting change. But when we provide services for free, we create dependence. Without realizing our impact, we do for people what they could do for themselves. Our actions strip people of their dignity and reinforce our own feelings of superiority.[13]

If a project depends on donations from overseas, it is not sustainable. Short-term missionaries often forget to think about sustainability – or to ask what happens when they go home. When visiting missionaries pour resources into projects that are not sustainable, they fail to make a lasting difference in local churches and communities. Ministries and projects that depend on donations from overseas have a high chance of hurting rather than helping.

Bringing donations

Visiting missionaries and volunteers typically bring stuff to donate to the churches, communities and orphanages they visit. These donations are intended to help meet very real needs.

---

13   Corbett, Steve, and Brian Fikkert. *When Helping Hurts.* 1st ed. Chicago, IL: Moody Publishers, 2009. Print.

The first time my husband and I visited Uganda, we brought three duffel bags – nearly 200 pounds – of stuff. We brought toys, clothes, books, diapers, art supplies, medicine, and candy. We left donations at every orphanage we visited. But we failed to consider if any of our donations would have a lasting impact. We did not stop to ask critically important questions: what impact will these donations have on the local economy? Will these donations equip the local church? Can these donations truly help the orphans we are visiting?

The truth is very little of the stuff we bring along on short-term mission trips has any lasting value. Nearly everything we put in our duffel bags could have been purchased locally. By providing these things for free, we unintentionally hurt the local economy. We did not realize that giving donations could disempower the local church. We did not understand that by giving donations to orphanages, we were supporting a system that separated children from their poor families.

Seeing poverty where it doesn't exist

When visiting a developing country for just a few weeks, we often see poverty where it doesn't exist. We think poverty is about a lack of money – about not having something. As North Americans or Europeans, we cannot imagine living like most people in Uganda, Nepal or Guatemala. We have a distorted and exaggerated perception of need that makes us unable to evaluate the poverty of others. Even when physical needs such as a lack of clean drinking water are obvious, we may be unable to see the deeper needs in a community, such as loneliness or despair.[14]

It is likewise possible to create the perception of a need where one did not exist. When we bring cell phones, computers, fancy clothes and wallets full of cash on mission trips, we create comparative poverty. People living in villages in the developing world may not have known what they were missing until we showed them.

I remember sitting with a group of women on a mission trip to rural Guatemala. I was wearing a bright pink raincoat, something these women had not seen before. They were wearing the traditional hand-woven shawls women had been wearing in Guatemala for hundreds of years. These women were fascinated with my coat,

14   Saint, Steve. 'Projecting Poverty Where It Doesn't Exist'. *Mission Frontiers* 2011. Web. 4 Sep. 2012.

asking how much it cost and where they could buy one. They did not know they wanted nor needed a raincoat until I sat with them – hoping to share the gospel – wearing a raincoat!

Supporting orphanages at the expense of families

Why do so many orphanages open their doors to visitors while at the same time acknowledging that hosting these visitors requires a lot of work? We think the answer is very simple. The orphanages know that giving visitors the opportunity to connect with orphans is a powerful fundraising tool.

Visiting Orphans is a ministry that was started by Christian adoption agency America World Adoption Association. The purpose of Visiting Orphans is to facilitate STM trips to orphanages around the world. In 2012, Visiting Orphans led more than 60 trips to orphanages in 13 countries.[15] In addition to sending teams, Visiting Orphans aims to build long-term relationships between orphanages and churches. One of the purposes of the partnership is fundraising for child sponsorship, medical care and improving the living conditions in the orphanage.

We have no doubt that the Visiting Orphans trips have had a profound influence on the hearts of those who have gone to serve. But we also have no doubt that these trips have been instrumental in helping raise thousands of dollars of financial support for orphanages all over the world – *and that is a big problem*.

Going on mission trips to visit orphanages supports a system that is ultimately harmful to children. Many STM trips focus on improving orphanages rather than emptying them. The hundreds of millions of dollars spent on trips to visit orphans could be used instead to give each child what they truly need: a family. Furthermore, visiting a child in an orphanage does nothing to solve the poverty at the root of the orphan crisis.

Exploiting orphans in order to attract generous donations

Sadly, some orphanages exploit children in order to earn money through donations or child sponsorship. We need to understand that when we visit orphanages, we may be participating in the exploitation of children. Some orphanages intentionally keep children living in horrible conditions, depriving them of food,

---

15   Amanda, Kerr. 'What Go. Be. Love. Means'. Visiting Orphans Blog 2012. Web. 26 Apr. 2014.

clothing and health care, in order to attract generous donations from visitors. Other orphanages will force children to beg on the streets or to perform in order to attract donations. Some orphanages do not require visitors to go through any sort of background check and potentially expose children to dangerous abuse.

Is visiting orphans ultimately harmful?

The Bible is clear. Christians are called to 'go' and to 'visit orphans.'

Eight million children in the world today live in orphanages. Many of these orphanages have truly appalling conditions. The things we have seen and the stories we have heard as we have researched this book have absolutely broken our hearts. Picture babies confined to cages in Haiti and children locked in crowded rooms where they face horrific sexual abuse during naptime in Democratic Republic of Congo. Imagine teenagers with special needs who have spent their entire lives in cribs in Eastern Europe.

There is absolutely a need for Christians to go to these hard places, to care for these hurting children, to shed light in the darkness – and to ultimately fight for justice for these orphans. But most STM trips to visit orphans hurt the children we're called to help.

To answer the question of whether it is good for Christians to go on mission trips to hold babies and play with children in orphanages, we have done three things. First, we have the considered research into best practices in child development. Second, we have talked with adoptive families who have seen in their own homes the impact of children growing up in orphanages visited by missionaries and volunteers. And third, we have talked with missionaries who have lived and worked with vulnerable children in the developing world.

What does the research teach us?

Elizabeth Styffe, Director of Orphan Care at Saddleback Church, is an expert in best practices in global orphan care. In a webinar for the Christian Alliance for Orphans, Elizabeth challenged Christians to ask a few key questions before planning a mission trip – especially to an orphanage. What do children living in orphanages really need? Are we in the best position to meet those needs? How can we help without hurting?

According to Elizabeth, Christians 'used to think that any kind of help was better than no help at all.' But in order to be effective in caring for orphans globally, 'we need to access all the resources God has for us.'[16] Research into child development and cross-cultural ministry can teach us how to relate to children who are growing up in difficult circumstances. Elizabeth recognizes that it is possible for Christians who go on mission trips to hurt the children we're called to help:

> If our help is not based on best practices for children there is potential harm developmentally, psychologically, relationally – and the most alarming part is there's a potential for harm for a lifetime.[17]

So what do children living in orphanages really need? Ultimately Elizabeth believes that every child needs a 'permanent, legal, safe, and loving family.'[18] In the last chapter, we learned about the importance of attachment to healthy child development. Children have a critical need for consistency and connection. Children need attention, affection and security. Children who have been orphaned or are vulnerable need special care. But are we – as short-term missionaries – in the best position to meet those needs?

Consider what a young child living in an orphanage has already endured. The child may have lost one or both parents. They may have been abused or neglected. They may have been abandoned or even left to die. Young children living in orphanages have faced difficult circumstances and this early adversity makes them vulnerable.

I remember the first time my husband and I visited an orphanage. The young children swarmed around us, pushing and shoving one another as they desperately fought for our affection. Young children in orphanages consistently display indiscriminate friendliness and an excessive need for attention. The children are likely to be one among many, fighting for attention and affection from too few caregivers. At many orphanages, the caregivers are poorly paid to do primarily domestic work. The caregivers often have little training in child development. The caregivers are not able to provide the children with the personal care or love they need to feel secure.

---

16   Styffe, Elizabeth. 'How to- help- without-hurting'. *Christian Alliance for Orphans*. 2 Jul. 2012. Webinar.

17   ibid.

18   Styffe, Elizabeth. Christian Alliance for Orphans Summit. 2012. Conference.

At many orphanages, volunteers are encouraged to love, connect and build relationships with previously neglected, abandoned and abused children. The visitors are encouraged to feed, bathe, hold, and play with the babies and toddlers. A close relationship is often formed between a missionary and a child. But after a few days or weeks, this attachment is broken when the visitor returns home. The volunteer likely feels she has made a positive contribution; however the child experiences another loss. When the next missionary visits, the child will form a new attachment, and so the cycle will continue.

Linda Richter is professor at the Human Sciences Research Council and an expert in the impact of the HIV/AIDS epidemic in Sub-Saharan Africa. In a paper investigating the rise of voluntourism in the region, Richter describes how visiting orphans puts already vulnerable children at risk of harm:

> We want to be needed – going and holding orphans meets an emotional need – and can be a life-changing experience for the volunteer. However this experience exploits children suffering from adversity as a result of poverty and HIV/AIDS.[19]

While there is insufficient research into the impact of short-term volunteers or missionaries caring for children in orphanages, there is evidence that disruptions in care are harmful to children. Studies from children in temporary or unstable foster care indicate that 'repeated disruptions in attachment are extremely disturbing for young children.'[20] Given that babies are designed to have the love and care of a mother and a father and children in orphanages have already experienced the loss of their family, this repeated cycle of attachment and loss is especially harmful.

What do adoptive parents think?

Grace House[21] is an orphanage in western Uganda surrounded by terraced hillsides and lush forest, more than 200 miles from the congested capitol city of Kampala. Grace House has long been involved in both caring for orphans and empowering the people of the nearby village to overcome poverty. The orphanage is led

---

19   Richter, L.M., and A. Norman. 'AIDS Orphan Tourism: A Threat To Young Children In Residential Care'. *Vulnerable Children and Youth Studies*. 2010. Print.

20   ibid.

21   Names have been changed for security.

by a Christian ministry that frequently invites volunteers and missionaries to serve for a few weeks or months at a time.

'I was one of those visitors to orphanages, so I know what it is like,' said Tina who adopted her daughter Ruth from Grace House in 2012. Before she traveled to Uganda to bring Ruth home, Tina was very grateful for visitors to the orphanage who would take photos and spend time with the toddler girl. She remembers, 'I liked knowing that she was special to a few of them who returned every year. But after seeing the impact first-hand, it definitely made me rethink whether sending teams to visit orphans was a good idea.'[22]

I first interviewed Tina when Ruth, who was two and a half at the time, had been home for just six weeks. She had noticed how the short-term missionaries had influenced Ruth's relationships. Ruth was shy and distant around Africans, but would seek the attention of white strangers, clinging to their legs or climbing into their arms.

'The missionaries and visitors were mostly white Americans and Europeans who came with gifts and showered her with love and affection while they were there,' Tina shared, explaining Ruth's behavior. 'The Africans were the caretakers and the authority figures. They obviously loved her very much, but were forced to spend their time cleaning, cooking and disciplining the children.'

Tina believes what her daughter experienced at the orphanage has made it more difficult for Ruth to bond securely with her new family. 'With so many loving visitors in and out of her life, Ruth now struggles with anxiety. She always needs to be reassured that Daddy is coming home from work and if Mama is out of sight, that she will be right back. She will begin growing closer to us, but then she pushes us away again, protecting herself for when we will leave her, as all of the loving white visitors before us have done.'

I interviewed Tina again after Ruth had been home for six months. The longer Ruth has been home from Uganda, the more Tina has witnessed the impact of the missionaries who visited Ruth's orphanage. 'She was a favorite among the missionaries who visited her orphanage,' Tina said, explaining how Ruth commonly puts on a show to earn the attention of strangers. She believes that for Ruth, performing to earn the attention and affection of strangers was a survival skill in the orphanage.

---

22 Anonymous. 'Interview about her daughter's experience in a Ugandan orphanage visited by short-term mission teams.' 2012. Email.

'It breaks my heart that she is in a constant state of trying to win people's approval, and even more that this comes as a result of people who I know were trying to love her the best they knew how.' Before adopting Ruth, Tina had been on numerous short-term mission trips. Reflecting on her experience, she now believes short-term mission trips to visit orphans are harmful: 'I had no idea how harmful it can be to orphans in the long run. I didn't fully understand it until I met my daughter. I kept thinking how glad I was that she had people come into her home and show her she was special – because every one of these kids needs to know they are special. But seeing the deep impact tells me that this is not the way to do it.'[23]

When we visit an orphanage for a day or a week, we may be able to be connect with a child – but we will not be there the next week. While we can meet the child's need for connection for a moment, we cannot be there consistently. Children living in orphanages do need love and attention, but short-term missionaries and volunteers are not in the best position to meet these needs. When we connect with a child in an orphanage and then leave, we may be hurting the child we are called to help.

What do long-term missionaries think?

Judy served as a missionary several years at Matu Baby Home, an orphanage in Uganda that welcomes and relies on volunteers.[24] Most volunteers stay at Matu for a few weeks or months at a time. The orphanage also invites teams to visit for a few hours or days. Judy recognizes why Christians enjoy holding babies and playing with children at an orphanage: 'I understand the feeling of "let's go give love." We feel like we are making a difference.'[25]

But Judy has also seen how children living in orphanages struggle after the visitors go home: 'I've been on the other side and I've seen the damage. We do not consider the impact on the kids.' Judy believes the cycle of attachment and loss is especially harmful to children who have already lost their families. While many teams visit orphanages with a goal of loving the children, Judy also

---

23   Anonymous. 'Follow up interview about her daughter's experience in a Ugandan orphanage visited by short-term mission teams.' 2013. Email.

24   Names have been changed for security.

25   Anonymous. 'Interview about orphan care and short-term mission trips in Uganda'. 2012. Phone.

believes that short-term visitors are not in a position to show the children what love is. 'Love should be about consistency,' but when visitors bring gifts and candy, 'the kids learn that love means "I get something."'

Tara Livesay is an adoptive mother, blogger and missionary with a passion for vulnerable mothers and children in Haiti. Tara and her family have lived in Haiti since 2006. Tara is a midwife who serves at a maternity center where pregnant women can find medical care and holistic support. Tara and her husband Troy work with Heartline, a ministry that empowers vulnerable families living in Port-au-Prince, Haiti.

How can it be that one of the poorest countries in the world is just 700 miles from the United States? To begin to understand the current situation in Haiti, it is important to learn a little about history. Haiti was once a wealthy French colony, known as the 'Jewel of the Antilles.' Located on an island between the Caribbean Sea and Atlantic Ocean, Haiti was once one of the most beautiful places on earth.

Haiti gained independence from France in 1804 as a result of a slave revolt. The last 200 years have been rife with political instability and violence. Haiti was once a lush, tropical paradise where forests covered most of the island. Over the last century, however, the Haitian people have cut down approximately 98 per cent of the trees to use for fuel for cooking. The deforestation has destroyed the ecosystem and once fertile farmland soils. Hurricanes have accelerated the soil erosion. Haiti is fast becoming a desert.

Haiti is the second poorest country in the world. Eighty per cent of the population lives in extreme poverty. In January 2010, Haiti was struck by a massive 7.0 earthquake. The earthquake has had a devastating impact on the people who were already struggling with poverty, injustice and hopelessness.

Nearly a half million Haitian children live in orphanages. According to Tara, there are 'hundreds and hundreds of orphanages.'[26] Most of these children have surviving families – and these families are typically living in abject poverty. Families often place children in orphanages hoping the children will be better off, but the opposite is often true. In a blog post about short-term mission trips to visit orphans in Haiti, Tara explains the situation:

---

26   Livesay, Tara. 'Interview About Orphan Care And Short-Term Mission Trips In Haiti.' 2012. Email.

Birth-families often place their children under the assumption and hope that their children will be fed and cared for better than they themselves could. Unfortunately that's not typically true. Show up unannounced at most orphanages and the conditions will shock you. Truly the children could have lived with greater dignity and protection from harm had they remained at home.[27]

Tara describes institutional care in Haiti as a 'broken system' and a 'corrupt business.' She feels the American church is in part to blame: 'because the American church is so willing to show up and fund orphanages, there are a lot of Haitian "Pastors" – that title is used but has little meaning – who will start an orphanage in order to have funding from America.'[28]

Because Haiti is located so close to the United States, it has become one of the most popular destinations for short-term mission trips. Many of these mission trips visit orphanages. Tara describes the situation:

Haiti is close and easy to visit from the USA. More STM trips happen here than any other country in the world. Since the earthquake teams have increased. Every week - all year long – team after team visits Haiti.[29]

As a missionary who has spent years in Haiti, Tara is frustrated with teams who fail to realize they are just 'one of thousands of STM groups that will come to Haiti this year.' She recognizes that while some teams come to 'sit and listen and learn,' others fail to think about the impact of their actions. She doesn't think groups come 'wanting to foster dependency or send a message that Haitians cannot do things for themselves,' but sadly, 'we've been doing just this. We need to realize that good intentions are often times not enough and in the end we might do more harm than good.'[30]

Burdened to help Christians help without hurting, Tara described what she is seeing in Haiti:

Since the earthquake Haiti has been inundated with new churches and missions groups ...that are seeking to help. Most of them probably have really great hearts and decent intentions. The

---

27   Livesay, Tara. 'A boat that needs rocking'. Livesay Haiti 2011. Web. 28 September 2012.

28   Livesay, Tara. 'Interview About Orphan Care And Short-Term Mission Trips In Haiti.' 2012. Email.

29   Livesay, Tara. 'Thinking Through STM.' Livesay Haiti 2012. Web. 29 September 2012.

30   ibid.

problem is that many (and I mean many) have come to build their own orphanages. That seems to be the hip thing to do right now.[31]

Tara recognizes that being against short-term missions is not a popular position, but after eight years in Haiti she has witnessed the unintentional harm caused by mission trips to visit orphans. She believes that mission trips cause 'abandonment issues to be compounded and create unhealthy children.' She has also seen first-hand how children are exploited and donations misused. When visiting missionaries donate to an orphanage, the 'donations walk out the door and into the hands of the employees or the orphanage director. Meanwhile, the kids sit with one caregiver per twenty kids and not enough to eat. It is horrible.'[32]

Good intentions are not enough

We believe in missions because the Bible calls Christians to 'go' and to 'make disciples of all nations,' (Matt. 28:19). We also believe in visiting orphans: the Bible is clear that we're called to 'visit orphans and widows,' (James 1:27). But at the same time, we're convinced that mission trips to visit orphans often harm far more than they help. We believe something needs to change.

Over the last few chapters, we've learned that good intentions are not enough. We've learned the reasons why building, supporting and visiting orphanages is not the best response to the orphan crisis. In our enthusiasm to do something about the orphan crisis, we may unintentionally hurt the orphans and vulnerable families we want to help. In the next chapter, we will look at what happens when we encourage adoption at any cost. In the second half of the book, we'll look at how God calls us to visit orphans differently – and how we can make a long-term difference even on a short-term trip.

QUESTIONS FOR DISCUSSION AND REFLECTION

1. Have you ever been on a short-term mission trip?

2. What impact did this experience have on your life? What impact did your trip have on the people you went to serve?

---

31   Livesay, Tara. 'Alleviate.' Livesay Haiti 2012. Web. 29 September 2012.

32   Livesay, Tara. 'Interview About Orphan Care And Short-Term Mission Trips In Haiti.' 2012. Email.

3. What are the risks of going on a mission trip to visit orphans?

4. What do children living in orphanages need?

5. Are visitors who volunteer at an orphanage for a few days or weeks in the best position to meet these needs?

International Adoption:
At what cost?

Amanda's Story: Coming home empty-handed

Coming from a long road of infertility, we wanted to be all in for Jesus and all in for the orphan, so long as we could get a beautiful, perfect, healthy infant.

We started the process to adopt from Democratic Republic of Congo in 2010. By the time we completed our adoption paperwork, we decided to adopt an older sibling group who were harder to place. In 2011, we said yes to a referral for a brother and sister. A few months later, we discovered the children had a big sister living at the orphanage. We said yes within days, and soon were in the process of adopting three children aged 9, 7 and 3.

The children's paperwork did not include any information about their biological family, except that the mother was unable to care for them and the father was unknown. We begged for more information and were told there was nothing. We naively accepted this, believing this was 'just Congo.' The lack of information was consistent with what we heard from other adoptive parents.

Looking back, we were drawn to the adventure and mystery of the unknown, and this contributed to our turning a blind eye to the signs of corruption. In the spring of 2012, we passed court in Democratic Republic of Congo. We became the children's legal parents, even though we had never met them or traveled to the country.

We chose our adoption agency because it was run by people who called themselves Christians and because they ran their own orphanage. At the time, we believed that meant the kids would be well-cared for, not seeing that it was a red flag for corruption. A few months after we passed court, the director of the orphanage in Kinshasa was fired due to allegations of corruption. When she fled the orphanage, our agency reported that she kidnapped three children.

No matter how many questions we asked, we never got a straight answer as to what was really going on in Kinshasa. Despite the chaos reported from other families who were in Kinshasa completing their adoptions, the agency staff acted like nothing was happening. Through it all and despite dozens of stories of corruption, the director of the agency refused to travel to Kinshasa to investigate.

Before we could bring our adopted children home to the United States, we had to apply for visas with the US Embassy in Kinshasa. In June 2012, the embassy raised questions about our visa application. The officer was concerned that the children we had adopted did not meet the legal definition of an orphan. In some ways, the investigation was a relief. We weren't crazy after all. There was something going on in Kinshasa. Our adoption agency failed to gather adequate evidence to support the story that the children were orphans. We withdrew our visa applications.

It was at this point that we began to stop and look at the red flags. We hired an independent attorney to research the children's birth family. The investigation revealed that the information the adoption agency had provided about the birth mother had been falsified. We also discovered that when the director had fled the orphanage, she had taken the three year old we were hoping to adopt. A careful review of the paperwork revealed that the birth mother of the children had the same last name as the fired orphanage director.

Fueled by a desire for the truth and a hope that maybe we were wrong, we decided to travel to Democratic Republic of Congo.

Before we were even able to unpack our luggage, we located the children's birth family. Our suspicions were true: the documents used to support the adoption were fraudulent.

The children were the nieces and nephew of the fired orphanage director. The director was using the orphanage and adoption agency to have children from her extended family placed for international adoption. The director, who had placed her own child for adoption, saw this as an opportunity to give these children a better life. The extended family expected to maintain contact with the children. They believed they would benefit from having American children. Their idea of adoption was nothing like ours.

The children were not orphans in any sense of the word. I recently traveled back to Kinshasa to meet the children, who live with their mother, aunts, grandmother, siblings, and cousins. They are attending school. I had lunch with the children and their extended family. With two living and involved parents and a family who love them, they were not the abandoned and orphaned children we sought to adopt.

Because the documents were fraudulent – and because the children were not orphans in need of a new family – we returned to the United States empty-handed. I never in a million years would have guessed that we would be defrauded by our Christian adoption agency. We now believe the adoption agency was aware of and involved in the fraud and corruption in our failed adoption – and dozens of others. Nevertheless, the agency has not been held accountable and has refused to refund any of the fees we paid.

A prominent adoption attorney in Kinshasa boldly told me, 'The line between child trafficking and adoption is very, very thin.' But we didn't get into adoption to traffic children into the US. We didn't want to be camp counselors or run a boarding school for children from DRC. We wanted to be parents. A child who has parents doesn't need new, wealthier parents.

Our desire to adopt a child who was healthy and well-adjusted was certainly part of the problem. After the fact, we asked ourselves, why were those kids so healthy? Is it because they came from a family who loved them and was caring for them? It's even worse that this is what we wanted: we wanted perfectly healthy, beautiful, happy, well-adjusted kids. But that's not generally what we should be seeking when we want to care for an orphan. There is no such thing. How could there be?

We walked away from this experience wondering why Christians are not adopting the street kids, the sick kids, the kids with truly no one to care for them. Why aren't they being adopted at the same rate as the healthy babies? Why are there waiting lists for healthy babies if there are 151 million orphans?

How did we get here?

We have never met an adoptive family that began the heart-wrenching, time-consuming and expensive process of adoption with a desire to take a child from another family. We all have good intentions. We believe there is an orphan crisis and millions of children who need families, children who would otherwise grow up on the streets or in horrible orphanages. But something is going wrong. Some Christians are unwilling to open their eyes to the truth that corruption is widespread in many countries popular for international adoption. A few believe so passionately that international adoption is the answer to the orphan crisis that they are pursuing adoption *at any cost* – even at the cost of destroying families in the developing world.

In this chapter, we will take a serious look at corruption in adoption. None of the popular books about adoption from a Christian perspective considers this issue. Adoption agencies don't tell you about corruption and fraud in their glossy brochures and websites full of smiling children. And no one wants to believe that corruption in adoption is anything but rare. The truth is hard and often heart-breaking.

But if we take God's word seriously, we need to understand what is at stake. Many Christians are following God's heart for the fatherless and making the decision to adopt. As Christians, we have a responsibility to seek the truth so that we can 'bring justice to the fatherless' (Isa. 1:17). There are millions of children who have been orphaned and abandoned and who desperately need new families. Yet on a worldwide scale, thousands of children are being adopted who are not in need of adoption.

Adoption can be a miracle

As Christians, we believe children are designed to grow up in families where loving parents protect and provide. People all over the world agree that children need the love and care provided by families. International adoption is a miracle for children who genuinely need it.

But taking a child from a desperately poor mother who fears there is no other way for the child to survive is exploiting the poor. In too many countries, poverty leads desperate families to place their children in orphanages or for adoption. Vulnerable families are at risk of being exploited by a system of international adoption that lacks safeguards against corruption.

How do we know whether a child is genuinely in need of international adoption? And if a child is in need of international adoption, how do we match the child with a forever family? How we answer these questions is critically important. Most corruption in international adoption is related to these two questions: who can adopt and who can be adopted.

Countries that have ethical international adoption programs have careful regulations regarding who can adopt and who can be adopted. The government works diligently to ensure the children placed for adoption truly need new families. Likewise, the government requires adoptive parents to be qualified and prepared. These decisions – who can adopt and who can be adopted – are made by government officials who have little to gain from the adoption process, other than the satisfaction of providing a better future for a child. The process is designed to protect vulnerable families and to prevent trafficking for the purpose of international adoption. *Ethical international adoption systems function to find families for children, not the other way around.*

Most corruption in international adoption takes place in countries where the adoption system lacks regulation. These countries typically let adoption agencies, lawyers, orphanages, officials, or adoptive parents influence the decisions of who can adopt and who can be adopted. For adoption agencies, lawyers, and orphanages, international adoption can be a lucrative business. While adoptions in these countries still go through judicial systems, these systems are often corrupt. Everyone responsible for deciding who can adopt and who needs to be adopted has something to gain. Without sufficient regulation, the process fails to protect vulnerable families from coercion and corruption in the adoption process. *These systems find children for families, rather than families for children.*

Too much red tape?

Many leaders in the Christian adoption and orphan care movement argue that red tape is the problem. They blame the decrease in international adoption over the last decade on regulation that has made the adoption process more difficult. It is true that red tape in some cases prevents or delays great families from welcoming home children who are truly in need of adoption. But appropriate regulation is necessary to protect vulnerable orphans and families and prevent trafficking.

In general, Christians have minimized the prevalence of corruption in international adoption. In the book *Adopted for Life*, which has had massive influence in the evangelical church, author Russell Moore wrote:

> Another risk involved in international adoption is that of shady operations in some countries, including baby-selling operations in which impoverished families are coerced, by their desperate circumstances, to give up their children for adoption...Going through a reputable, licensed agency will avoid putting oneself in this kind of ethically reprehensible situation...such situations are much more rare than one might think from watching television news reports.

Is Moore right? Is corruption in international adoption rare? Is working with an adoption agency that has a good reputation all you need to do to avoid corruption? Are poor families coerced by their circumstances to place children for adoption – or are they sometimes coerced by lies, bribes or threats of violence? While *Adopted for Life* has inspired many Christian families to adopt, the book has also led families to believe that avoiding corruption in adoption is as simple as working with a reputable, preferably Christian adoption agency. As Amanda's story shows us, this is far from the truth.

Adopted for Life also characterizes adoption as a spiritual battle. Moore argues that 'the universe is at war, and some babies and children are on the front line,' and that Satan works through human authorities to achieve his objectives. While we agree that adoption and orphan care involve a spiritual battle, we have also seen a disturbing trend among Christian adoptive families. Some Christians argue that anything standing in the way of an 'orphan' coming home to America is the work of the enemy. For example, when a child's case is under review by the US Embassy, some Christian families say that anything that slows down the case is spiritual warfare – rather than the work of government officials who are trying to protect a child from trafficking.

From 2004 to 2013, the number of international adoptions in the United States fell from 23,000 to just over 7,000.[1] The number of internationally adopted children worldwide fell from 45,000 in 2004 to 30,000 in 2010.[2] Some Christians call this decline a crisis – and blame both governments and international organizations for preventing orphans from being adopted.

In 2010, adoptive father Craig Juntunen founded Both Ends Burning, a movement 'dedicated to defending every child's right to a permanent loving family.'[3] As part of its mission to 'mobilize public outrage' about children living in institutions and being denied their right to a family, Both Ends Burning produced a documentary chronicling the journey of several adoptive families whose children were 'stuck' in orphanages allegedly because of bureaucratic red tape.

The documentary, *Stuck*, was widely successful among Christians in the United States. The movie premiered in sixty different locations across the country and ignited an 'Unstuck' movement. By 2014, Both Ends Burning was involved in political advocacy calling the United States government to make international adoption easier – or possible at all – from many countries including DRC, Nepal and Kyrgyzstan.

To address what it sees as a red tape problem, Both Ends Burning has promoted legislation entitled the Children in Families First Act, often called CHIFF. CHIFF seeks to ensure that children grow up in loving, permanent families. The legislation was before the United States Congress at the time we were writing this book. While CHIFF seeks to increase protection for vulnerable families and children, its primary aim is to simplify the process of international adoption, thereby increasing the number of children adopted internationally.

While CHIFF addresses the red tape problem, it does little to improve regulation of the international adoption system. It is unclear how this legislation would help, rather than exacerbate, the weak and vulnerable systems that allow for pervasive corruption and exploitation of families within the adoption process.

In recent years, journalists including Kathryn Joyce, author of *The Child Catchers*, and Erin Siegal McIntyre, author of *Finding*

---

1   Bureau of Consular Affairs, US Department of State. 'Statistics | Intercountry Adoption'. 2014. Web. 6 Sep. 2014. See also Crary, David. 'Foreign Adoptions By Americans Decline Sharply'. Associated Press 2014. Web. 6 Sep. 2014.

2   Selman, Peter. *Global Trends In Intercountry Adoption: 2001 - 2011*. 1st ed. National Council for Adoption, 2012. Web. 18 May 2012.

3   Bothendsburning.org. 'Our Mission & Approach'. 2014. Web. 6 Sep. 2014.

Fernanda, have documented the widespread corruption in international adoption. A growing number of families are bravely speaking up about the corruption they have experienced in the adoption process. Likewise, many adult adoptees and experts in children's rights agree: there is something deeply wrong with our current system of international adoption.

Yet many adoption advocates fear that bringing corruption into the light will cause more countries to close to international adoption. Families fear that what happened in Guatemala or Vietnam will happen in Ethiopia or Uganda. As a result, Christians are minimizing corruption in international adoption with the hope of not making things worse. Christians are closing their eyes to the truth – often in their own adoptions – because they believe the ends justify the means. Likewise, few Christians are deeply engaged in the fight to reform international adoption.

Although it is complicated, we need to take steps to understand this issue. The Christian community is largely in denial about widespread corruption and problems in international adoption. If we want international adoption to continue to be an option for orphans, we need to open our eyes to the truth.

Is there widespread corruption in international adoption?

How we answer this question is critically important. If the answer is yes, then we have a responsibility to step up. The Bible makes it clear that Christians have a responsibility to defend orphans and widows.

To begin to answer this question, we will take a look at the recent history of international adoption. Over the last fifteen years, Cambodia, Vietnam, Guatemala and Nepal, among a handful of other countries, have become hot spots for international adoption. Each of these countries ultimately closed as a result of widespread corruption.

Examining recent history will help us understand that the current system of international adoption does not protect or provide for the best interests of children. Many countries that are currently popular for international adoption – including Ethiopia, Uganda and Democratic Republic of Congo – are vulnerable to corruption. These countries share common risk factors and are following a similar pattern of growth in adoptions compared to the countries where corruption became widespread.

Before we dig into some difficult stories, please hear our hearts. We are not claiming that every adoption from Cambodia, Vietnam, Guatemala or Nepal was unethical. Likewise, we are not suggesting that closing adoptions from Uganda, Ethiopia and Democratic Republic of Congo is the answer. Rather, we want you to open your eyes to the truth – to see that the risk of corruption is real – so that we can fight for justice for orphans and widows. Christians need to think critically about God's word, what's happening in the world, and how to respond.

Cambodia: Selling a child for a bag of rice

In the late 1990s, adoption agencies began to arrange international adoptions from Cambodia to the United States. Cambodian adoptions were faster and less expensive than adoptions in other countries and American parents rushed to adopt children from Cambodia. International adoptions from Cambodia increased rapidly. In 1999, 161 children were adopted to the United States. Americans adopted 797 and 811 Cambodian children in 2000 and 2001 respectively. The vast majority of these children (88 per cent) were under the age of three.[4]

When most children being placed for adoption are younger and healthier than the children living in institutions in the country, this is a red flag for corruption:

> When a country's abandoned and institutionalized children are predominantly older, HIV-positive, or otherwise sick or disabled, and yet the international adoptions are predominantly of infants and toddlers, it can be a signal that entrepreneurs are illegally or unethically attempting to find the children that Westerners want to adopt.[5]

As adoptions increased, there was intense competition between agencies and facilitators for the babies and toddlers who were in demand. The majority of adoptions in Cambodia were arranged by Lauryn Galindo, a US citizen. By 2000, Cambodian newspapers and human rights organizations were suspicious of international adoption. They claimed Lauryn Galindo was paying families and orphanages for babies who were placed for international adoption,

---

4   Bureau of Consular Affairs, U.S. Department of State. 'Statistics | Intercountry Adoption'. 2014. Web. 6 Sep. 2014.

5   Schuster Institute, Brandeis University. 'Cambodia Adoption'. Web. 6 Sep. 2014.

while also bribing government officials to create false documents and to approve their adoptions. Around the same time, the US Embassy became aware of fraud in orphan visa applications. In 2001, following months of allegations that children were being trafficked for adoption, the US government closed adoptions from Cambodia.[6]

Hundreds of American parents were left in an uncertain position, unable to bring home children whom they had already legally adopted in Cambodia. Eventually, most of these children were allowed to go to the United States with their adoptive parents. This did not mean their cases weren't fraught with questions about corruption. Despite evidence of wrongdoing, most children were given visas because it was nearly impossible for the US Embassy to deny visa applications.

Several years later, the US began a criminal investigation into the dealings of adoption facilitator Lauryn Galindo and her sister, Lynn Devin, who was the owner of an adoption agency. The corruption discovered in the investigation, called *Operation Broken Hearts*, is almost unbelievable.[7]

Lauryn Galindo directed baby recruiters to approach birth families in their local village to see if they were willing to sell their child. The recruiters were paid $50. Galindo then worked with baby buyers to acquire adoptable children. The buyers were typically orphanage directors and taxi drivers. They had several methods to obtain children from their families. Some families were told their children would be placed in an orphanage where they would have food and medical care and be able to go to school. They were told they could have their child back at any time and that they could visit the child. Other families were told a rich family would raise the child in the United States and that when the child became an adult, he would petition for the parents to become citizens. In other cases, the baby buyers offered desperate parents compensation. Children were sold for as little as a bag of rice worth $20.

After children were purchased, the next step was to create a false paper trail. The children's identities were erased, and they were given new names and histories. These false identities were used on legal documents, including the adoption papers and passport. This made it almost impossible for the embassy to do investigations.[8]

---

6   Maskew, Trish. 'Child Trafficking And Intercountry Adoption: The Cambodian Experience'. *Cumberland Law Review*, 2004. Print.

7   ibid.

8   Oreskovic, Johanna, and Trish Maskew. 'Red Thread Or Slender Reed: Deconstructing Prof. Bartholet's Mythology Of International Adoption'. *Buffalo Human Rights Law Review*, 14, 2008. Print.

From January 1997 to December 2001, Galindo and her conspirators helped American families adopt more than 800 children from Cambodia. Galindo and Devin received 9.2 million dollars from adoptive parents and used the profits to fund lavish lifestyles. Some supporters of international adoption argue that corruption in international adoption is limited and rare. In Cambodia, Lauryn Galindo was involved in 80 per cent of the international adoptions. Corruption in Cambodian adoptions was pervasive and systematic.

Though this was a conspiracy to traffic children for the purpose of international adoption, no charges of child trafficking were filed. Under US law, the buying and selling of children is not considered child trafficking if the children are adopted rather than exploited. Galindo and Devin pled guilty and were convicted of conspiracy to commit visa fraud and conspiracy to commit money laundering. Galindo was sentenced to eighteen months in prison, and Devin was sentenced to six months of house arrest.

Vietnam: When children and families become collateral damage

Between 2006 and 2009, Americans adopted 2,220 children from Vietnam.[9] By 2008 when the United States shut down American adoptions from Vietnam, the State Department had discovered systematic corruption that resulted in the trafficking of children. A network of adoption agency representatives, orphanages, hospitals, police officers, and government officials were profiting through baby buying, coercing or defrauding families, and even stealing Vietnamese children to sell them to unsuspecting Americans.[10]

Though US Embassy officials in Vietnam were aware of corruption, they did not have 'the right tools to shut down the infant peddlers while allowing the truly needed adoptions to continue.'[11] In Vietnam, as in Cambodia, the government officials were not able to respond effectively to stem corruption without closing adoptions entirely.

Vietnam had a long history of corruption in international adoption. In the late 1990s and early 2000s, Americans were adopting hundreds of Vietnamese babies and toddlers each year despite

---

9   Graff, E.J. 'Anatomy Of An Adoption Crisis'. Foreign Policy 2010. Web. 6 Sep. 2014.
10   ibid.
11   ibid.

reports that children 'were being bought, coerced, defrauded, or even kidnapped from their birth families.'[12] The United States banned adoptions from Vietnam entirely and Vietnam tried to reform the system. In 2005, Vietnam and the United States signed a three-year bilateral agreement so that adoptions could begin again between the countries.

The extensive fraud and corruption in Vietnamese adoptions between 2006 and 2009 were documented by the US State Department. The truth is shocking. As soon as adoptions resumed, there was a dramatic increase in the number of infants who were abandoned at orphanages and hospitals involved in international adoption. These hospitals and orphanages were actively engaged in bribing and lying to birth mothers to secure children for international adoption.

The US Embassy discovered 'safe houses' where women were offered housing, medical care and money to 'start a new life' in exchange for their child. Mothers were often lied to and intimidated. The women were required to sign documents promising to relinquish their child for international adoption and were separated from their child immediately after birth. One hospital essentially kidnapped infants from their parents by refusing to release the child until they paid their medical bills. When poor parents could not pay the bills, the hospital declared the children abandoned and placed them for adoption without the parents' knowledge or consent.

The US State Department and Embassy were aware of these problems, but in many ways their hands were tied. Vietnamese officials objected strongly to American officials investigating the circumstances of the adoptions. The embassy believed the problem lay with the Vietnamese officials who were profiting from wrongful adoptions: 'If Vietnamese children were being wrongfully taken, it was Vietnamese families that were being harmed, usually by Vietnamese citizens on Vietnamese soil.'[13] Vietnamese officials, however, believed the real problem was that American adoption agencies were putting pressure on orphanages to 'find' more adoptable babies. In their opinion, agencies' humanitarian donations were really advance deposits on adoptable 'orphans.'[14]

---

12   ibid.
13   ibid.
14   ibid.

The problems in Vietnam were so serious and systematic that by the end of 2009, the United States decided it could not permit adoptions from Vietnam to continue. When parents were informed of the changes in adoptions from Vietnam, they were devastated. Many were stuck in Vietnam for months, caring for children they had legally adopted but were unable to bring home. They called their congressional representatives who put pressure on the State Department to let the families bring 'their' babies home.

Under the law, the US government had only three tools to respond to its suspicions about corruption in Vietnamese adoptions. The first was for the US government to pressure Vietnam to enforce the law and crack down on unethical adoptions. Second, the United States could stop accepting adoptions from Vietnam altogether. But this would stop legal adoptions together with corrupt ones, and the United States government hesitated to take this step.

The third option was for the U.S. government to investigate the circumstances behind American adoptive parents' applications for orphan visas. The limited tool of immigration law was the only legal authority that the United States had to oversee adoptions in Vietnam. After parents adopted a child in the Vietnamese courts, they would file an application for an I-600 orphan visa to bring the child home. Legally, the United States couldn't hold the American adoption agencies or Vietnamese orphanages that may have done something wrong accountable. Instead, the only way the US government could prevent corruption in Vietnamese adoptions was to hold American adoptive parents responsible for whether or not their child was in fact a legitimate orphan. If the United States did find fraud in the investigation and their child's visa was denied, adoptive parents were devastated. Both the child and the well-intentioned adoptive parents became collateral damage. The parties responsible for the corruption were not held accountable.

When Vietnam opened to international adoption, some orphanages reported a 2,000 per cent increase in abandonments. After Vietnam closed to lucrative international adoption, many orphanages that had been full of healthy infants closed or only had a small number of babies and toddlers. When the money stopped flowing in, so did the supply of 'abandoned' babies. Orphanages not involved in international adoption continued to care for older and special needs children.

Guatemala: The lucrative business of finding babies

Guatemala's long civil war ended in 1996 with the signing of a peace treaty. The same year, 731 Guatemalan children were adopted by American parents. By 2007, Americans adopted 5,577 children, mostly healthy infants and toddlers.[15] This represents one in every 110 babies born in Guatemala. From 1997 to 2007, Americans adopted more than 30,000 children from Guatemala, which is widely considered to have had the most pervasive corruption in international adoption.[16]

In Guatemala, large numbers of healthy infants were bought, coerced or kidnapped away from their parents in order to be adopted overseas. The older children who were abandoned or waiting in orphanages were not typically placed for adoption. A study in 2007 at the height of the adoption boom found 5,600 children and teenagers living in Guatemalan orphanages; one third of those were free for adoption. Fewer than 130 infants were available for adoption. Yet each month, more than 270 Guatemalan babies under one year of age were being placed for international adoption.[17] Americans were not adopting orphans who truly needed families; they were adopting babies who had been placed by – or taken from – their parents.

The problem was private attorneys were able to solicit children directly from individuals or families, with the prospect of earning very large profits. These adoption attorneys often worked through child-finders to acquire children for international adoption. The attorneys offered no assistance to support struggling birth families. In some cases, families were offered money for their children or women appear to have been getting pregnant and giving birth repeatedly to earn money. In others, women were coerced to give up their children. For example, women were offered free housing and medical care while pregnant, but later were told that they owed rent and medical fees—and could either give up the newborn or owe impossible amounts of money. In still other verified cases, children were kidnapped for adoption.[18]

15   Schuster Institute, Brandeis University. 'Cambodia Adoption'. Web. 6 Sep. 2014.

16   Brandeis.edu. 'US Embassy Cables Reveal Adoption Fraud In Guatemala, Erin Siegal | Adoption | Schuster Institute For Investigative Journalism | Brandeis University'. Web. 6 Sep. 2014.

17   Schuster Institute, Brandeis University. 'Cambodia Adoption'. Web. 6 Sep. 2014.

18   Brandeis.edu. 'Responses To Criticisms | Adoption | Gender & Justice | Schuster Institute | Brandeis University'. Web. 6 Sep. 2014.

As in Vietnam, the U.S. Embassy in Guatemala struggled with limited tools to fight the trafficking of children for the purpose of adoption. The U.S. government knew as far back as the 1980s that Guatemalan children 'were being bought, sold, and kidnapped so that American families, believing the children were orphans, could adopt them.'[19] The officials were aware of criminal activities associated with international adoptions, but at the same time they faced pressure and demands from American adoptive families who were desperate to bring 'their' children home. Though the US government was aware of illegal practices in Guatemalan adoption, American families who were in the process of adopting Guatemalan children were not informed about the extent of the problem.[20]

Nepal: How did we end up here?

For many years, Nepal allowed very few children to be adopted internationally. Traditionally very few Nepalese children were abandoned. Orphans and children separated from their parents were cared for by grandparents or others in the extended family. In 2001, several international adoption agencies discovered Nepal, and adoptions to the United States increased from a total of 8 in 2000 to 394 in 2006.[21] This was a massive jump in a small country experiencing a civil war.

Between 1996 and 2006, Nepal experienced a civil war between the ruling Nepalese monarchy and Maoist fighters who sought to establish a People's Republic.[22] The conflict had two important consequences. First, many poor, rural families were desperate for a brighter future for their children. Second, the war multiplied opportunities for corruption and fraud. In this environment, orphanages were founded to focus specifically on international adoption. Desperate, illiterate parents left their children in these institutions, believing the children would receive shelter and an education. The parents expected to bring their child home a few months later, only to discover the child had been adopted abroad. Apparently, unscrupulous people discovered that large amounts of money could be made through international adoption. They began

---

19   Brandeis.edu. 'US Embassy Cables Reveal Adoption Fraud In Guatemala, Erin Siegal | Adoption | Schuster Institute For Investigative Journalism | Brandeis University'. Web. 6 Sep. 2014.

20   ibid.

21   Bureau of Consular Affairs, U.S. Department of State. 'Statistics | Intercountry Adoption'. N.p., 2014. Web. 6 Sep. 2014.

22   BBC News. 'Nepal Country Profile'. 2014. Web. 8 Sep. 2014.

to 'find' the healthy infants and toddlers Americans most wanted to adopt.[23]

One underlying factor problem is that Nepalese law only allowed adoption if a child had been abandoned. Some desperate birth families may have made the decision to create documents that made their child look 'abandoned' in order to give her a better home. But other families were bribed or coerced into placing children in orphanages or for adoption. Almost all the documents used for international adoption were fraudulent. Many inconsistencies were found in adoptive children's official documents. The individual lies about a child's age or circumstances seemed minor; however they fit a pattern that indicated baby buying, fraud, coercion or even kidnapping. The falsehoods were often intended to conceal the truth and make a child more marketable for international adoption. The fraudulent documents made it very difficult for the embassy to confirm the circumstances around the child's abandonment.[24]

Furthermore, the US Embassy was concerned that orphanages were offering children for adoption not out of concern for the children's welfare, but because adoption brought in money through fees and bribes. The government of Nepal charged an official fee of $300 for international adoption. Adoption agencies instructed American parents to bring large amounts of cash into the country, though this was against Nepalese law. After parents arrived in Nepal, orphanages and officials demanded surprise fees, ranging from $500 to $20,000. The embassy was concerned that Americans were being taken advantage of and that children were being offered for adoption so corrupt orphanages and government officials could profit, not because the children genuinely needed families.

Nepal lacked the resources to protect vulnerable children and to combat the problems created by poverty and corruption in international adoption. Plagued by accusations, the government of Nepal shut down its international adoption program in 2007 for reform.[25] Two years later, Nepal began to allow international adoptions once again. Many of the agencies and orphanages that had been involved in earlier corruption were allowed to resume the lucrative business of international adoption.

---

23   The Huffington Post,, 'Orphaned Or Stolen? The U.S. State Department Investigates Adoption From Nepal, 2006-2008'. 2011. Web. 6 Sep. 2014.

24   ibid.

25   ibid.

In February 2011, dozens of American families found themselves stuck in Nepal, unable to take their adopted children home. Under Nepalese law, the families had adopted and taken responsibility for the children. However, the US Embassy in Kathmandu had not yet issued visas that would allow these families to bring their children home. The Embassy and American immigration authorities were asking for more information to determine whether each child was truly in need of adoption. The Embassy was concerned that false documents had been submitted to declare children free for adoption. There was a growing concern that the children had been trafficked for the purpose of adoption.[26]

Stuck: What do these countries have in common?

> The situations in Guatemala, Vietnam and Cambodia raise significant concerns about whether these systems found homes for children in need or instead, created paper orphans whom, absent payments, might not have been available for adoption.
>
> Red Thread or Slender Reed[27]

In these and many other countries, there have been serious concerns about *irregularities* – signs of fraud, coercion, corruption, baby buying, and other serious problems – in international adoptions. Once the US Embassy or government in the sending country is aware of corruption, officials must make the difficult decision to subject individual cases to a high level of scrutiny or to close adoptions from the country entirely. In many cases, adoptive parents who were completely unaware of corruption are held responsible for problems created by adoption agencies and their representatives. These families end up stuck, unable to bring home their adopted children, and often bewildered as to how they got there.

Cambodia, Vietnam, Guatemala, and Nepal are all countries where there is desperate poverty and widespread corruption. Both Guatemala and Nepal opened to international adoption shortly after the end of civil war.

All of these had privately controlled adoption systems where adoption agencies and their representatives were involved in

---

26   ibid.

27   Oreskovic, Johanna, and Trish Maskew. 'Red Thread Or Slender Reed: Deconstructing Prof. Bartholet's Mythology Of International Adoption'. *Buffalo Human Rights Law Review*, 14 (2008): 71. Print.

finding children for adoption and matching them with adoptive parents. Families believed there was an overwhelming need for international adoption from these countries. All of these countries were also known for quick, easy adoptions of healthy babies and toddlers.

In all of these countries, the numbers of children placed for adoption increased rapidly in response to the demand from adoptive parents. In Cambodia, Vietnam, Guatemala and Nepal, most children who truly needed adoption – who were typically older or who had special needs – remained in orphanages while large numbers of healthy babies and toddlers were separated from their families. In other words, these systems were efficient at finding children for families, not families for children. Eventually, in response to widespread corruption, these countries closed entirely for international adoption.

Cambodia, Vietnam, Guatemala, and Nepal have much in common with many of the countries popular for international adoption today. The pattern of corruption found in these countries is likely to be repeated elsewhere around the world if the United States and other nations do not take steps to reform international adoption. Many countries that are growing in popularity for international adoption, including Ethiopia, Uganda and Democratic Republic of Congo, are highly vulnerable to corruption in adoptions.

The Democratic Republic of Congo is located in sub-Saharan Africa and is one of the poorest, most corrupt, and most violent nations in the world.[28] Although the civil war in DRC officially ended in 2003, armed conflict continues across the country, especially in the East. The country has a staggering rate of infant and child mortality: one in seven children dies before the age of five. Nearly half of the population does not have clean drinking water[29] and three quarters struggle with malnutrition.[30] There are approximately four million orphans in DRC.

Over the last few years, Democratic Republic of Congo has become the latest hot spot for international adoption. Until recently, DRC was one of the only countries where you could adopt a healthy infant in less than a year. In 2008, there were 9 international

---

28   BBC News. 'Democratic Republic Of Congo Profile'. 2014. Web. 6 Sep. 2014.

29   Unicef.org. 'UNICEF - Countries | Democratic Republic Of Congo'. Web. 6 Sep. 2014.

30   Soschildrensvillages.ca. 'Democratic Republic Of The Congo'. Web. 6 Sep. 2014.

adoptions to the United States. Two years later in 2010, there were 41 adoptions. By 2013, there were 311 adoptions of Congolese children by American citizens.[31] This represents a growth of more than 3,000 per cent over the last five years. The per capita income in the DRC is around $300 a year – yet some adoption agencies charge upwards of $50,000 to complete an adoption.

In September 2013, the immigration authorities in DRC suspended the issuance of exit letters, the final and crucial document that allows for the child to leave DRC. By May 2014, close to 100 families who had legally adopted children in DRC were unable to bring them home. These children had been adopted by American families, and they had received immigration visas allowing them to enter the United States, but without the exit letter they were unable to leave DRC.

Holly Mulford is an adoptive mother, blogger and expert on adoptions in DRC. On her blog, Holly explained the reasons why the DRC immigration authorities might have suspended the issuance of exit letters. Between 2010 and 2014, journalists published 'reports of child trafficking, orphanage raids, and illegal border crossings.' Families who are adopting from DRC describe the abuse of children in orphanages, the coercion of birth families, and unethical fees and bribes paid to those who are responsible for deciding whether or not a child needs adoption. US Embassy announcements reveal 'concerns of corruption, false documents, bribery, illegal border crossings and backdated court documents... all of it paints a very clear picture of endemic corruption and fraud in the international adoption business in DRC.'[32]

Immigration authorities in DRC suspended the issuance of exit letters in response to very serious concerns about the adoption process. Nevertheless, this created an impossible situation for parents who were in the process of adopting children who truly needed new families.

In 2013, Hannah received the judgment of adoption for her son Michael, from DRC.[33] Michael is HIV positive. In the United States and other developed countries, HIV is considered a treatable condition, not a death sentence. In the DRC where life-saving

---

31   Bureau of Consular Affairs, US Department of State. 'Statistics | Intercountry Adoption'. N.p., 2014. Web. 6 Sep. 2014.

32   Kitumaini.blogspot.com. 'An Open Letter To Both Ends Burning'. 2014. Web. 6 Sep. 2014.

33   Names have been changed to protect privacy.

antiretroviral treatment is not widely available, however, HIV and AIDS are life-threatening. Michael's only treatment consists of a combination of Tylenol and vitamins. In September 2013, Hannah travelled to DRC to pick up her son only to have the immigration authorities in DRC refuse to issue an exit letter.

After three long months filled with dashed hopes and expectations, Hannah was forced to leave Michael with a foster family and return home to wait for the suspension to be lifted or an exception to be made. Other DRC adoptive families have packed up their lives, left spouses and children in the United States, and moved to Kinshasa for the foreseeable future while they hope and pray.

For the American families stuck in DRC, this has been a heartbreaking and frustrating disruption of their lives – to say the least. Yet these families are not alone and their story is painfully familiar. Since 2001, hundreds of families hoping to adopt from Cambodia, Vietnam, Guatemala, and Nepal have found themselves in a painfully similar position.

Pattern of Corruption in Adoptions

Poverty, corruption and the lure of large amounts of money from international adoption create a dangerous situation where officials, lawyers and others involved in adoption are willing to exploit desperately poor families to create the supply of orphans demanded by adoption agencies and their clients. In country after country, a remarkably similar cycle plays out.

There is an 'orphan crisis'

A large number of children are orphaned, abandoned or separated from their families by HIV/AIDS, conflict, injustice, poverty, and brokenness. As a result, thousands of children are living in orphanages. There are few resources to support orphans and vulnerable families. When people learn about the crisis, they want to help.

The country opens to international adoption

A small number of families adopt children from the country. These adoptions are difficult, but pave the way for future families to adopt. A growing number of families recognize the need and begin the adoption process. Initially there are many children waiting for adoption and the adoption process is quick and inexpensive.

Adoption agencies start new programs

Adoption agencies see the opportunity to place more orphans in families and launch new adoption programs. The adoption agencies form partnerships with orphanages, offering financial assistance in exchange for the opportunity to place children for adoption.

International adoptions grow quickly

The numbers of families adopting from the country increase rapidly. There are many children in need of international adoption, but few are the healthy, young children desired by most adoptive parents. There is growing demand for fast, easy adoptions of healthy babies and toddlers. Families hoping to adopt young children often wait for years on wait lists. Meanwhile, orphans who are older or have special needs continue to wait for families.

The demand for adoptable children fuels corruption

As adoptions increase, the orphanages, lawyers and government officials involved in adoptions recognize that there is a lot of money changing hands. International adoption fees are high compared to the cost of living in many sending nations. Motivated by the lure of money, orphanages, lawyers and government officials begin to do whatever it takes to find adoptable children. Vulnerable, poor families are coerced into placing children in orphanages or for adoption.

Corruption becomes widespread and systemic

In many countries popular for international adoption, bribery and fraud are common practices. It becomes difficult or impossible to do adoptions the right way because orphanages and government officials have financial incentives to ignore corruption in adoptions. Those who break the law are not held accountable for their actions.

The government struggles to respond to corruption

The government of the sending country may struggle to reform the adoption system and prevent corruption. At the same time, receiving country officials become aware of a growing pattern of fraud and corruption in adoptions. They must decide between closing adoptions entirely and subjecting individual cases to a higher level of scrutiny.

Families and children get stuck

Eventually government officials from the receiving or sending country decide that corruption has gone too far and close the country to adoption. As a result, families in the adoption process become stuck, unable to complete their adoptions or to bring home children whom they have adopted overseas. Likewise, children who are truly in need of new families end up stuck, waiting in orphanages. Adoptive families are held responsible for the actions of agencies and their representatives overseas. Meanwhile, the adoption agencies that were involved in corrupt adoption practices are not held accountable. They typically shift their operations to another country that is opening to international adoption and the cycle begins again.

While this cycle plays out a little differently in every country, this is the basic pattern that was repeated in recent years in many countries popular for international adoption, including Cambodia, Vietnam, Guatemala, and Nepal, and is now playing out in DRC, Uganda and Ethiopia. Without changes in international adoption law, this pattern is likely to be repeated again and again.

What makes international adoption risky?

The international adoption system lacks the tools and resources needed to protect vulnerable children and families. Some international adoption programs are particularly vulnerable to abuse. This is true for both sending and receiving countries. Countries that are particularly vulnerable to abuse in international adoptions have several things in common. Sending countries where corruption in adoption becomes widespread typically struggle with poverty, violence and corruption. These countries have weak justice and social services systems that fail to protect and provide for vulnerable families. Receiving countries where corruption becomes common allow families to adopt from these sending countries. Likewise, these receiving countries fail to hold adoption agencies accountable for their actions overseas.

Poverty

Most sending countries are struggling with extreme poverty or have recently emerged from conflict or civil war. These countries lack all but the most basic structures for child welfare. Their governments do not have the resources to provide social services or to ensure access to healthcare and education. Likewise, the countries lack infrastructure to protect vulnerable families. The government may not know how many children are living in orphanages or on the streets.

Corruption

Many developing countries struggle with a culture of corruption, where government officials routinely accept or demand bribes. In countries facing widespread corruption, such as Democratic Republic of Congo, there is a lack of respect for laws and regulations. Justice favors the wealthy and the powerful. Without the means to pay bribes, the poor have no voice. Corrupt judges and government officials may be willing to rule a certain way or to falsify documents in exchange for a bribe. When the culture of corruption is pervasive, lawyers and adoption agencies may find it is difficult to do the right thing, as officials are unwilling to do their jobs without something in return. Together, poverty and corruption create a context that is dangerous for marginalized families.

Money

Adoptive families are willing to pay relatively huge sums of money in order to bring a child home. Adoption fees are very high, often outlandishly so when compared with the per capita income of sending countries. The total cost of an international adoption is typically between $20,000 and $50,000. Often a significant amount of these fees are for in-country expenses or humanitarian donations. The money involved in international adoption creates incentives for governments and others who are responsible for the welfare of children to encourage adoption or tolerate corruption.

For example in Ethiopia, international adoption has become a big business. An LA Times article in 2004 memorably titled 'Ethiopia's Latest Export: Adoptable Children' explained the economic reasons why the government was making international adoption easier. The desperate country was struggling to care for the estimated 5 million children orphaned by famine, war, disease, and AIDS. Allowing children to be placed for international adoption was considered a last resort to provide for vulnerable children.[34]

Over the last decade, the growing international adoption industry has brought in millions in adoption fees and humanitarian donations

---

34   *Los Angeles Times*. 'Ethiopia's Latest Export: Adoptable Children'. 2004. Web. 6 Sep. 2014.

to Ethiopia. In 2010, American adoption agencies contributed $14 million in services for orphans and vulnerable children.[35] This represents the equivalent of 10 per cent of Ethiopia's annual health budget. Has the Ethiopian government become dependent on international adoption agencies to care for the country's orphaned and vulnerable children? This would create a dangerous incentive for government officials to ignore inconsistencies indicating problems in international adoption.

Furthermore, international adoption can be highly lucrative for lawyers, orphanages, adoption facilitators, and corrupt government officials in developing countries. The chance to earn a large amount of money in exchange for placing a child for adoption creates a significant incentive for people, especially in poor countries, to obtain children by any means possible.

Consider the example of Guatemala. Between 2002 and 2008, nearly 25,000 Guatemalan children were adopted by families in the United States. The typical fee paid to Guatemalan adoption attorneys ranged from $15,000 to $20,000 per child. This is a total of 371 to 495 million dollars over seven years.[36] To put this in perspective, the per capita income in Guatemala was around $2,000 in 2005.[37] In the United States, the per capita income the same year was roughly $40,000.[38] The $20,000 paid to a Guatemalan attorney is equivalent to paying $400,000 to an American attorney for every child placed for adoption. In Guatemalan adoptions, attorneys paid orphanages and facilitators to locate adoptable children and bribed government officials to fake documents and approve adoptions. When this much money is involved, it is hardly surprising that corruption is a problem.

There is an acute lack of transparency at the most critical points in the adoption process: when a child is separated from their parents and how the decision is made to place the child for international adoption. In countries with private adoption systems, it is virtually impossible to determine how a child came into care and whether the process was free of coercion, deception or payments to induce relinquishment.[39]

35 David M. Smolin and Elizabeth Bartholet. Intercountry Adoption: Policies, Practices, and Outcomes. Ed. Judith L. Gibbons & Karen Smith Rotabi. Williston, VT: Ashgate, 2012.

36 ibid.

37 Data.un.org. 'Undata Country Profile: Guatemala'. Web. 6 Sep. 2014.

38 Data.un.org. 'Undata Country Profile: United States of America'. Web. 6 Sep. 2014.

39 Oreskovic, Johanna, and Trish Maskew. 'Red Thread Or Slender Reed: Deconstructing Prof. Bartholet's Mythology Of International Adoption'. *Buffalo Human Rights Law Review*, 14, 2008. Print.

Supply and Demand

While many assume the orphan crisis means there are orphanages full of babies who need to be adopted, this simply is not true. There is a significant need for international adoption, but there are very few healthy babies and young children waiting in orphanages. This reality goes against the image popularized by the media of millions of children desperately in need of adoption.

We are not entirely comfortable talking about supply and demand as if there were a market for adoptable children, but the reality is there is a mismatch between the families who want to adopt and the children who need adoption. The 'supply' of children who need international adoption is primarily children who are older, in sibling groups, or have special needs. At the same time, most families who want to adopt 'demand' healthy babies and toddlers.

There may be 151 million children who have experienced the death of one or both parents, but very few of these children are available for international adoption. Most live with their families. There are around 8 million children living in orphanages, but four out of five of these children have at least one surviving parent. It is common in many developing countries for poor parents to send children to orphanages to receive an education or for care while the parent works. These children have contact with their families and should not be made available for adoption, as the parents have no intent to relinquish the children permanently.

There may always be children who are orphaned, abandoned or who cannot be cared for by their families for social or cultural reasons – but in some countries these numbers are decreasing. For example in South Korea, fewer babies are being abandoned as a result of greater support for single mothers and domestic adoption. In many countries across the world, children who are orphaned and in need of new families may be adopted in their home country. For example in India and China, there is a growing interest in domestic adoption. Even in developing countries, many families are willing and able to adopt.

Of those children who need international adoption, most are older or have special needs. UNICEF estimates that 88 per cent of the world's orphans are over the age of five. Between 1996 and 2006, however, 89 per cent of the children adopted by American families were under the age of five.[40] Many more orphans have

---

40   ibid.

special needs, such as medical conditions, developmental delays or physical disabilities. There is no shortage of older or special needs children waiting for adoption. The number of families willing to adopt older or special needs children remains significantly lower than the number of children in need.

At the same time, the demand for international adoption is increasing for several reasons. There is an increase in infertility in the developed world. An estimated 15-20 per cent of married couples struggle with infertility, sometimes as a result of delaying having children until later in life. Likewise, there is a growing movement within the evangelical church encouraging Christians to get involved in adoption and orphan care. As a result, many families who do not struggle with infertility are interested in adoption. The vast majority of couples and families, understandably, want to adopt healthy young children.

There is a significant mismatch between the supply of children in need of adoption and the demand of parents who want to adopt. Most parents in the United States or Europe view only a small fraction of children in orphanages overseas as adoptable. In many countries, children wait in orphanages because there is not demand to adopt older and special needs children.[41] While prospective adoptive parents wait for years to be matched with healthy, young children, older and special needs children wait because they are not wanted.

This mismatch between the supply and demand of adoptable children creates a dangerous situation, especially in countries where poverty and corruption are present. As a result, there is an incentive for those who can profit from international adoption to find children for families – rather than families for children.

Legal loopholes

Internationally there are two broad types of adoption systems: government-controlled and private. These systems have an important difference at two critical points. The first is when a child enters care and the second is when a child is matched with an adoptive family. These systems answer the questions who can adopt and who can be adopted very differently.

Some countries have a government-controlled system where a central authority facilitates and controls adoption. The government creates rules about who can adopt and be adopted, as well as how

---

41   ibid.

children are matched with adoptive parents and placed in families. Countries with strong central authorities overseeing the adoption process generally have stable, ethical adoption programs that effectively find families for children.

Some countries that have strong central authorities, such as Russia and Republic of Korea, are not a part of the Hague Convention on Inter-country Adoption. But all countries that are party to the Convention are required to have a central authority. Adoptions from Hague Convention countries such as China, Colombia and Latvia are subject to laws designed to protect children from trafficking and facilitate international adoption. Countries that are party to the Convention are required to have a central authority capable of regulating international adoption.

Countries that have not implemented the Hague Convention and that do not have a strong central authority have private adoption systems. In these countries, international adoptions are often handled by adoption agencies and their representatives who form relationships with private orphanages and attorneys. Adoption agencies may build or provide financial support to orphanages for the purpose of placing children for international adoption. The orphanage, lawyer and adoption agency may all be involved in deciding who can be adopted and matching the children with adoptive parents. Agencies may have direct contact with birth families and may be involved in the paperwork to file for termination of parental rights and adoption. In many countries lacking a central adoption authority, laws regulating international adoption are poorly defined. In these countries, the adoption system is driven by the market, and the people who are responsible for deciding who can adopt and who can be adopted have something to gain from international adoption.

Most instances of corruption in international adoption are from countries that have private adoption systems. The countries that are particularly ripe for abuse in international adoption are those that have widespread poverty and corruption. Where no foreign controls prevent adoption abuse, the burden falls to the receiving country, often the United States or another developed country, to regulate international adoption.

Adoption agencies lack accountability
Both the United Kingdom and the United States have signed the Hague Convention, yet the two countries approach adoption very

differently. In the United Kingdom, all adoptions – both domestic and international – require families to be approved through their local government. There are very few international adoptions in the United Kingdom, and it is nearly impossible for British citizens to adopt from countries that are not a part of the Hague Convention.

In contrast, all international adoptions in the United States are handled by private adoption agencies. American adoption agencies are subject to minimal regulation. International adoption is much easier in the United States than in the United Kingdom. American citizens can adopt from many countries that are not a part of the Hague Convention, including Ethiopia, Uganda and Democratic Republic of Congo.

We believe current laws in the United States do not adequately protect adoptive families or children from corruption and trafficking. The legal requirements placed on adoption agencies are insufficient and as a result, agencies are seldom held accountable when they are involved in corruption. To understand why, we will look at the role of adoption agencies in international adoption and immigration law.

Some adoption agencies in the United States have long traditions of providing ethical adoption services and supporting child welfare. The best agencies work diligently to find families for orphans while also working to support vulnerable families and prevent corruption. Keeping these standards, however, is a choice the agencies make, not something required by law.

While many adoption agencies function as non-profit organizations, adoption agencies are also allowed to function as for-profit businesses. Adoption agencies have no legal obligation to document how so-called 'in country expenses' or 'humanitarian fees' are spent. Frequently, there is no legal accountability if the agency is bribing orphanages, facilitators, judges, or other officials in connection to the adoption. Furthermore, many agency fees are non-refundable, whether or not the adoptive family completes an adoption.

When a family begins the process to adopt, they are required to sign a contract with the adoption agency. This contract lays out the risks of adoption and the responsibilities of the adoptive parents and the agency. Adoption agency contracts, however, shift most of the risk and responsibility from the agency to the adoptive family. These contracts make it difficult for adoptive families to hold adoption agencies accountable for fraud or corruption. Adoption agencies have no legal obligation to act in the best interest of the adoptive parents or adopted children. The private agency system is structured to maximize profit potential while minimizing risk and shifts legal responsibility to adoptive families and children.

Immigration law is not designed to regulate adoption

In countries like Ethiopia, Uganda and DRC, adoption agencies rely on their overseas representatives. These representatives are often not employees of the agency and therefore the agency will not take any legal responsibility for their actions. Adoption agency representatives are involved in almost every aspect of the process in country, including finding children, counseling birthmothers and completing adoption paperwork. Adoptive parents have little to no recourse against facilitators when things go wrong and likewise have been unsuccessful holding adoption agencies accountable for the actions of their facilitators. Current regulations have failed to hold most adoption agencies accountable for their actions or the actions of their representatives overseas.

The United States has signed and implemented the Hague Convention. This means that when American parents are adopting from another Convention country, the adoption is regulated by the provisions in the Convention. The Convention penalizes child buying and other forms of coercion in adoptive placements. The Hague, however, only applies to adoptions where both countries are parties. This is a big problem.

Outside the Hague Convention, the primary federal law overseeing international adoptions to the United States is the Immigration and Nationality Act. At its core, immigration law is not designed to regulate adoption. Under immigration law, parents must meet certain requirements in order to adopt, including having a home study completed by a qualified social worker. After parents adopt a child overseas, they must apply for a visa in order to bring the child home to the United States. The US Embassy and immigration authorities (USCIS) conduct an investigation into the adopted child's history to determine if the child fits the legal definition of an orphan.

As we learned in reading about the history of international adoptions, it's nearly impossible for the Embassy to complete thorough investigations. Officials must rely on documents created by adoption agencies, lawyers, orphanages, and officials, who may have been involved in falsifying paperwork to make the child look like an orphan. Adoption lawyers transport birth family members to interviews, thus providing them with opportunities to threaten and coerce them to provide certain answers. Embassies in countries like DRC and Ethiopia have only a few staff members to process all visas – not just those for adoption purposes – and have little ability to travel to rural areas to conduct investigations. Moreover, these investigations may happen months or years after court judgments are pronounced.

Furthermore, immigration law does not include any legal requirements or responsibilities for adoption agencies. Adoption agencies and their representatives are not held legally accountable for ensuring the children they place for adoption are genuinely orphans, and the investigations conducted by the U.S. Embassy cannot be relied upon as proof that the international adoption was in the child's best interest.

Adoptive parents are ultimately responsible to USCIS to prove that their adopted child is really an orphan. When the Embassy and USCIS discover that a child is not legally an orphan or that the birth parents were coerced or bribed in the adoption process, the only possible penalty is the denial of an immigration visa. This is one of the reasons why parents get stuck in countries such as Nepal, having adopted children whom they cannot bring home.

Under the current law, the adoptive children and parents are punished with the denial of an immigrant visa while the responsible parties - the adoption agencies and their in-country representatives - suffer no consequences at all.

Ultimately, if there is corruption in countries that have not enacted the Hague Convention, local US Embassies have very little power to respond. Government officials can increase investigations or close adoptions entirely. Closing adoptions may protect hundreds of vulnerable families from wrongfully losing their children, but it does so at the cost of preventing children who genuinely need new families from being adopted.

Poverty, corruption, money, supply and demand, and legal loopholes: together these issues put vulnerable children and families at risk. The current system punishes vulnerable children as well as adoptive and biological parents. It does not hold accountable those responsible for corruption, fraud and trafficking children for the purpose of international adoption.

The ongoing corruption in international adoption has three painful consequences. First, when corruption becomes so widespread that countries are forced to close to international adoption, children who are truly orphaned are denied the opportunity to be adopted. Second, abusive adoption practices destroy vulnerable families in the developing world. Third, when a child's documents are altered to make them a 'paper orphan' eligible for international adoption, the truth about the child's story is concealed.

Bring justice to the Fatherless

We hope this chapter persuades you that there is a pattern of corruption in international adoption that is both widespread and likely to be repeated – and that as Christians we have a responsibility to take this issue seriously.

Our sincere hope is that Christians will stand up together to seek justice, to defend widows and bring justice to the fatherless. If we want adoption to be an option for children who are truly in need, we need to fight against corruption in international adoption. We need to support reform that protects orphans and vulnerable children and biological and adoptive families. We need to take steps to hold adoption agencies and their overseas representatives accountable for trafficking children for international adoption.

The rest of this book will focus on how to respond to what you have learned in the first four chapters. First, we will examine what the Bible teaches about God's heart for the fatherless and what we are called to do in response. Then we will look at how we can 'do good' without harming the vulnerable children and families we are trying to help.

QUESTIONS FOR DISCUSSION AND REFLECTION

1. Have you or anyone you know been involved in an adoption where a child was 'stuck?'

2. Do you think there is too much 'red tape' in international adoption? Why or why not?

3. Do you agree with the authors that corruption in adoption is widespread?

4. How would you respond to a friend who was hoping to adopt a child from Uganda, Ethiopia, Democratic Republic of Congo, or another country struggling with a corrupt adoption system?

5. Do you know anyone who has adopted a child only to discover later that what they were told about the child's history was false or misleading?

Seeking God's Heart for the Fatherless

*The people who walked in darkness have seen
a great light; those who dwelt in a land of deep
darkness, on them has light shone.*
(Isaiah 9:2)

At night when I (Sara) tuck my daughter into bed, when it is still and quiet in her room, we often talk about her adoption. Sometimes she asks to lie on my chest where she can hear my heartbeat – and asks if she grew in my tummy. I gently tell her no and remind her of the story of her adoption. As an adoptive parent, one of my heaviest burdens is that of carrying my daughter's story. She has experienced the loss of her first family and culture. While we love our daughter unconditionally, we cannot replace what she has lost. We can comfort her as she grieves and do our best to answer her questions about her adoption.

We will not only stand before God to answer for the choices we made in our adoption process, we will stand before our adopted daughter. Will we be able to say that we did everything we could to make sure her adoption was necessary?

Over the last four chapters, we've learned that there is an orphan crisis, but that it's not as simple as millions of children who will to go sleep tonight with no one to say *you are mine* and *I love you*.

We've learned that most of the world's orphans are living with their families – and many of these families are desperately poor and at risk of exploitation. We've learned that building, supporting and visiting orphanages often hurts the children we're called to help. We've learned how the system of international adoption takes advantage of vulnerable families to find adoptable babies and toddlers, while simultaneously failing to find adoptive families for orphans who are truly in need of adoption.

If you have read the last four chapters, I imagine you feel the same heaviness that I do. You may want to give up on caring about orphans and poverty and injustice, or to shut your eyes and carry on as if you had not learned the truth. As Christians involved in the adoption and orphan care movement, we have made mistakes. With the best of intentions, we have hurt the vulnerable orphans and widows we are called to help.

But there is good news.

The good news is not that we can fix what we have messed up. The good news is the Gospel. There is no reason for us to be discouraged by our failure to do what God has called us to do. We don't need to give up or to shut our eyes.

In the next chapter we will look at who God calls us to be – and how He calls us to respond to the orphan crisis. The Bible is full of practical wisdom for how to care for the poor and oppressed. The rest of this book will empower you to do adoption and orphan care differently. But before we go there, I want to pause. Before we dig into the how to redeem international adoption and orphan care, let's dig into the why.

Knowing God must be at the heart of caring for the fatherless. If we want to follow the example of the Father of the Fatherless, we must first get to know Him. If we want to know God, we need to study the Bible. The Bible tells us who God is and who we are. It shows us how God reveals Himself – and what He cares about. In the words of Dan Cruver, we want to align our hearts 'missionally with the heart of the Father.'[1] In order to understand our Father's agenda – what He is calling us to do – we need to understand His heart.

The Bible teaches Christians to defend the fatherless. We're called to visit orphans and widows. As Christians we believe that every verse in the Bible is God-breathed and is helpful, and

---

1   Cruver, Dan. *Reclaiming Adoption.* 1st ed. Adelphi, Maryland: Cruciform Press, 2011. Print.

Isaiah 1:17 and James 1:27 are no exception. But plucking a few Bible verses out of context is not enough. If we want to know God's heart, we need to study the Bible from the beginning to the end.

God's heart is ultimately revealed in the Gospel. From Genesis to Revelation, the Bible is a story about God creating a people who will be His people.[2] The Gospel is a rescue mission. It's a war. It's also an adoption story. The Gospel provides a deep foundation for orphan care and adoption.

The Gospel can be summarized in two words: but God.

But God...

Let's start at the beginning. God creates the heavens and the earth. He makes the night and the day. He creates the sun and the moon and fills the universe with stars. He gathers the oceans and forms the dry land. He fills His creation with life: plants, animals, fish, and birds. Finally He digs His hands into the mud and creates man in His image. Men and women are created to live in relationship with God, with one another, and with creation. We are created to be God's family: to love Him and to love one another. We are formed to worship God and to enjoy God's kingdom. Made in the image of God, we are designed to create culture and steward creation – to be His representatives reflecting His glory to the world.

When the serpent tempts Adam and Eve in the Garden of Eden, he asks a question that has defined human history: is God really good?[3] The serpent portrays God as oppressive. Adam and Eve believe the lie, and they reject God. But when Adam and Eve rebel against God, everything changes. Sin enters the world. The consequences of the fall shape every area of life.

We were created to live as God's children, but we reject God as our father. We were created to worship God, but we serve idols. We were designed to love one another, but sin breaks our relationships. We were made in the image of God to reflect His glory, but our identity is distorted and we glorify ourselves instead of God. We were created to represent God to the world, but we fail to be who God calls us to be.

The story continues. As people begin to fill the earth, there is increasing corruption:

---

2   Chester, Tim. Together for Adoption 2011. Conference.

3   In Genesis 3:1-4, the serpent questions the truth of God's word and the goodness of God's character.

The Lord saw that the wickedness of man was great in the earth, and that every intention of the thoughts of his heart was only evil continually. And the Lord was sorry that he had made man on the earth, and it grieved him to his heart. (Gen. 6:5-6)

God sees the earth, and it is full of corruption and violence. He sends a flood to destroy nearly everything. The flood has consumed the peoples of the earth. No one is left but Noah and his family, who are drifting alone in a wooden boat full of animals.

But God remembered. (Gen. 8:1)

This is the turning point in the story. God could have destroyed everything He made. He could have started over from scratch. But God has a plan. He makes a promise to Noah that He will never send another flood to destroy the earth. He gives Noah a rainbow as a sign of this covenant. God has a plan to redeem everything He has made.

Another 'but God' moment happens a few chapters later. God shows up to Abraham and promises that he will be the father of a multitude of nations. This is laughable because his wife Sarah is a barren, old woman. But God remembers Sarah, and she gives birth to a son named Isaac. In the same way, God remembers Rebekah and Rachel in their barrenness.

God makes a covenant promise to Abraham, Isaac and Jacob that He will be their God – and they will be His people. God is promising to be with His people. He promises to protect and provide for them like a father. He promises to work through them – and often despite them – to accomplish His plans.

This promise hints at the end of the story: God will make a great nation that will be a blessing to all the nations of the earth. God promises that in the end He will redeem a people who are His people, a people who will know God, a people who will bless and worship Him. God promises that redemption will be through grace.

The story continues. Joseph is the son of Jacob and Rachel, the second youngest of twelve brothers. The older brothers despise Joseph and conspire to kill him. They eventually decide to sell him into slavery. Joseph ends up in an Egyptian prison, but God is with Joseph. God works through what seems like an impossible situation to give Joseph a position of power serving the Egyptian Pharaoh.

Meanwhile, there is a severe famine over all the earth. Jacob and his family are starving. They hear that there is grain for sale in Egypt. Jacob's sons travel to Egypt hoping to buy food. There, the brothers are met by Joseph, their second youngest brother whom they sold into slavery. The brothers do not recognize Joseph, but eventually Joseph tells them the truth. In another 'but God' moment, Joseph realizes this was all in God's hands:

> As for you, you meant evil against me, but God meant it for good, to bring it about that many people should be kept alive, as they are today. (Gen. 50:20)

God renews His promise with Israel to be with His people and to deliver them again to the Promised Land. For hundreds of years, the people of Israel have been slaves in Egypt. But God sees their suffering and remembers His covenant and leads the people out of Egypt and into Canaan. As God delivers the people of Israel out of bondage, He makes a promise:

> I will take you to be my people, and I will be your God. (Exod. 6:7)

God delivers the people of Israel out of Egypt, through the Red Sea and into the desert wilderness between Egypt and Canaan. When the people arrive at Mount Sinai, Moses goes up the mountain to spend time with God. There God delivers an even more astounding promise:

> If you will indeed obey my voice and keep my covenant, you shall be my treasured possession among all peoples, for all the earth is mine; and you shall be to me a kingdom of priests and a holy nation. (Exod. 19:5-6)

God's people are saved from something to something. The people of God are to live in a distinctive way that makes God known. God's law shows His people how to set up their lives to show others the glory of God. God's way of ordering life is good: a source of blessing, freedom and life. God gives the law for the sake of mission. God's people are blessed to be a blessing.[4]

Though God graciously brings His chosen people into the Promised Land, God's people ultimately fall into sin and idolatry. God chose His people to worship and be in community with Him, but Israel rejects God. The people of Israel forgot God's law, and everyone does as they see fit. Instead of being a blessing to the nations around them, the people of Israel become more evil than the nations surrounding them. The people of God do not structure their lives to show others the glory of God.

---

4   ibid.

God's people fail to protect and provide for the vulnerable. Instead of loving mercy and justice, God's people exploit the poor.[5]

But God is not done with His people. Through the prophets, God renews His promise to create a people who will be His people. This promise will be fulfilled ultimately in the coming of Christ.

Jesus is the true Son of God. The way He lives proclaims the glory of God. In His perfect, sinless life Jesus fulfills the requirements of the law. He loves God and He loves His neighbors. Jesus demonstrates the goodness of God's kingdom. He heals the sick and feeds the hungry. Jesus' ministry never separates the proclaiming of truth from the meeting of needs. Jesus reveals God's heart as he executes justice, offers mercy, and walks humbly with God the Father.

Though Jesus is the Messiah for whom they have been waiting, Israel's religious leaders don't believe Him. Jesus calls them to repentance for missing the point of God's law:

> Woe to you, scribes and Pharisees, hypocrites! For you tithe mint and dill and cumin, and have neglected the weightier matters of the law: justice and mercy and faithfulness. (Matt. 23:23)

Threatened by His powerful influence and radical teaching, the religious leaders plot to have Jesus killed. Jesus is betrayed by one of His best friends. He is mocked, tortured and nailed to a cross. Jesus dies in our place for our sin. Jesus is crucified, 'but God raised him from the dead' (Acts 13:30).

> But God shows his love for us in that while we were still sinners, Christ died for us. (Rom. 5:8)

When Jesus dies on the cross, He becomes the sacrifice who atones for our sin. He is the priest who mediates between man and God. Through Jesus, we are adopted into God's family. We are reconciled into relationship and community with God and with one another.

The gospel can be summarized in two words: but God. The world is full of poverty and injustice, brokenness and sin. But God sent Jesus to forgive sin and to heal brokenness, to proclaim freedom and usher in God's kingdom:

> The spirit of the Lord God is upon me, because the Lord has anointed me to bring good news to the poor; he has sent me to bind up the brokenhearted, to proclaim liberty to the captives, and the opening of the prison to those who are bound. (Isa. 61:1)

---

5   See Isaiah 10:1-2, Jeremiah 5:28 and Ezekiel 22.

God's mission is fulfilled in Jesus. He reveals the glory of God to the nations. Jesus is the servant King who proclaims the coming of God's kingdom. Jesus is the King who came in humility; He is also the King who will come again in glory. Throughout His ministry, Jesus teaches that God's kingdom is good news.

God is making all things new. He is making a new heaven and a new earth. He is adopting a people who will be His people:

> Behold, the dwelling place of God is with man. He will dwell with them, and they will be his people, and God himself will be with them as their God. He will wipe every tear from their eyes, and death shall be no more. (Rev. 21:3-4)

The Heart of a Father

At the end of the day when my husband Mark comes home from work and knocks on the front door, our adopted daughter Ella runs to open the door. She throws down her toys and reaches up for her daddy's arms, squealing *daddy, daddy, daddy*. He scoops her up and cuddles her close. She rests her head on his shoulder and snuggles her thick black curls into his neck.

Ella has a daddy. This is good news for a little girl who lost her biological father to AIDS. Made fatherless by AIDS, this little girl would have grown up without a daddy to care for her, feed her, love her, or protect her. But my husband Mark was overjoyed to adopt Ella as his own daughter, to be a father to this fatherless girl. Now Ella has a daddy who adores her, who will protect and provide for her.

Adoption is a beautiful picture of the gospel. What does it mean that God calls Himself a father?

When God describes Himself, He uses words of relationship. God reveals Himself as the Father to His Son. He also describes Himself as the Father of His chosen people and the Father of the Fatherless. God has always been a father. Long before He created the heavens and the earth, God was a father.

God is a Father to his Son

> And when Jesus was baptized, immediately he went up from the water, and behold, the heavens were opened to him, and he saw the Spirit of God descending like a dove and coming to rest on him; and behold, a voice from heaven said, 'This is my beloved Son, with whom I am well pleased.' (Matt. 3:16-17)

In this moment, we are invited to peek into the eternal relationship of love between the Father and Son. The Father declares Jesus is His beloved son. The voice from heaven confirms the eternally existing relationship of divine love that the Son and Father share.

The voice also confirms Jesus' identity as the Son of God in fulfillment of prophecy. The Jewish people have been waiting for the Son of God. In 2 Samuel 7:14, Nathan the prophet predicts the coming of the Son of God: 'I will be to him a father, and he shall be to me a son.' This beloved Son is the triumphant King, but He is also the humble Servant who will lay down His life to bring salvation to all nations.

In Mark 14, we get another glimpse into the relationship between the Father and the Son. It is late at night after the last supper. Jesus has been betrayed by Judas. He knows He is about to be arrested, beaten and murdered. Filled with sorrow, Jesus falls to the ground and prays to God the Father:

> And he said, 'Abba, Father, all things are possible for you. Remove this cup from me. Yet not what I will, but what you will.' (Mark 14:36)

Jesus calls God the Father *abba* – literally daddy – and yet He submits His will to His Father. Jesus, who was God and was with God from the very beginning, 'did not count equality with God a thing to be grasped, but emptied himself, by taking the form of a servant, being born in the likeness of men...he humbled himself by becoming obedient to the point of death, even death on a cross' (Phil. 2:6-8).

On the cross, Jesus became fatherless for us. He was forsaken by God the Father so that we could be adopted into God's family:

> But when the fullness of time had come, God sent forth his Son, born of woman, born under the law, to redeem those who were under the law, so that we might receive adoption as sons. And because you are sons, God has sent the Spirit of his Son into our hearts, crying, 'Abba! Father!' (Gal. 4:4-6)

Jesus died on the cross so that we would be welcomed into the family of God. Now we who through Jesus are children of God can – by the power of the Holy Spirit who lives in our hearts – call God the Father our daddy.

God is a Father to His People

> From the beginning to the end the Bible is the story of God creating a people who will be his people.
>
> Tim Chester[6]

I did not grow up believing that God was my Father. The summer I turned fifteen, I had to read most of the Bible for a British Literature class. I read through Genesis and Exodus, the Psalms and Isaiah, all the way through Matthew and Mark laughing. I wondered how anyone could believe that the Bible was true.

But then God did something amazing. When I read the story of the Prodigal Son in Luke 15, God opened my eyes and changed my heart. I could see myself in the Prodigal Son, and here was a Father willing to welcome me home. In that moment, I was adopted into the family of God.

The Parable of the Prodigal Son reveals God's heart for His people. Dan Cruver, author of *Reclaiming Adoption*, brilliantly describes God's passion for His chosen people:

> But the beauty and wonder of the Parable of the Prodigal Son(s) is that it puts the father's love on display—a love that embraces the younger son with uninhibited joy...the father comes to the rebels to bring them into *his* joy, *his* home. This father loves prodigals.
>
> We are the prodigals whom Jesus, the true and eternal Son, came to bring home.[7]

God is an adoptive Father. Adoption is God's idea. Adoption was the plan from the very beginning:

> He chose us in him before the foundation of the world, that we should be holy and blameless before him. In love he predestined us for adoption as sons through Jesus Christ, according to the purpose of his will. (Eph. 1:4-5)

When God chose Israel, He adopted them into His family.[8] And when God chose us, He predestined us to be adopted into His family.

We were fatherless. We were rebels. We were prodigals. But God, because of His deep love for us, sent His Son to die in our

---

6   Chester, Tim. Together for Adoption 2011. Conference.

7   Cruver, Dan. *Reclaiming Adoption*. 1st ed. Adelphi, Maryland: Cruciform Press, 2011. Print.

8   Romans 9:4.

place for our sin – so that we could be reconciled to God. God's love is relentless and endless. Adoption is the point of the gospel.

Even now as we live as the adopted children of God in a broken world, we are surrounded by injustice and poverty. We have experienced a taste of what it's like to be God's people and we long for more. We join all of creation in groaning 'inwardly as we wait eagerly for adoption as sons, the redemption of our bodies,' (Rom. 8:23). We are waiting for the day when, in the words of Dan Cruver:

> The heavens and the earth will be transformed into our Father's house. The renewed earth will become the place where we forever enjoy our Father's love as his sons and daughters.[9]

God is a Father to the Fatherless

> Realize, then, how significant it is that the Biblical writers introduce God as 'Father of the fatherless, defender of widows' (Ps. 68:4-5, NIV). This is one of the main things he does in the world He identifies with the powerless. He takes up their cause.
>
> Tim Keller, *Generous Justice*

God is the creator and ruler of the universe. He is perfect in holiness, wisdom, power, and love. God is powerful and strong, and yet He identifies with the weak. God seems to have a special compassion for the fatherless.

Throughout the Bible, we see God's heart for all who are powerless. In ancient Jewish culture, orphans, widows, immigrants, and the poor would have been vulnerable to exploitation.

Who are the fatherless in the world today? We live in a world where there are 115 million desperately poor widows caring for more than half a billion children, a world where eight million children are growing up in orphanages. We live in a world torn by violence and conflict, where 25 million people have been forced from their homes.[10] We live a world where every year more than 1.2 million children are trafficked and forced into slavery. We live in a world where 1.4 billion people live in extreme poverty, a world where 1,000 women die every day in childbirth and 26,000 children die every day because of poverty.

9   Cruver, Dan. *Reclaiming Adoption*. 1st ed. Adelphi, Maryland: Cruciform Press, 2011. Print.

10   'UNHCR Global Appeal 2013 Update - Populations Of Concern To UNHCR'. *United Nations High Commissioner for Refugees*. 2013. Web. 8 Sep. 2014.

We live in a broken world, a world where we desperately need God. When God tells us who He is, He is teaching us what is close to His heart. God calls Himself the Father of the Fatherless.[11] As the perfect Father, God protects and provides for His children.

We live in a world where the poor have no voice, but God is passionate about justice:

> He executes justice for the fatherless and the widow, and loves the sojourner, giving him food and clothing. (Deut. 10:18)

> Father of the fatherless and protector of widows is God in his holy habitation. (Ps. 68:5)

> You hear the desire of the afflicted; you will strengthen their heart; you will incline your ear to do justice to the fatherless and the oppressed, so that man who is of the earth may strike terror no more. (Ps. 10:17-18)

> The LORD watches over the sojourners; he upholds the widow and the fatherless, but the way of the wicked he brings to ruin. (Ps. 146:9)

We live in a world in crisis, but our God is our merciful Redeemer:

> In you the orphan finds mercy. (Hosea 14:3)

> But you do see...you have been the helper of the fatherless. (Ps. 10:14)

> Do not move an ancient landmark or enter the fields of the fatherless, for their Redeemer is strong. (Prov. 23:10)

Living in the light of the gospel

From beginning to end, the Bible is a story about God, who calls Himself a Father, adopting a fatherless people. God's people are called to protect and provide for the fatherless in response to what we have received and as a reflection of the Father's heart.

For those of us who believe in the gospel, God is our Father, our Redeemer, and our King. In the light of the gospel, we have a new identity.

We were fatherless, but we have been adopted by God. We are precious children welcomed into the family of God. We were lost, but we have been redeemed by God. We are missionaries sent by

---

11   Psalm 68:4.

God. We were in slavery, but we have been set free by God. We are disciples who live under the glorious and good reign of God.

When we understand who God is and what He has done for us, we want to align our hearts with His. God is merciful, and so we are called to offer compassion to a hurting world. God hates injustice, and so we are called to defend the fatherless. In the next chapter, we will look at how God calls His people to respond to the orphan and widow crisis.

QUESTIONS FOR DISCUSSION AND REFLECTION

1. The author claims the Gospel can be summarized in two words: but God. Do you agree? Why or why not?

2. Can you describe a 'but God' moment in your own story?

3. What does it mean to you that God is Father?

4. How does what God has done change our identity?

5. How does the Gospel provide a foundation for adoption and orphan care?

The Father's Hands

What does the Old Testament have to do with orphans and widows?

The book of Exodus begins with the story of a mother who is in a desperate situation. She is a Hebrew living in Ancient Egypt. The ruthless king of Egypt has forced the people of Israel to work as slaves. In fear of future rebellion, the Pharaoh commands all male children born to Hebrew mothers to be killed at birth.

When this young woman gives birth to a son, she must make a heartbreaking choice. She hides her child for three months. Knowing she cannot hide the boy much longer, she tenderly makes a basket. In an act equal parts faith and desperation, she places her baby in the basket and puts it among the reeds on the edge of the river.

In God's providence, the daughter of the Pharaoh finds the baby boy who is crying by the edge of the river. She has mercy on him and intervenes to protect his life. The woman rescues the boy and names him Moses. He grows up as an Egyptian prince in the house of the Pharaoh.

Meanwhile, the Pharaoh continues to oppress the people of Israel. They are forced into slavery.

> 'And God heard their groaning, and God remembered his covenant... God saw the people of Israel – and God knew.'
> (Exod. 2:24-25)

When Moses is a young man, he sees and is grieved by the oppression of his people. After he kills an Egyptian whom he found beating one of his people, he flees Egypt in fear of the Pharaoh.

But then God appears to Moses in a burning bush. God calls Moses to go back to Egypt and to bring the children of Israel out of slavery. Through a series of miraculous events, this promise is fulfilled. God's people have suffered through hundreds of years of slavery, yet they were defined by their covenant relationship with the God who heard their cries and remembered His promise. God is faithful to His chosen people.

God appears to Moses and gives him the Law. The law is not a set of rules to be followed to earn the favor of God. The law represents how to set up life with gospel intentionality. To live as who they are. The people of Israel are already chosen by God. This was by grace, not because of anything they did.

The whole of the law is concerned with Israel being holy before a holy God. Much of the law is devoted to how Israel should worship God. The law also provides moral and ethical commandments that shape how the people of God should relate to one another and to the world around them. The law affects every aspect of life – including protection and provision for the fatherless and the widow.

> 'You shall be holy, for I am holy.'
> (Lev. 11:44, 1 Pet. 1:16)

But is the Old Testament law – including the requirements to protect and provide for orphans and widows – relevant to us today? The sacrificial system of Leviticus has ceased for the people of God. It has been fulfilled in the coming of Christ. Studying the law remains important because it enables us to understand sin and how Jesus saves us. By studying the Old Testament, we discover what it means that Jesus is our great High Priest, our Sacrificial Lamb, and our King.

Furthermore, studying the Old Testament not only allows us to understand Christ's work on the cross; it teaches us how we should live as the people of God. The Old Testament law deals with what it looks like for God's people to be holy, set apart from the world around them. Like the Israelites, we are called to be holy. The law's moral requirements reveal the kind of conduct that is acceptable and unacceptable to a holy God.

In the book of Leviticus, the law makes it clear that God's people are called to protect and provide for the poor and oppressed. Widows, orphans, foreigners and the poor represent people who would have been vulnerable to oppression. When the people of Israel were sojourners

> *'You shall not mistreat any widow or fatherless child.'*
> (Exod. 22:22)

in Egypt, they were exploited through slavery. God's people are called to remember how they suffered in Egypt and to care for the needy with justice and mercy.

What are the specific requirements of the law? The people of Israel are prohibited from harvesting to the edge of their fields and vineyards. They are required to leave the gleanings and fallen grapes for the poor (Lev. 19:9-10). In this way, God commands His people to provide for those who, in an agrarian society would have had no means to provide for themselves. Likewise, God forbids oppression and calls for justice amongst His people and their neighbors (Lev. 19:13, 15). In particular, God prohibits His people from mistreating orphans and widows (Exod. 22:22).

> *'When a stranger sojourns ... in your land, you shall not do him wrong ... you shall love him as yourself, for you were strangers in the land of Egypt.'*
> (Lev. 19:33)

These laws flesh out what it means for the people of Israel to love their neighbors as themselves. God continually reminds Israel that they were sojourners and that He brought them out of slavery. The people of God are to show mercy because they have received mercy. They are to love justice because they have received justice.

But God's people forget. They forget that God is God. They forget that He chose them, that He brought them out of Egypt, that He made them His own. Even while Moses is meeting with God on Mount Sinai, the people of Israel build an idol out of gold, worshiping created things rather than the Creator. Not long after the law is given, as the people of God begin the journey from Mount Sinai to Canaan, they grumble and complain. They forget that God has redeemed them from slavery so that they could live as His children – so that they could represent God to a broken world. As a result of their idolatry and disobedience, God sentences the people of Israel to spend forty years wandering through the desert before entering Canaan.

Getting to the heart of the law

Forty years later, Moses is an old man. The people of Israel are camped near the Jordan River. They can see the Promised Land. Moses knows this is his last chance to tell his people what is most important. Try to imagine everything he has experienced in his lifetime. Moses grew up as a Prince of Egypt. He met God in a burning bush. Moses witnessed the miraculous power of God and led his people out of Egypt. He was chosen by God to receive the law, to call his people to repentance from idolatry and sin. Moses has led his people through forty years wandering in the wilderness, waiting for the promise to be fulfilled. Deuteronomy is the final three sermons Moses would preach to the people of Israel before he died – and before the next generation entered the Promised Land.

Deuteronomy is one of my favorite books of the Bible. If the law in Exodus and Leviticus can be a little hard to understand, Deuteronomy puts it all in perspective. Deuteronomy is a rich commentary on the law that reveals the heart of God. Moses loves God, and he loves his people. He knows deep in his soul that God has been faithful despite Israel's ongoing sin. He is pleading with the people he loves to walk in faithful obedience. What does Moses want his people to remember?

Moses pleads with his people over and over again to remember: they were slaves. They were foreigners. They were poor. They were orphans.

'I am the LORD your God who brought you out of ... Egypt, out of the house of slavery.'
(Deut. 5:6)

Moses reminds the people they were not chosen by God because of righteousness. They were a stubborn people, but God chose the nation of Israel as an act of grace, of undeserving love. God has made them His holy people, His treasured possession.

And then Moses reminds the people who God is: 'know therefore today and lay it to your heart that the Lord is God in heaven above and on earth beneath; there is no other,' (Deut. 4:39). A few chapters later in Deuteronomy 10:17-18, Moses goes deeper: 'For the Lord your God is God of gods and Lord of lords, the great, the mighty, and the awesome God, who is not partial and takes no bribe. He executes justice for the fatherless and the widow, and loves the sojourner, giving him food and clothing.'

Finally, Moses focuses on the very heart of the law: 'You shall love the Lord your God with all your heart and with all your soul and with all your might' (Deut. 6:5). The law was never a rule book to follow in order to gain God's favor. God has already given Israel His blessing, even though they are undeserving. Israel is not saved through the law, but through grace. Moses calls the people to faithful obedience in response to God's grace.

Israel has been chosen by God to represent Him to a broken world. The purpose of the law is to reveal how to live in response to who God is and what He has done. The law is not about outward obedience. It is about being aligned missionally with the heart of the Father. When people love God in response to God's love for them, they are transformed – and this is the means by which the rest of the world is to learn about the true God. This is the very reason for which Israel was chosen.

Justice and Mercy at the Heart of the Law

God's people are called to protect and provide for the least of these. They are intended to fight for justice for – and to offer mercy to – the fatherless, the widow, the poor, and the sojourner.

Ancient Israel was an agrarian society. The Levites, who had a unique position leading Israel in worship, owned no land and had no means to produce grain, wine or oil, or to raise animals. The other tribes were required to provide for the needs of the Levites. Like the Levites, orphans, widows and sojourners would not own land and would have no way to provide for their needs. In Deuteronomy 14:29, Moses commands the people not only to care for the Levites, but also to care for the vulnerable: 'And the Levite... and the sojourner, the fatherless, and the widow, who are within your towns, shall come and eat and be filled, that the Lord your God may bless you in all the work of your hands that you do.'

Take a minute to see how radical these words are. Moses is saying that widows and orphans deserve the same protection and provision as the Levites, the tribe of priests who held an important position in the community. The rest of Deuteronomy lays out how God's people are to protect and provide for orphans and widows.

Protection: Fighting for Justice

Moses calls the people to remember they were slaves and God has redeemed them. They have been rescued by a God who heard their groaning and who intervened to bring them justice. In response, God's people are to love justice. Moses commands the people to appoint righteous judges and forbids them from showing partiality or accepting bribes, which 'blind the eyes of the wise.' The law specifically commands the people to protect widows and orphans:

> 'Give justice to the weak and the fatherless; maintain the right of the afflicted and the destitute.'
> (Ps. 82:3)

> You shall not pervert the justice due to the sojourner or to the fatherless, or take a widow's garment in pledge. (Deut. 24:17)

> 'Cursed be anyone who perverts the justice due to the sojourner, the fatherless, and the widow.' And all the people shall say, 'Amen.' (Deut. 27:19)

Provision: Offering Mercy

Moses likewise reminds the people to remember they have been blessed to be a blessing. God has graciously provided for their needs. In response, they are to be generous with the poor, the widows, the fatherless, and the sojourner who are in their midst: 'You shall give to him freely, and your heart shall not be grudging when you give to him, because for this the Lord your God will bless you in all your work and in all that you undertake' (Deut. 15:10). In the next verse, we see that the people are called not to cling to what God has given, but to let go and be merciful: 'You shall open wide your hand to your brother, to the needy and to the poor, in your land' (Deut. 15:11).

The law commands the people to care for widows, orphans and other people who are in desperate need in four specific ways.

Tithes

Tithes were set down before God as an act of worship and then given to the sojourner, the fatherless and the widow: 'When you have finished paying all the tithe of your produce in the third year, which is the year of tithing, giving it to the Levite, the sojourner, the fatherless, and the widow, so that they may eat within your towns and be filled' (Deut. 26:12).

Sabbatical Year

At the end of every seven years, the people of Israel were called to forgive one another's debts. Likewise, the law forbids people from refusing to lend to one another just because the sabbatical year is coming. These are in effect commands to be generous. The purpose of the Sabbatical year is that 'there will be no poor among you' (Deut. 15:4).

Gleaning

Like sojourners or the poor, widows and fatherless children were vulnerable in ancient Israel because they did not own land. This meant they could not grow food or raise animals to provide for their own needs. The people of Israel were required to leave a margin in their lives to care for orphans and widows:

> When you reap your harvest in your field and forget a sheaf in the field, you shall not go back to get it...When you beat your olive trees, you shall not go over them again...When you gather the grapes of your vineyard; you shall not strip it afterward. It shall be for the sojourner, the fatherless, and the widow... (Deut. 24:19-21)

Worship and Feasts

God's people are required to invite widows, the fatherless, the poor and the sojourners to join them in celebrating and worshiping God. Unable to afford the cost of food or wine, widows and orphans would have been excluded from participating in feasts where Israel was to rejoice before God. The Israelites are required to welcome the least of these into their celebrations: 'And you shall rejoice before the LORD your God, you and your son and your daughter, your male servant and your female servant, the Levite who is within your towns, the sojourner, the fatherless, and the widow who are among you, at the place that the LORD your God will choose, to make his name dwell there' (Deut. 16:11).

What happens when we fail to care for orphans and widows?

God's people are called to reflect God's heart for orphans and widows, the poor and needy. They are called to protect and provide for the least of these. They are called to pour out the love and mercy that they have received. They are called to remember: who God is, what He has done, who they are.

But God's people forget.

Israel rebels against God. They do not know Him or understand His heart. The words of Isaiah cut deeply: 'Sinful nation, a people laden with iniquity, offspring of evildoers, children who deal corruptly! They have forsaken the Lord, they have despised the Holy One of Israel, they are utterly estranged' (Isa. 1:4). As a result of their sinful rebellion, Israel is sent into exile. Jerusalem is burned with fire. The temple that was built as the dwelling place of God on earth is destroyed.

Israel has continued to offer a 'multitude of sacrifices' (Isaiah 1:11), but God has had enough of their empty rituals. God grows weary of Israel's 'vain offerings' (Isa. 1:13-14). He refuses to listen to the prayers of the people because when they spread out their hands, they are 'full of blood' (Isa. 1:15).

Why are their hands full of blood? The words of the prophets are clear. Israel has failed to protect and provide for the fatherless, the widows, and the poor. I will let these verses speak for themselves.

- How the faithful city has become a whore, she who was full of justice...everyone loves a bribe and runs after gifts. They do not bring justice to the fatherless and the widow's cause does not come to them. (Isa. 1:21, 23)

- Woe to those who decree iniquitous decrees, and the writers who keep writing oppression, to turn aside the needy from justice and to rob the poor of my people of their right, that widows may be their spoil and that they make the fatherless their prey! (Isa. 10:1-2)

- For wicked men are found among my people...they judge not with justice the cause of the fatherless, to make it prosper, and they do not defend the rights of the needy. (Jer. 5:26, 28)

- Thus says the Lord of hosts...do not oppress the widow, the fatherless, the sojourner, or the poor, and let none of you devise evil against another in your heart. But the people refused to pay attention and turned a stubborn shoulder and stopped their ears that they might not hear. They made their hearts diamond-hard lest they should hear ... (Zech. 7:9-12)

- Father and mother are treated with contempt in you; the sojourner suffers extortion in your midst; the fatherless and the widow are wronged in you. (Ezek. 22:7)

Ezekiel 22 goes on to catalog how the people of God are breaking every commandment. Israel has utterly failed in its mission to live like the children of God. Every area of life is defiled. The people of Israel are guilty of rape, murder, worshiping idols, taking bribes, oppressing the poor, neglecting justice, and 'destroying lives to get dishonest gain' (Ezek. 22:27).

God's people have forgotten.

> 'Cease to do evil,
> learn to do good;
> seek justice,
> correct oppression;
> bring justice to the fatherless.
> plead the widow's cause.'
> (Isa. 1:16b-17)

This is profound. God is saying that our faithfulness – the genuineness of our faith, our hearts – is revealed in how we care for the least of these. We cannot claim to love God while ignoring the needs of the poor or depriving widows and orphans of justice.

God's people have failed to protect and provide for orphans and widows. But this is not the end of the story. The prophets call the people of Israel to repentance. They call God's people to protect and provide for the fatherless, the widow and the poor. The prophets also promise the coming of Jesus:

The Spirit of the Lord GOD is upon me,
    because the LORD has anointed me
to bring good news to the poor;[a]
    he has sent me to bind up the brokenhearted,

to proclaim liberty to the captives,
and the opening of the prison to those who are bound;
to proclaim the year of the LORD's favor. (Isa. 61:1-2a)

Several hundred years later, a poor, young woman gave birth to a baby. Like Moses' mother, Mary faced a difficult decision. King Herod is looking for the baby Jesus, seeking to destroy Him. Jesus, Mary, and His earthly father Joseph flee to Egypt. After the death of Herod, Jesus' family returned to Israel.

Nearly thirty years later, a humble, Galilean peasant entered the synagogue in Nazareth. Jesus opened the scroll and read these words from Isaiah 61. Every eye in the room was fixed on Him as He said, 'Today this scripture has been fulfilled in your hearing' (Luke 4:21). Jesus is the Messiah for whom the people of Israel have been waiting.

Jesus did not come to abolish the law or the prophets, but to fulfill them (Matt. 5:17). To properly understand Jesus' mission on earth, we need to see that the Old and New Testaments are part of the same story. The Old Testament law was given to teach the people of Israel how to live as the children of God. They were called 'to act justly and to love mercy and to walk humbly with [their] God' (Micah 6:8, NIV). Why? Because God had given them justice, poured out His mercy and adopted them as His own. But the people of God have failed.

And this brings us to Jesus: Jesus will be the true Son who will teach the nations about God's heart. Jesus fulfills the requirements of the law. He loves God. He loves His neighbors. He heals the sick. He feeds the hungry. He executes justice. He offers mercy. He walks humbly. He goes to the cross. He redeems. He reconciles. Jesus' ministry never separates the proclaiming of truth from the meeting of physical needs.

Like the people of Israel who have been redeemed out of slavery but not yet delivered to the Promised Land, we are wandering in the wilderness waiting for our eternal home. Like the people of Israel who were longing for the coming of the Messiah who would triumph over their enemies, we are longing for Jesus to come back and to destroy sin and death.

Like the people of Israel, we are called to live with gospel intentionality while we wait for the return of the King and the coming Kingdom of God. Like Jesus, we must not separate the proclaiming of truth from the meeting of physical needs. We have been redeemed. We have been adopted into the family of God. We are called to reflect the heart of our Father – and to be His hands to a broken world.

How does Jesus summarize the requirements of the Old Testament Law?

> You shall love the Lord your God with all your heart and with all your soul and with all your mind. This is the great and first commandment. And a second is like it: You shall love your neighbor as yourself. On these two commandments depend all the Law and Prophets. (Matt. 22:37-38)

Quoting the words of Moses from Deuteronomy, Jesus is saying that the law is not about outward obedience to a list of rules. The law is about total devotion to God. When we understand who God is and what He has done, our right response is worship. This is how we love God. And when we love God, we will love our neighbors. If we truly love our Father, our lives will reflect His heart for the least of these:

> 'For I was hungry and you gave me food, I was thirsty and you gave me drink, I was a stranger and you welcomed me, I was naked and you clothed me, I was sick and you visited me, I was in prison and you came to me.' Then the righteous will answer him, saying, 'Lord, when did we see you hungry and feed you, or thirsty and give you drink? ... And when did we see you sick or in prison and visit you?' And the King will answer them, 'Truly I say to you, as you did it to one of the least of these my brothers you did it to me.' (Matt.25:35-40)

In this passage, Jesus is talking about the final judgment. He will sit on His glorious throne and the nations of the world will be gathered in front of Him. He will separate the sheep from the goats, the righteous from the cursed. The righteous will inherit the Kingdom of God; the cursed will depart into the eternal fire. This image should cause us to pause and reflect on the significance of Jesus' words. Is Jesus teaching that we can earn salvation by caring for the least of these?

No. The righteous will not inherit the Kingdom because of the compassionate works they have done; righteousness is a gift from God. Believers are called righteous because their hearts have been transformed in response to Jesus. The evidence of this is their compassion for the least of these. In other words, if you do not care for the least of these, you have not been transformed by God.

This same idea is echoed by the leaders of the early church. James exhorts Christians to be 'doers of the word, and not hearers only, deceiving yourselves' (James 1:22). In other words, we are lying to ourselves if we claim to love the word of God but we do not do what it says. Later in the same passage, James describes true religion:

> Religion that is pure and undefiled before God, the Father, is this: to visit orphans and widows in their affliction and to keep oneself unstained from the world. (James 1:27)

Likewise John makes it clear we are called to love people as we have been loved by God.

> See what kind of love the Father has given to us, that we should be called children of God... (1 John 3:1)

> By this we know love, that he laid down his life for us, and we ought to lay down our lives for the brothers. But if anyone has the world's goods and sees his brother in need, yet closes his heart against him, how does God's love abide in him? Little children, let us not love in word or in talk but in deed and in truth. (1 John 3:16-18)

What does this mean in the world today?

God is the Father of the Fatherless, the Defender of Widows. We are created in God's image. We have been redeemed from sin and adopted as the children of God. As a result, we have a responsibility to the fatherless. Christians are called to protect and provide for orphans and widows. The rest of this book will inspire you to be the hands of the Father in the world today.

In the first half of this book, we asked questions that challenged the assumptions of the Christian adoption and orphan care movement. You recognize that most of the world's orphans live with families and these families are often vulnerable to poverty and injustice. You understand why building, supporting and visiting orphanages can be harmful to orphans. You appreciate how corrupt adoption practices can destroy poor families. In the last two chapters, we have examined the truth in the Bible to gain a deeper understanding of God's heart for the fatherless and how we're called to respond.

The second half of this book will empower you to fight for an end to harmful adoption and orphan care practices. You will learn effective ways to protect and provide for orphans and vulnerable children by addressing the root causes of the crisis. You will be inspired by stories from families, ministries and churches who are involved in international adoption and orphan care.

Before we get very practical, we want to summarize what we have learned about whom God is and what we are called to do.

What does it mean to bring justice to the fatherless?

We live in a world today where orphans and vulnerable children are often denied justice. Thousands of children are forced to be child soldiers. Millions of children are trafficked and exploited through the sex industry. More than one thousand children will experience the death of their mother during childbirth today, and every day. These women die because they do not have access to medical care – and this is unjust. Likewise, more than twenty-five thousand children die every day because they lack food. This too is an injustice. Christians are called to protect orphans and vulnerable children from exploitation and poverty.

At the deepest level, bringing justice to the fatherless is about fighting for the right of every child to have what every child most deeply needs: a family.

As Christians, we believe that God created us to live in families. God designed mothers and fathers to protect and provide for their families. Children who are fatherless are vulnerable precisely because they lack the very people intended to keep them safe. Widows are vulnerable because they have lost their husband, who was intended to defend them from harm. Bringing justice to orphans means protecting the right of children to grow up with loving, safe families.

In the world today, there are millions of children who have been orphaned, abandoned, or separated from their families. These children have a right to grow up with a family. They do not need government programs or institutions. They need mommies and daddies. But all across the world, restrictive government policies keep children from having new families through adoption. Governments with limited resources seldom prioritize the needs of orphans and vulnerable children.

As a result, millions of orphans are confined to institutions where they often suffer abuse and neglect. They wait for years in foster care. They end up stuck indefinitely in countries that close to international adoption as a result of concerns over corruption.

Good families who would love to welcome a child into their home through adoption cannot. Adoption often costs tens of thousands of dollars and takes years. Meanwhile, children are growing up without the love and care of a family – often with devastating consequences for their hearts, minds and bodies.

Christians in the Evangelical adoption and orphan care movement are rightly outraged. Denying children the opportunity to grow up with loving families through adoption is an injustice. But it is also an injustice to destroy a desperately poor family in order to find a child for international adoption.

Principles for Caring for Orphans and Widows

Remember

From beginning to end, God calls us to remember who He is and what He has done. We were slaves; God has redeemed us from slavery. We were fatherless; God has adopted us into His family. We were poor; God has made us heirs of the Kingdom. We were dead in our sin; God made us alive in Christ. Everything we do should be grounded in our experience of mercy. The adoption and orphan care movement should be deeply rooted in the Gospel. Our motivation should not be guilt inspired by the overwhelming need, but rather love.

God tells us to care for orphans and widows

God's people are called to protect and provide for orphans and widows. If we love God, we should care for the fatherless and the poor out of obedience to Him. The authenticity of our faith is revealed in how we care for the least of these.

Caring for orphans and widows is missional

God calls Himself the Father of the fatherless and the Defender of widows. When Christians protect and provide for orphans and widows, we demonstrate God's heart. There is something about adoption and caring for orphans that gives us a deeper experience of the Gospel. In the words of Jedd Medefind, the President of the Christian Alliance for Orphans, caring for orphans makes 'grace touchable'.

What is God's design? The family and the church

God's plan is straightforward. There are two institutions that God has designed to protect and provide for orphans and widows: the family and the church. The most powerful thing we can do to fight the orphan crisis is to empower the local church. If you empower the church, you can empower families.

Providing for orphans and widows

Our primary goal should be providing orphans and widows a path out of poverty. Remember that poverty is about more than a lack of money or resources. Poverty is about broken relationships that affect every area of life. Poverty is separation from God. Poverty is broken relationships with others. Poverty is a wrecked relationship with creation. The way God's people were called to provide for the poor deals with all of this brokenness.

In the Old Testament, God's people were called to provide for orphans and widows by letting them glean in their fields, sharing their food through the tithe, inviting them to join in feasts, lending freely and forgiving debts. To put it simply, the poor were invited to worship and to work in community with God's people.

What does this look like in a world today where few of us have fields where we could let the poor glean? We are called to be generous – to leave a margin for the needs of orphans and widows. We are invited to be open-handed with our wealth: to realize everything we have is a gift from God and that we are simply stewards of His resources. Furthermore, we must consider how our efforts to provide for orphans and widows offer a path out of poverty. Vulnerable families should be invited to work and worship in community with God's people.

Protect orphans and widows from injustice

Christians are called to protect orphans and widows from exploitation. In the Old Testament, God's people were called to set up a legal system that protected vulnerable families from injustice. They were also prohibited from accepting bribes, dealing corruptly and exploiting the fatherless, the widow, the sojourner and the poor. Christians today are called to uphold these same principles.

QUESTIONS FOR DISCUSSION AND REFLECTION

1. What does the Old Testament have to do with caring for orphans and widows?

2. How does God call His people to protect and provide for the fatherless?

3. What happens when God's people fail to care for orphans and widows?

4. Are these things relevant to us today?

5. What does it mean to bring justice to the fatherless?

Families
not Institutions

When Charlotte and Charles[1] decided to adopt from DRC, they wanted to help children who needed a family. They signed on with a Christian adoption agency and agreed to adopt a sibling group of three children who, according to the agency, had been abandoned by their mother who could not afford to care for them. Well into the adoption process, after Charlotte and Charles became the children's legal parents in DRC, Charlotte received an email from the agency informing her that her son had broken his leg and needed surgery.

Out of concern for the boy, Charlotte asked a Congolese friend to visit him in the hospital to ensure he was safe. At the hospital, she made a startling discovery. The boy's mother sat at his bedside. Through this friend, Charlotte learned that the children's mother, Grace, had not abandoned the children. Rather, a person who worked at an orphanage had convinced Grace to bring the children to the orphanage. She was told that Americans would come and take

---

1   Names have been changed for security.

them to America for education, after which time they would return to build her a house and take care of her. Shortly after handing over three of her children, she gave birth to a baby girl. The orphanage staff convinced Grace to place this child for adoption as well, telling her that 'Americans love babies.' Grace's newborn daughter was matched with another adoptive family.

Charlotte had the opportunity to speak with Grace on the phone using a translator. Weeping, Grace told her that she would be heartbroken if she never saw her children again. She begged Charlotte not to take them away from her. When Charlotte told her that she would help Grace get her children out of the orphanage and back into her care, Grace wouldn't stop thanking her. Because the children were not orphans needing adoption, Charlotte and Charles pulled out of the adoption. They then worked to remove the children from the orphanage and place them back into the care of their mother. I (Amanda) traveled to Kinshasa at Charlotte's request to help accomplish this goal.

When I arrived at the orphanage, I discovered that Grace was living there with her four children. She was caring for them while they waited for their new American parents. I asked to meet them at Charlotte's request. After speaking with Grace through a translator, it became clear that Grace loved and cared for her children deeply. She was in her early twenties, extremely poor and had no safety net, but she was a devoted mother. While she desired to give her children a different life, she did not intend to relinquish her children for a permanent, legal adoption as we in America understand it.

Because the orphanage would lose the $1,200 per month they were receiving from Charlotte, Charles and the baby's adoptive parents, Charlotte had to hire a local attorney to remove the children from the orphanage. Ultimately, this effort was successful. Today Grace is living with her four children along with her sister and family.

A Family's Heartbreaking Choice

Grace is not the only mother to place her children in an orphanage with the hope of providing them with a better life. As a single mother living on a razor's edge in the large city of Kinshasa with little support, she was easily lured by the romantic idea of her children growing up in America. She imagined they would have a comfortable life and a bright future, which she feared she could not provide in DRC.

Adoptions from DRC became popular in 2010. Since 2010, over 700 children have been adopted to the US.[2] It's estimated that over 800 adoptions are currently in process.[3] Based on the countless stories we have heard from families who have adopted from DRC and other developing countries, we are certain there are many mothers like Grace who make the heartbreaking choice to place their children in an orphanage or for adoption out of desperation caused by poverty. And whether or not Grace's story is typical, we believe that these families deserve our attention and protection.

There are an estimated four million orphans in DRC. As we've learned, orphan does not necessarily mean alone and unloved. Children need the love, security and sense of belonging provided by a family to thrive, but desperate families struggle to provide food, clean water, education, medical care, shelter, and safety from violence. Vulnerable families have been given two options: place their children in an orphanage or relinquish them for adoption. Neither one does anything to address the reasons why the family is vulnerable. While adoption provides the child with a new family, it leaves the first family no better off. Adoption is not in the best interests of a child who has a loving family.

Christians have built orphanages all over DRC with good intentions, but building more orphanages is not the answer. Institutional care is harmful to children and should always be the last resort. Building orphanages takes children out of families and does little to fight poverty.

Children are designed to live in families. As Christians, we should defend the right of every child to grow up with the love and care of a mother and father. It is inexcusable to take children from desperately poor families in the name of Christ – regardless of whether the child will live in an orphanage or with an adoptive family.

In countless villages and slums around the world, few voices are speaking up for what is best for children or defending the rights of vulnerable families. The decision to place a child in an orphanage is rarely made in the best interests of a child or with complete

---

2   U.S. Department of State. Bureau of Consular Affairs. Intercountry Adoption. Country Information – Democratic Republic of Congo. Web. 20 June 2014.

3   Both Ends Burning.'The DRC Crisis by the Numbers – as of June 19, 2014.' Web. 8 September 2014.

information about the effects of such a decision. Likewise in DRC, the decision to place a child in an orphanage is often driven by the desire to provide the child with food, shelter and education. Orphanage staff, government officials and social services are focused on the traditional solution of institutionalization. Rarely does anyone ask whether family preservation is an option.

How do we care for orphans without orphanages?

The truth is that there are countless orphans and vulnerable families in the developing world that need help. As Christians have opened their eyes to the orphan crisis in the developing world, building and supporting orphanages has become the primary solution. Before we propose an alternative, let's quickly review why this solution falls short.

Most of the world's orphans are living in families, and these families are often vulnerable to poverty and exploitation.

There are millions of children who have been orphaned, abandoned, or separated from their families, but comparatively few live in orphanages or on the streets. Most of the world's orphans continue to live with their families. Most of the children living in orphanages or on the streets have been separated from their families not by death, but by poverty. Children and families living in extreme poverty are among the most vulnerable people in the world.

When you build an orphanage in a poor community, you create orphans.

There are hundreds of millions of families who – *just like the mothers in DRC* – face impossible decisions. Mothers consider selling their bodies to pay for medical care for a sick child. Fathers struggling to provide for their families consider selling themselves or their children into slavery. For families living in desperate poverty, the margins are slim. Children living in poverty are at risk of being separated from their families because desperate parents may feel they have no other choice.

When just a few dollars can mean the difference between life and death, families are vulnerable to exploitation. Christians who build orphanages or encourage international adoption may take children from their desperate parents, unintentionally exploiting these vulnerable families.

Orphanages are harmful to children.

While orphanages may provide shelter and safety in a time of crisis, long-term institutional care is harmful to children. Many orphanages fail to meet children's basic needs. Children living in orphanages are at risk of abuse and neglect. Even the best orphanages cannot replace families. Children have a critical need for connection and even good orphanages cannot provide children with the love, security and identity offered by a family.

Orphanages will never be able meet the needs of most of the world's orphans or end the orphan crisis.

Building orphanages is not sustainable. Caring for children in institutional care is far more expensive than caring for children in families. Furthermore, building orphanages does nothing to address the poverty, injustice and brokenness at the root of the orphan crisis.

We've learned that orphanages are not good for children – but how do we care for orphans without building orphanages?

As Christians who are convinced that the Bible calls us to protect and provide for orphans, how do we do orphan care differently? Can we care for orphans without institutions? When is building or supporting an orphanage the right thing to do? Are the families and churches in the developing world willing and able to care for the orphans in their communities?

From Orphanages to Families

Here's the good news: it is possible to care for vulnerable children and orphans without building orphanages. Every expert we have spoken with – from Ethiopia and Uganda to Haiti and Costa Rica – agrees. There is no need to build more orphanages. We are not suggesting we abandon the eight million children who live in institutions today. Rather, we have an amazing opportunity to reform these institutions while also advocating for what children truly need.

There may be millions of orphans in the world today, but there are billions of people who worship Jesus. This means there are billions of people who have been called to protect and provide for the least of these. The church has heeded the call to care for orphans, turning out in droves at adoption conferences and raising money for adoptions. Christians have proven that they care about orphans and want to see them in families. There are more than enough families in the world to care for orphans without building more orphanages. It is time we start investing in families, businesses and churches rather than institutions.

The first part of this chapter will dig into principles for reforming orphan care. We believe that families are the solution to the orphan crisis. We likewise believe that the global church has an incredibly important role to play in supporting vulnerable families, protecting children, and addressing the brokenness at the root of the orphan crisis. We are not alone in this vision. A growing number of Christians involved in the adoption and orphan care movement share this vision. Likewise, international organizations involved in alternative care, including UNICEF, believe it is possible to care for most of the world's orphans without orphanages.

This chapter will challenge you to think about orphan care differently and will focus on three important topics: family preservation, family- and church-based orphan care, and reforming institutional orphan care. It will also empower you with knowledge to build an orphan care ministry that will make a lasting difference. This chapter also serves as an introduction to the rest of *In Defense of the Fatherless*. The ideas we develop in this chapter are at the heart of the principles and methods in the rest of this book.

Throughout this chapter, we will look at examples of organizations that are putting these principles into practice. Each has been a tremendous encouragement to us as we have researched this book. We know these stories will inspire you that it is possible to care for vulnerable children without building orphanages.

What is Alternative Care?

The United Nations has developed Alternative Care Guidelines, which set best practices for when children need to be removed from parental care and the provision of a range of care options to meet individual children's needs. The guidelines prioritize permanent, family-based care over temporary or institutional care for children who have been orphaned, abandoned or separated from their families. The goal of the guidelines is to give 'these children a better opportunity to reach their full potential and transition successfully into adulthood.' In other words, the goal is what is best for each child.

The Alternative Care Guidelines are already influencing orphan care in countries around the world, from Uganda to Guatemala. While Christians in the orphan care and adoption movement may disagree with how the United Nations sometimes works, we believe the Alternative Care Guidelines will serve to protect children from exploitation and harmful practices in institutional care.

As Christians, we believe we can build on the framework of the Alternative Care Guidelines. In this chapter, we are proposing a continuum of family- and church-based orphan care that is based on a Biblical conviction that God designed families and churches to protect and provide for orphans and widows.

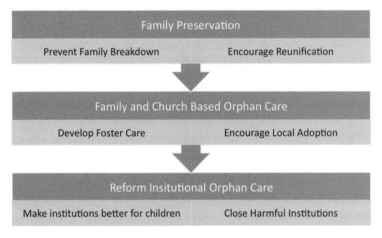

What is family preservation?

Family preservation is about empowering families to prevent children from being orphaned or abandoned. It is also about reuniting families that have broken down. Strengthening families and communities is the best way to meet the needs of orphans and vulnerable children. It is important whenever possible to encourage families and communities – even those burdened by conflict, poverty and disease – to continue caring for orphans. Our first priority in serving orphans and vulnerable children living in their families must be helping these families thrive.

What is family- and church-based orphan care? In a broken world, we know there will be times when children are orphaned, abandoned or separated from their families. Family- and church-based orphan care is about creating alternatives to institutional care for children who are in crisis. The goal of family- and church-based orphan care is to provide children with what they truly need: a permanent, loving, safe family. The family and the church are the two institutions designed by God to protect and provide for children.

First Families First

In the developing world, poverty is often the main reason why parents abandon or relinquish their children. Our first priority in orphan care must be strengthening vulnerable families to prevent children from being orphaned or abandoned. To decide what interventions will prevent family breakdown, consider the reasons why the family is vulnerable. The Africa Child Policy Forum was a meeting of African leaders in 2012 to discuss the future of orphan care and adoption in Africa. The leaders agreed that supporting first families is a central priority in orphan care:

> As much as possible, and when in their best interests, children should grow up in their biological family environment – which includes their extended family – and in their country of origin.[4]

A family may be vulnerable as a result of a crisis, such as a natural disaster, conflict or illness of a parent. In these circumstances, families who were previously self-sufficient may have acute needs. In a time of crisis, children are at high risk of being separated from their families and placed in orphanages or even relinquished for international adoption. In the aftermath of conflict or disaster, families may need relief, such as food, shelter, medical care and education. If a family is vulnerable because of a crisis, we can provide temporary assistance to meet these acute needs, empowering families to support their children and stay together.

Other families are vulnerable as a result of poverty or injustice – deeply rooted issues that cannot be solved by relief alone. These families may need food today, but they also need to be empowered to provide food for their children tomorrow. Breaking the cycle of

---

4   ACPF. 'Intercountry Adoption: An African Perspective'. Addis Ababa: *African Child Policy Forum*, 2012. Print.

poverty requires development. Likewise, breaking the bonds of injustice requires transforming the systems that oppress the poor. Later in the book, we will consider in more depth how we can fight poverty and injustice to strengthen vulnerable families.

One of the best examples of work with first families we have seen is Abide Family Center in Jinja, Uganda. In 2013 Megan Parker and Kelsey Nielsen began the work of Abide after they had both volunteered at an orphanage. While working at the orphanage, they witnessed the power of family reunification and the reality that many of the children living at the orphanage had families that loved them, but were considered 'too poor' to care for them.

Megan and Kelsey wanted to give families an alternative to placing their children in an orphanage. Seeing babies growing up without families, Megan became 'frustrated that [she was told] families were too poor to take care of their children,' for something as simple as not being able to provide formula after a mother's death.

Abide has developed a model for keeping children in families. They have seen how poor families who reach out to social services are often sent home without help or referred to an orphanage. Abide seeks to break this cycle by 'offering services that empower caregivers to keep their kids at home instead of removing a child from a poor family.'[5] Abide believes that poverty should never be a reason that children are separated from their families.

Abide offers three levels of family preservation services. First, when Abide becomes aware of a family that is at risk of breaking down, they begin an investigation to determine what support the family needs.[6] Second, Abide provides direct services to families. Third, Abide offers referrals to other aid organizations when necessary. Abide offers the following direct services depending on each family's situation and needs:

- Case management by trained social workers
- Emergency and transitional housing for a maximum of three months
- Early childhood education for children up to six years of age
- Business classes for caregivers with certificates upon graduation

---

5   Abide Family Center. 'How We Help.' N.d. Web. 24 June 2014.
6   ibid.

- Small grants for business class graduates
- Pastoral counseling and Bible studies with a full-time pastor
- Parenting Discussion Group for caregivers currently in the programs[7]

Janet is one of those mothers who was considered 'too poor' to care for her child. When Janet's husband became seriously ill, his family came and took him home to his village, leaving his young pregnant wife with their three year old child to fend for themselves. Weeks after he left, Janet gave birth to Queen, a sweet healthy girl with a big personality. Janet spent months living with relatives and friends until she ran out of options. When she finally found a job, her employer told her that she would need to leave the children behind before coming to work. Seeing no other option, Janet went to a baby home to leave her children. She planned to return once she had enough money.

By God's grace, instead of accepting the children, the baby home referred Janet to Abide. Abide took them in, provided them with basic necessities, and offered Janet training in business and tailoring. A few months ago, Janet was able to move into her own house with the children. When she graduates from the tailoring class, Abide will give her a sewing machine so that she can start a business and earn income.

Janet says that she 'came to Abide crying and now I have hope.' She dreams of 'getting a sewing machine so I can pay for school fees and provide a good life for my children.'

What happens when a child is separated from their family?

Children who have been orphaned, abandoned or separated from their families have experienced a crisis. Children may be orphaned as a result of HIV/AIDS or conflict. Desperate parents may abandon their children when they have no way to provide or fear violence. Some children have been removed from their homes by authorities as a result of abuse or neglect.

When a child has lost their family, we need to ask two important questions. The first is why the child has been orphaned, abandoned or separated from their family. The second is whether there is

---

7   ibid.

someone in the child's family or community who loves and is able to care for the child. The answers to these questions will influence what type of care is best for the child.

There is amazing human capacity – if not economic capacity – across much of the developing world to care for orphans and vulnerable children.[8] At the same time, however, there is very little support for needy families caring for orphans and vulnerable children. While developing alternatives to institutional care is not easy, it is a good investment.

The From Faith to Action Initiative is a coalition of faith-based organizations involved in orphan care. The leaders of the initiative are passionate that children grow best in families and communities. According to From Faith to Action:

> Children who are well cared for by families within communities are more likely to thrive than those in orphanages. Children growing up in families generally receive the kind of love, attention, and care essential to their wellbeing.[9]

The idea that children thrive when growing up in families and communities is common sense. It is what we would want for our own children. Melissa Fay Green is best known for her book *There is No Me Without You*, about the orphan crisis in Ethiopia. According to Melissa:

> Adoption only touches a tiny fraction of orphans and vulnerable children. To reach millions upon millions more, let us reach out to the children's home communities, enabling these little ones to grow up among friends and relatives who knew their parents, speak their language, know their history, and already love them. Isn't this what we would wish for our own children?[10]

Encourage Family Reunification

What is family reunification? Family reunification is the process of restoring a child who is living in an institution to her biological family. Children may be reunified with their parents or with another caring family member. When a child is reunited with a relative, this is called kinship care.

---

8   Richter, L.M., and A. Norman. 'AIDS Orphan Tourism: A Threat To Young Children In Residential Care.' *Vulnerable Children and Youth Studies*. 2010. Print.

9   From Faith to Action. Strengthening Family and Community Care for Orphans and Vulnerable Children in Sub-Saharan Africa. Firelight Foundation. N.d. Web. 8 September 2014.

10   Journeys of Faith. A Resource Guide for Orphan Care Ministries Helping Children in Africa and Beyond. Faith to Action Initiative. N.d. Web. 8 September 2014.

Globally, four out of five of children living in orphanages have at least one surviving parent. Many more have extended family. So while we often believe that children who are living in orphanages or on the streets are all alone in the world, the truth is more complicated. Most children living in orphanages or on the streets have families who want to love and care for them. What is often missing is a commitment to reunify children who are living in orphanages with their families.

In deciding if family reunification is in the best interests of the child, it is important to consider carefully the reasons why the child was separated from the family. We must also determine if the separation is temporary or permanent. For example, if a child was placed in an orphanage as a result of abuse, it may not be in the best interests of the child to return to the abusive parent. On the other hand, if the child was placed in the orphanage as a result of temporary crisis such as a natural disaster, returning the child to the family should be the first priority.

Most children are living in orphanages as a result of poverty. For reunification to be successful, a family living in poverty may need support, such as help with the cost of school fees or access to health care. Over time, efforts to help should shift from relief to economic development.

To ensure children are thriving, parents need education, support and accountability. Parents need support to change harmful ways of thinking. When a child is resettled, it is essential that social workers follow up with the family for at least a year to ensure the family is healthy.

Support extended families caring for orphans

Kinship care is when someone from a child's extended family, including an older sibling, aunt or uncle, or grandparent, provides temporary or permanent care for a child who has been orphaned, abandoned, or separated from her parents. As Americans, it is important to remember that our extended families are small compared to the extended families across much of Africa, Asia and Latin America.

Research across Africa has found that the extended family takes care of 9 out of 10 children who have experienced the death of both parents, or who have experienced the death of one parent and are not living with the surviving parent.[11] In communities in Africa that

---

11   ACPF. 'Intercountry Adoption: An African Perspective'. Addis Ababa: *African Child Policy Forum*, 2012. Print.

have been affected by HIV and AIDS, grandparents are caring for 20-60 per cent of orphans.[12]

While providing holistic support to vulnerable families is not easy, it is a good investment. Providing support to the vulnerable family is much less expensive than caring for the child in an orphanage. Furthermore, research from all over the world 'proves that, when implemented well, care provided by a family in a child's own community is generally the best option for that child.'[13] Supporting extended families that are caring for orphans and vulnerable children represents a tremendous opportunity for the Church.

It is also important to understand that for kinship care to be in the best interests of the child, the family must want the child. Depending on the family's culture and situation, the child may grow up feeling different. They may be more likely to suffer abuse or neglect. The child may not go to the same schools or wear the same clothes as other children in the family. In some cases, the child may be exploited. Likewise, financial support offered to the extended family may create an incentive for families to offer to take children they don't truly want to parent. These risks do not mean it is better for a child to grow up in an orphanage, but it is important to consider the motivation and capability of the family when deciding if reunification or kinship care is in the best interests of the child.

Child's I Foundation and Malaika

According to some experts, there is no orphan crisis in Uganda. Rather, there is a crisis of broken families. There may be more than 2 million children who have experienced the death of a parent, but traditionally orphans in Uganda would be cared for by their extended families. This traditional system is under threat – and not just by AIDS and poverty. Tens of thousands of children have been abandoned to orphanages by desperate families who are given no other choice. Every week, babies and children are abandoned in Uganda, thrown in trash heaps or left alone in empty houses. These abandoned children often grow up in orphanages. But most children who are abandoned are not orphans: 80 per cent of abandoned children have families.

---

12   From Faith to Action. Strengthening Family and Community Care for Orphans and Vulnerable Children in Sub-Saharan Africa. Firelight Foundation. 2006. Web. 8 September 2014.

13   ACPF. 'Intercountry Adoption: An African Perspective'. Addis Ababa: *African Child Policy Forum*, 2012. Print.

Child's I Foundation is an organization that works with abandoned babies and vulnerable families in Uganda. The organization's mission is to find families for children instead of sending them to orphanages. They believe all children should grow up in loving families, not institutions. Child's I Foundation's first priority is to resettle children with their biological families. When this is not possible, the organization places children with adoptive families in Uganda.

Child's I Foundation operates Malaika, a transitional care center that provides care for abandoned babies before they can be placed with families. When babies have been abandoned, they are often weak, malnourished and in need of medical care.

As soon as a child arrives at Malaika, the organization begins the process of looking for the child's family. When a baby is abandoned, Child's I Foundation begins an immediate investigation, placing ads on the radio and in the newspaper. Their social workers talk with people in the neighborhood where the child was found to try to locate the family. When a family is located, the social workers determine if the child can be safely reunited with their parents or another relative.

The organization has been incredibly successful in encouraging family reunification. While most orphanages in Uganda do not resettle 10 per cent, Malaika has been able to resettle 66 per cent of children in their care. To ensure the safety and wellbeing of children who are reunited with their families, social workers provide support to families for one year. Whatever types of assistance are offered to families, the goal is sustainability.

In addition to caring for abandoned babies, Child's I Foundation focuses on supporting mothers. When a mother is forced to decide between letting her child starve to death or placing them in an orphanage, she feels she has no choice. By supporting mothers, Child's I Foundation is able to empower women to keep their babies and prevent them from making a decision they may regret. Malaika cares for the babies of moms who are in crisis situations while they get back on their feet. The social workers also provide support to mothers who are facing difficult situations such as the birth of triplets.

When it is not possible to resettle a child with their biological family, Child's I Foundation begins the process of looking for an adoptive family. Only when domestic adoption is not possible would they consider international adoption – and in its first three years, Child's I Foundation found families through resettlement and domestic adoption for 100 of the 130 children that came through Malaika.[14]

One of the challenges Child's I Foundation faced was that the idea of adoption outside the extended family is uncommon in Uganda. This resulted in many children who were orphaned or abandoned growing up in orphanages. Over the last two years, Child's I Foundation has launched a media campaign to encourage Ugandan families to adopt. With the partnership of the Ugandan Government, Child's I Foundation has developed a process to assess families for adoption. The Ugandans Adopt media campaign has been successful and there is now a wait list of Ugandan families who want to adopt. Malaika has been able to place nearly every child in their care who could not be reunified with their biological families with an adoptive family in Uganda.

Reunite Uganda

Welsh missionary Keren Riley founded Reunite Uganda in 2010. Reunite is committed to restoring children to their families and empowering families instead of institutionalizing children. Keren founded Reunite after her experience with a baby boy living in an orphanage in Kampala. The boy spent months living in the orphanage because no one investigated his story. Keren looked into the situation and was able to resettle the baby boy with his father. This experience became the inspiration to launch Reunite Uganda.

Keren serves children by going into orphanages and locating children who might have families and would benefit from reunification. Reunite has also worked with a number of American families who discover fraud in their international adoptions in progress and helps reunite these children with their families. Investigators work to locate family members and determine whether reunification is possible. Reunite then provides emergency support when necessary and then social work services and economic empowerment to 'ensure a sustainable and successful resettlement.'[15]

When it's not possible to resettle a child with his parents, Reunite will look to kinship care. Beatrice[16] is the grandmother

---

14   New Vision. 'Ugandans Adopt 100 Babies.' 19 May 2013. Web. 24 June 2014.

15   Reunite Uganda. 'About'. N.d. Web. 24 June 2014.

16   Name has been changed for security.

of two Ugandan children. The children spent two years in an orphanage before being reunited with their grandmother thanks to the work of Reunite. In Beatrice's grandchildren's case, Keren went to the orphanage and retrieved the children's file. Based on information in that file, Keren was able to locate the place where the children came from and travelled there to investigate further. When she arrived to meet with the local leader and showed him the photograph of the boy, he exclaimed, 'I know his father, he looks exactly like him!'

A visit to the father's home led Keren to Beatrice. Keren recalls, 'she was overcome with excitement when we showed her pictures of her grandchildren. Beatrice shouted in her native tongue, "they've found my babies, they've found my babies!"' Riley watched the community react:

> The people in the community said it was like the children had come back from the dead and that day was like a miracle for them. They got their children back; they got their futures back.

The children have been resettled for nearly three years and are happy and healthy at home with Beatrice and other extended family.

Some Christians involved in global orphan care and adoption argue that presently there are no alternatives to orphanages and international adoption in developing countries. The success of Child's I Foundation and Reunite makes it clear that when we invest resources in supporting families and encouraging adoption, there are better alternatives. Even if it was possible to build enough orphanages to care for the world's orphans, we must remember this isn't the best solution. God designed children to grow up in loving and caring families surrounded by communities. This approach needs to be the primary response.

Caring for Orphans in Families and Churches

Develop Foster Care

What is foster care? Foster care is family-based care for children who have been orphaned, abandoned or separated from their families. Foster care is better for children and less expensive than institutional care. Foster care is typically temporary while adoption is permanent. When a child is fostered, they remain a legal part of their biological family. Adoption, on the other hand, makes the child a legal member of a new family.

In the United States and the United Kingdom, as in most developed nations, foster care is supervised and supported by the government. Foster parents are required to go through training and licensing. This process is designed to protect foster children from abuse and neglect. Likewise, the government provides financial support and services to help foster families thrive.

Most of the world's orphans not living with their surviving mother or father are living in informal foster care. Often families caring for orphans live in communities deeply affected by poverty, conflict or HIV/AIDS. Family and community resources are stretched thin, but there is little support for vulnerable families caring for orphans in informal foster care.

As a result, there is a risk that children living in informal foster care will suffer neglect or be denied the opportunity to attend school. There is also a real risk these children will be exploited or abused. While children who are in informal foster or kinship care are usually well-loved and cared for, their risk of discrimination, neglect, abuse and exploitation is far greater than those who live with their parents. This situation is often exacerbated by poverty.[17] This does not mean, however, that these children would be better off in orphanages. We believe that holistic support for vulnerable families, especially vulnerable families who are caring for orphans, can reduce this risk.

In most circumstances, foster care should be temporary, providing a safe and caring family for a child while working towards the goal of a permanent family. Ideally children should be in foster care no more than six months to a few years. As soon as possible, the child should be reunited with her biological family or placed in an adoptive family. Children who live in foster care are often separated from the families who love them for longer periods than needed. When making the decision of whether a child can return to her biological family or be adopted, the focus must be what is best for the child.

Church-Based Foster Care
The priority in developing foster care is to make sure foster children will be safe and families supported. This can be done through

17   United Nations General Assembly. Factsheet on Alternative Care of Children. 2009. Web. 8 September 2014.

the government; however in many developing countries there is limited government support for foster care. We believe this presents a tremendous opportunity for the Church to make a difference in the lives of orphans and vulnerable families.

One of the key challenges in global orphan care is reaching the millions of orphans and vulnerable children who live in rural, isolated communities. But in almost every community around the world there is a church! Churches are full of families. Churches can play a vital role in encouraging families to care for orphans. By sharing what the Bible teaches about God's heart for orphans and widows, church leaders can challenge their congregations to meet the needs in their own communities. Churches can also be involved in protecting children living in foster care. The church has an amazing opportunity to partner with governments in caring for orphans in this way.

If you are the leader of an American church considering how to get involved in orphan care overseas, partnering with local churches to encourage local Christians to care for the orphans in their own communities is one of the most powerful and sustainable strategies.

Saddleback Church's P.E.A.C.E. Plan

Mary Kamanzi has fostered children in her home for as long as she can remember. As a Rwandan Christian missionary in her home country, she believes it is her responsibility to care for the children in her community who need help. Mary and her husband recently adopted a ten-year old boy who had been living in an orphanage in Rwanda. She reflects, 'While it has been a challenge for us, I am so happy to see him thriving outside of the institution.'

Using her expertise in caring for children, Mary works as the Director of Family and Orphan Care for Saddleback Church's P.E.A.C.E. Plan in Rwanda. As will be discussed in more detail later in the chapter, the Rwandan government has proactively been reforming care for orphans and vulnerable children for the last two years with an ultimate goal of emptying orphanages. The Rwandan government has welcomed partnership with churches in caring for orphans. Mary's team works to mobilize the local church to care for vulnerable children in their communities.

While international adoption was popular in Rwanda for a few years, it is now closed. Jana, a former American missionary in Rwanda, once facilitated international adoptions. This past experience with international adoption gave her a unique perspective. In Rwanda, it is illegal to relinquish a child for adoption, so most adoptions were of children who were abandoned. You would think greater numbers of children being adopted would mean fewer children living in orphanages. 'But for every kid we got out,' she shared, 'another baby was abandoned. Adoption didn't decrease the number of kids in orphanages.' As a result of her experience, Jana has a passion for domestic adoption – something she sees as the most sustainable approach to caring for orphans in Rwanda. Jana's dream is being realized through people like Mary.

Saddleback Church, based in California, promotes a vision of local churches taking the lead in caring for orphans with churches in the developed world providing support when necessary. As many of the remaining orphanages in Rwanda are not allowed to take in new children who have been abandoned, Saddleback challenges families in the local church to consider fostering abandoned babies. Mary shared, 'we want to put babies into families right away.' The Saddleback team has a list of families who can be called in an emergency to take children in as short-term foster children while investigations are done and permanent solutions are sought.

Placing a child with a foster family instead of in an institution serves multiple goals. Jana explains, 'When Rwandans see a foster child in their church or community, they can't ignore it. And some of the stigma is broken.'

One of the goals of Saddleback's P.E.A.C.E. Plan is to see babies and children who cannot be reunited with their biological families adopted by Rwandan families. Legal adoption, as we in the West understand it, is a new concept in Rwanda, but over time both the leaders of Saddleback and their Rwandan church partners hope to see domestic adoption flourish.

Reforming Institutional Orphan Care

Whether you call them orphanages, baby homes or children's villages, institutions are not a sustainable response to the orphan crisis. Orphanages should be considered the last resort. Nevertheless, approximately eight million children worldwide live in institutions. Simply closing these orphanages is not realistic. Christians need to stop building new orphanages and to invest in family- and church-based alternative care while also considering how to best meet the needs of children who are already living in institutions.

While orphanages are not the best for children, it is possible to improve them. If there are no other options that meet the needs of the child, every effort should be made to improve the quality of the institution. We have researched many organizations to identify what good-quality institutions have in common. Some orphanages seek to meet children's physical, emotional and developmental needs. Orphanages that do a good job of the meeting children's needs aim to do the following:

Respect the rights of children.

Good orphanages serve children by respecting their rights. What are the rights of a child? The United Nations Declaration on the Rights of the Child is a good place to start. The Declaration provides that a child has the right to a family and an education, to be free of employment, to be safe and free from cruelty or abuse, and to be free from discrimination.[18] In addition, a child has the right to have clean water and healthy food, the right to play, and the right to be heard.

Care for children in a family environment.

Orphanages that are less harmful to children are typically small, home-like facilities designed to serve children. A small group home is in a better position to meet a child's need for security and affection than a large institution. Likewise, village-model orphanages where small groups of children live together in family groups with consistent caregivers or 'parents' are better for children.

Hire excellent caregivers.

The caregivers who are responsible for loving and leading children should be well trained and well paid. Caregivers should be hired based on skill and experience. Caregivers must be paid well so that they remain committed to their work and can provide consistent care. Caregivers should receive training in how to care for children, including nutrition, child development and psychology, and spiritual formation. Orphanages should try to retain excellent staff who can provide consistent affection to the children in their care. Above all else, caregivers need to have the ability to connect with children.

---

18   United Nations Declaration on the Rights of the Child. UN General Assembly Resolution 1386 (XIV) of 10 December 1959. Web. 24 June 2014.

Protect children from abuse.

It is essential for institutions to create a child protection policy in order to prevent and respond to sexual and physical abuse. A high level of accountability and supervision of staff, volunteers and children is critical to avoid abuse.

Help babies and toddlers form healthy attachments.

Babies and toddlers from birth to three have a critical need to attach to a consistent, loving caregiver. To encourage children to develop healthy attachments, baby homes need a low caregiver to child ratio, to provide consistent caregivers, and to train these caregivers in what is needed for attachment. Orphanages should not allow volunteers or visitors to care for babies or toddlers.

Build a connection to the community.

Many orphanages are located away from communities and are led by missionaries from the United States or other developed countries. Yet when children age out of the orphanage, they must live in the community. Teenagers who are close to aging out of the orphanage have a unique set of needs. When they leave the orphanage, they are all alone: without a family it only takes one crisis for a child to fall through the cracks. It is important, therefore, for orphanages to prepare children for the transition to living independently in the community.

Ensure every child has an exit strategy.

Orphanages should very rarely be considered a permanent solution for a child. Good orphanages are not focused on raising the next generation of leaders for a country. Rather, they are focused on providing good-quality, temporary care to children so that they can either return to their biological families or be placed with permanent adoptive families. This focus on encouraging reunification and supporting adoption requires good social work with a consistent focus on what is best for each child.

When is institutional care appropriate?

Institutionalization should always be considered the 'last resort response for children with no other means of support.'[19] Despite our best efforts to care for children in families, there are some

---

19   From Faith to Action. Strengthening Family and Community Care for Orphans and Vulnerable Children in Sub-Saharan Africa. Firelight Foundation. 2006. Web. 8 September 2014.

circumstances where institutions are necessary or in the best interests of children.

It is important to differentiate between short-term and long-term institutional care. Short-term care for children in an orphanage may be appropriate as a temporary response to a crisis. While long-term institutional care is rarely in the best interests of a child, there are exceptional situations where it is the best choice given the actual alternatives. For example, institutional care may be appropriate for street children, children with special needs, and children who are vulnerable to exploitation.

Street Children

Homes for street children exist all over the world. The best offer a temporary residential program that aims to rehabilitate children so that they can resettle with their families. In Rwanda, Children of God is a temporary home for boys who have been living on the street because of poverty, abuse or neglect. Children of God provides educational opportunities and a stable environment where boys can learn how to live as part of a functioning group. Living on the street can be violent and scary. Street children grow up too soon, living only to survive. Children who have experienced life on the street must learn how to be a child and live in a family. Social workers from Children of God also work with each boy's family to address the reasons why he ended up on the street. Whenever possible, boys are resettled with their families. For boys who come from homes with significant neglect or abuse, reunification is not possible. The boys are educated and supported, and once they reach adulthood, they are resettled into a home of their own.

Children with Special Needs

Children living with special needs may experience neglect or discrimination. When a poor family lacks support and knowledge to meet the needs of the child, some families turn to orphanages. Ekisa Ministries in Jinja, Uganda stands in the gap for struggling families with children with disabilities. Ekisa provides residential care for children with special needs, but they do not support residential care as the only solution. Ekisa believes that children belong in families. As soon as a child comes in to care, they begin an investigation into the family's situation. Ekisa immediately puts in place a plan aiming for reunification or domestic adoption. Ekisa has been quite successful in reuniting children with their families and since 2011 three children have been adopted by Ugandans.

Ekisa also works in the community to prevent children from being relinquished or abandoned by providing support and training to families of children with disabilities.

Ekisa has seen firsthand how children with disabilities grow and flourish when they move from institutions into families. But sometimes, it is not possible to find an adoptive family or to meet the needs of a severely disabled child in a family environment. For some children who have significant disabilities, Ekisa has been unable to identify families willing and able to meet their needs. When this is the case for a specific child, the staff of social workers, teachers, caretakers, and physical therapists do their best to provide the child with love and care knowing that it still falls short of what a family can provide. Ekisa hopes that these children will eventually be adopted, but for now they remain in care.

Children who are Vulnerable to Exploitation

Some vulnerable families face unique challenges in protecting children from violence and abuse. As Our Own is an organization in western India that 'protects vulnerable children from certain enslavement and exploitation, caring for them as our own.' The ministry provides two homes for girls who are at risk of being trafficked into the sex industry. Some of the girls rescued by As Our Own have biological mothers who are enslaved in the red-light district; however it is not safe for children to grow up in brothels. Research shows that as many as 95 per cent of the children who grow up in brothels become enslaved as sex workers themselves.[20] As Our Own protects girls while allowing them to stay in contact with their mothers when possible. When mothers are safe, they are able to visit their daughters.

As Our Own believes that children belong in families and that institutional care must replicate the family environment as closely as possible. Girls live in small groups with house mothers. As Our Own employs men who serve as father figures for the girls, building relationships with the girls and providing support and guidance as they grow up. Instead of using the term orphan, the girls are referred to as daughters. As Our Own believes in providing lifelong aftercare. There is no aging out of the program. As Our Own

20   As Our Own. Stats and Facts. 2013. Web. 29 June 2014.

remains a part of the girls' lives even when they grow up. They have daughters now in college, and when the young women marry, As Our Own provides financial support for their weddings as parents would traditionally do in the local culture.

Loving Shepherd Ministries works with orphans and vulnerable children in Haiti, a country where many children are exploited as domestic slaves. In Haiti, it is common for a desperately poor family to send a child to live with a wealthier family as a *restavek*. Families hope their children will receive an education and livelihood in exchange for household help; however many *restaveks* are treated as slaves.

Like As Our Own, Loving Shepherd Ministries builds Homes of Hope to care for vulnerable children in new Haitian families. This provides an alternative to the most vulnerable children ending up in institutions or as *restaveks*. Children live in small groups of twelve boys or twelve girls in a home with a mom and a dad who make a lifelong commitment to the children. The ministry operates in close partnership with local churches who commit to supporting and walking alongside the new parents.

Both As Our Own and Loving Shepherd Ministries recognize the importance of children growing up with parents – both mothers and fathers. Both work with children who are highly vulnerable to exploitation or abuse. The ministries seek to provide deep lifelong support to the children they serve, seeing them as a part of their families. Both believe that God designed children to live in families and aim to help children not only live, but to thrive in the world.

Close the Worst Orphanages
Across Africa, Latin America, Asia, and Eastern Europe, there are far too many orphanages. Sometimes the answer is not making these institutions better. Many of these orphanages should be simply shut down. Orphanages that severely abuse or neglect children and institutions that exploit children, such as orphanages in Cambodia that profit from children begging on the streets, should be closed. The leaders of orphanages that recruit children from vulnerable families in order to earn money from donations or international adoption need to be held accountable. As Christians, we have supported many of the orphanages that have been built over the last decade. We now have a responsibility to hold these orphanages accountable, to close orphanages that exploit children and to support children in families rather than institutions.

In Rwanda, the government has placed a high priority on closing orphanages. During the genocide, approximately one million people were killed in 100 days, tearing apart hundreds of thousands of families and leaving half a million children orphaned. The traditional system that had cared for orphans in Rwanda was destroyed. In the aftermath, institutions were built in response to an overwhelming orphan crisis. Orphanages were needed as a temporary measure to protect and provide for children. As Rwanda has rebuilt, the approach to caring for orphans and vulnerable children is changing. While international adoption was popular from 2008-2010, the Rwandan government has sought to make closing orphanages and supporting local solutions the priority.

After the genocide, there were nearly 100 orphanages. Today only 34 remain. The government and its partners have encouraged church-based foster care, family reunification and domestic adoption. While it is a small country, Rwanda is paving the way for other countries to provide local solutions to the orphan crisis.

What should you do if you are supporting an orphanage?

Many Christian families and churches are already involved in supporting an orphanage or sponsoring children living in an orphanage. If you find yourself in this situation, we encourage you to start by asking the orphanage the following questions:

- **Legal Registration**: Is the orphanage registered with the government, if that is required? Is the orphanage authorized to care for children?

- **Family Preservation**: Are they focused on family care whenever possible? What do they do to support poor families who seek to place their children in the institution? Do they employ social workers to try and place children in families? Are the orphanages used as temporary emergency care or are children placed on a more permanent basis?

- **Standards of Care**: Does the orphanage adhere to minimum standards of care as set forth by the local government or by recognized standards for child care? Is there a written child protection policy? Are staff members screened and well-trained?

- **Community Life:** Are the children learning life skills to prepare them to exist in community? Do they have regular interaction with the local community? What has happened to the children who have already aged out of care?[21]

You may be able to come alongside the orphanage to improve the quality of the care for children and to help more children be reunited with their families. If through this process you discover that the orphanage is exploiting children or failing to protect children from abuse, it is important to withdraw financial support and to alert the local authorities.

From Orphanages to Families

Our primary goal in orphan care is simple. Our goal is not to provide orphans with clothing, food or an education. Our goal should always be to make orphans into sons and daughters.

Our first priority must always be empowering parents to care for their own children. Families in the developing world are vulnerable to poverty and injustice. Every effort must be made to support vulnerable families to prevent children from being orphaned or abandoned. Likewise, every effort must be made to reunite children who are living in institutions with their families.

But ultimately, if it is not possible for a child to grow up with their biological family, the child needs a new family. Adoption – either domestic or international – can provide children with permanent, loving, safe families. Chapter Nine will focus in much more depth on how Christians can encourage domestic adoption while also reforming international adoption. Adoption, when done ethically, is a vital part of global orphan care.

God designed children to grow up in families. If even a tiny fraction of the world's Christians open their hearts to care for the millions of children who are growing up in orphanages, these institutions would no longer be needed. The Church is made up of the children of God living in every country in the world. Together we have a tremendous opportunity to equip and disciple families to care for orphans and vulnerable children in our communities and around the world.

---

21   Konnected, Keeping Kids in Families. Orphanage Checklist. ACC International Relief. N.d. Web. 8 September 2014.

We cannot do this alone

These principles provide a foundation for how to do orphan care that will make a lasting difference in the life of a child. But we cannot do this alone. This is critically important. As Americans, we have no right to go into countries in the developing world to tell people how to care for orphans and vulnerable children. We are outsiders. We have resources, but this does not mean we know what is best for children, families and communities different than our own.

It is critically important for Christians who want to be faithful and fruitful in doing orphan care to develop partnerships with local churches, communities and governments. Our orphan care projects will fail if they do not have local ownership. If we want to make a lasting difference in the lives of orphans, we need to change not just what we are doing – but also who we are working with.

Governments have a responsibility to protect orphans and vulnerable children. As Christians, we need to partner with governments in fighting against corruption and protecting children from trafficking. We also have a tremendous opportunity to partner in providing services that will support vulnerable families and tackle the root causes of the orphan crisis.

As Christians in the developed world, our most important partners in the fight to end the global orphan crisis are churches and families in the developing world. Church- and family-based orphan care has many benefits when compared to institutional orphan care. By strengthening families and equipping churches, we are encouraging local ownership and sustainable development. Family-based orphan care is less expensive than institutional orphan care, so investing in families is wise stewardship. Growing up with the love of a family surrounded by a church community is better for children. By partnering with local churches and communities, we are respecting the dignity of people made in the image of God.

This chapter has introduced you to a few organizations and ministries that prove there are alternatives to orphanages. It is possible to encourage people in Rwanda, Uganda, Ethiopia, and beyond to get involved in caring for orphans. Many communities in the developing world are already doing an incredible job caring for orphans. Most of the world's orphans are already living with families. Equipping extended families and communities to care for orphans is not without challenges, but it is worth the effort.

Questions for Discussion and Reflection

1. What circumstances may lead a family to place their child in an orphanage? Can you imagine how you would feel in a similar circumstance?

2. Is it possible to care for orphans without orphanages? What can we do to strengthen the capacity of communities to care for orphans and vulnerable children?

3. When is institutional care in the best interests of a child? When this is the case, what can we do to make orphanages better for children?

4. How can we support churches in developing countries to care for orphans and vulnerable children?

5. Do you feel challenged to do something differently as a result of what you have learned in this chapter?

Make a Lasting Difference

Jenni's first short-term mission trip to El Salvador was in 2009. At the time, she and her husband Mike were in the process of adopting a child from El Salvador. There are approximately 20,000 children living in orphanages in El Salvador, an impoverished country in Central America.[1] Jenni had a heart for orphans, was fluent in Spanish, and had served as a leader in her church's missions department for more than a decade.

'When our adoption agency asked me to lead a mission trip to visit orphans in El Salvador, I said "yes",' Jenni remembers. 'I was told there were desperate needs, and that I could help. I thought I would go care for orphans – and possibly meet the child we would soon be adopting.'[2]

When Jenni and her team traveled to visit the orphanage, they brought donations that were intended to meet needs of the

1   Gordon, Karen, et al. 'Whole Child International Latin American Children's Home Project'. Whole Child International, 2006. Print.

2   Ramsey, Jenni. Personal Interview. 2014.

orphans: 'We showed up with lots of cash. We naïvely brought the leaders of the orphanage lots of stuff.' Jenni quickly realized that everything she had been told about the orphanage was false. Although Jenni was not new to missions, she had been naïve to assume the donations would make it to the children: 'We had never been there. We didn't know the real needs. There were red flags everywhere, and there was no accountability.'

This first mission trip was a powerful learning experience for Jenni, who continues to lead short-term mission (STM) trips. Jenni now serves as the Director of His Hands His Feet, a ministry that serves orphans and vulnerable children in El Salvador and Guatemala.[3] His Hands His Feet sends teams to serve alongside local churches and ministries. Jenni is passionate about working in close partnership with local believers who understand the needs of their communities.

In El Salvador, His Hands His Feet partners with Sus Hijos, an orphan care ministry led by primarily local believers who are supported by North American missionaries. The organization serves in government orphanages, where most children have been placed due to abandonment, abuse or neglect. The government centers and transition homes also care for children who have been rescued from trafficking and children with severe special needs. In addition to serving in the centers, Sus Hijos works to empower poor families, helping to provide jobs and to build houses, to prevent family breakdown. The ministry has a transition home for children who age out of the government care centers, and a ministry that feeds homeless street kids.

The leaders of Sus Hijos know the needs of their local community inside and out. They have built a strong relationship with the local government, and they know the children and families whom they serve. These local believers are in the best position to meet the needs of the vulnerable children in their community. His Hands His Feet has formed a long-term partnership with Sus Hijos, and visiting short-term missionaries come alongside the local leaders to support and encourage their work. Jenni is passionate that the role of a short-term missionary is to submit, to listen and to learn from the local believers.

In July 2012 Jenni led her seventh mission trip to El Salvador. This trip had a special purpose. The team was planning to throw

---

3   His Hands His Feet is a ministry of All Blessings International Adoptions.

a big birthday party – a *quinceanera* – for dozens of teenage girls living in a government transitional care center. According to Jenni:

> A *quinceanera* is a traditional birthday celebration for Latin American girls who are turning fifteen. It is a 'rite of passage' and families often spend thousands of dollars on this momentous event for their daughters. Sadly, the teenage girls in the government orphanages miss the opportunity to celebrate their *quinceaneras*. In July 2011, our team learned how this heart-breaking reality affected the teenage girls and committed to return the following year. We remembered these girls, honored our word and returned to host an unforgettable *quinceanera* for forty-three beautiful, young women.

The visiting missionaries worked alongside the local leaders of Sus Hijos to put together a wonderful party. The visiting team brought dresses, jewelry and make up, and spent the day with the girls helping them prepare for the celebration. Many of the young women who were honored in the *quinceanera* had been victims of abuse, violence or trafficking. For some, this was the first time anyone had celebrated their birthday. The *quinceanera* had a profound impact on these young women.

Two years later, government officials who oversee children in protective custody asked Sus Hijos to throw a second *quinceanera* for nearly 100 more girls. In 2014, Jenni led a team to El Salvador to do just this. The first and second ladies of El Salvador attended the celebration along with judges and officials. According to Jenni, the *quinceanera* made a significant impact:

> The government leaders were impressed by the event and the team met their ultimate goal of supporting the Sus Hijos foundation and improving their influence and relationship with the government.[4]

We think there is something beautiful about this story. Many mission trips focus on projects, but this mission trip focused on people. The trip was about building relationships, with the visitors serving alongside the local leaders. On the surface, the trip wasn't about evangelism or alleviating poverty. The focus of the trip was simply a party – and there's something deeply Biblical about throwing a party. God's kingdom will be a glorious celebration, and this *quinceanera* gave these women a taste of God's lavish love, and the truth that He has not forgotten them.

---

4   Ramsey, Jenni. 'Update on 2014 mission trip to El Salvador'. Personal Interview. 7 September 2014.

In chapter three, we discussed how STMs have the potential to do more harm than good. But at the same time, we believe there is a role for Christians to go and serve in cross-cultural ministry. God calls Christians to go and make disciples. He calls us to protect and provide for the poor and oppressed. He calls us to visit orphans and widows. We want to go because the Bible says go, but we want to go without hurting the people we're called to help. In this chapter we will explore how to do STMs differently.

Before we get to our vision for short-term mission trips, however, we want to clarify a few things.

We don't have to go to be on mission.

We don't have to spend thousands of dollars and travel halfway around the world to visit orphans. No matter where you live, there are children and families in your community who need Jesus. You can be the hands and feet of Christ to the hurting and vulnerable who are your neighbors. By loving and serving single parents, foster kids, or refugees in your community, you can live out James 1:27. You are called to make a lasting difference in the places where you live, work and worship. Before you go to another country to serve, you should be engaged in what God is doing all around you.

There is nothing wrong with wanting a life-changing experience.

If you want to have your eyes opened, few things are more powerful than traveling to another country. Spending a few weeks or months in a developing country can change your heart, values and perspective. If you want to go learn and experience life in another culture, by all means go. But when we go to minister cross-culturally, especially to care for orphans and vulnerable children, we must not go for selfish reasons. We must go because we are called. We must think less about the impact on ourselves and more about the impact on the people we are called to serve.

Where We Want To Go

Over the last few chapters, we've shared our vision for family- and church-based orphan care. We've learned that there are more than 100 million widows caring for a half billion orphans living in extreme poverty. We've seen that there are eight million children living in orphanages, and most of these children have been separated from their families by poverty and injustice.

We've looked at God's heart and how we're called to respond. We believe that Christians are called to protect and provide for orphans and widows in response to and as a reflection of the Gospel.

Our aim throughout this book is to encourage Christian families and churches to embrace a different kind of orphan care ministry. We believe God calls His people everywhere to protect and provide for vulnerable children and families. This includes the billions of Christians who live in Africa, Asia, Eastern Europe, and Latin America. We want to move away from supporting children in orphanages and toward empowering Christians in the developing world to care for the orphans and widows in their communities.

So where do short-term mission trips fit into this vision?

Short-term mission trips have an important role to play in supporting the people who are doing kingdom work in difficult places, day in and day out. This means long-term missionaries. It also means the local church that is on the ground in nearly every community in the world.

In writing this chapter, we have heard from missionaries and local leaders that short-term missions can be helpful and encouraging if approached in the right way. While some STMs unintentionally hurt the communities they seek to help, it does not have to be this way. Few people advocate doing away with STMs entirely, but many want them to change.

While there is potential to hurt rather than to help, the Bible makes it clear that Christians are called to go and serve. With intentionality and awareness of the potential for harm, an informed church, leader and team can make a powerful difference.

By coming alongside local churches and ministries, we can have a long-term impact – even on a short-term trip. We can use our resources and skills to empower Christians to make a difference in their local communities. By building relationships, we can encourage the people who are on the ground making disciples and caring for orphans and widows. Through thoughtful partnership, we can protect vulnerable children from harm.

Go and Make Disciples

Go therefore and make disciples of all nations, baptizing them in the name of the Father and of the Son and of the Holy Spirit, teaching them to observe all that I have commanded you. And behold, I AM with you always, to the end of the age. (Matt. 28:19-20)

We believe in missions because Jesus tells us to go. These words – often called the Great Commission – are Jesus' final instruction to His followers. God the Father sent Jesus His Son on a mission to reach the people He loved. We are called to do the same.

In Luke 5, Jesus calls His first disciples. He comes alongside a group of fishermen who are packing up their empty nets after a long night of work. Jesus is surrounded by crowds who want to hear the word of God, and so He climbs in a boat and asks Simon to push out from the land. When Jesus is done teaching the people about God, He invites Simon to put his nets down into the deep water. Simon, who was likely exhausted after fishing all night but catching no fish, lets down the nets. What happens next is remarkable. Simon catches so many fish that his nets are breaking and his boat is sinking. His partners James and John come to help him bring in the catch. Jesus then calls these men – His first disciples – to leave everything, follow Him and become fishers of men.[5]

Mission is a response to mercy. In a message on Luke 5 preached at The Gospel Coalition 2013 National Conference, David Platt rightly observed that Jesus called His disciples to go on mission after they received His mercy. In the same way, we are called to go in response to the mercy we have received.[6]

We are not just called to go share the Gospel in all corners of the world. We are called to make disciples *who make disciples*. Discipleship is about building relationships with people, inviting people to receive the mercy of God. It is also about empowering people to live differently in light of God's mercy.

We cannot do this in a few days or a few weeks. When we go to serve cross-culturally for a few weeks or months, we must remember that building relationships takes time. Likewise, new believers need relationships with other Christians in their communities. If we go and make disciples in Uganda or India or El Salvador, we need to think about who will be there when we go home. Successful short-term missions partner with indigenous churches and missionaries who can build long-term relationships.

Protect and Provide

Christians are called to protect and provide for the vulnerable in response to God's mercy. We heal the sick, feed the hungry, care

---

5   Luke 5:1-11.

6   Platt, David. 'Every Disciple Making Disciples, Every Church Multiplying Churches.' The Gospel Coalition. 2013. Webinar.

for the poor, and fight injustice because we want the people of the world to know that Jesus loves them and cares for them.

Just as Jesus never separated the meeting of physical needs from the preaching of truth, discipleship is not just about teaching the Bible. When we are sharing the good news, we are inviting people to be a part of a counter-cultural community that reflects God's kingdom.

After Jesus called His followers to go and make disciples, they went from Israel to modern-day Turkey, Greece, Italy and beyond planting churches. Discipleship is about church planting – and churches are intended to be families that reflect God's priorities.

The call to protect and provide for the vulnerable is not limited to the American or European church. This calling is not constrained by our material wealth. There are profound needs across much of the developing world. There is material poverty and there is also spiritual poverty. But we aren't the answer – and our money isn't the answer. Discipleship is about planting churches full of people who care for orphans and widows in response to and as a demonstration of God's mercy.

Cross-cultural missions offer a unique opportunity to come alongside local believers in the developing world. We can challenge our brothers and sisters in Christ to see that God wants them to be the answer to the problems in their communities. We can then equip and empower them to help solve these problems.

Visit Orphans and Widows

One of the most significant problems in many communities in the developing world is the orphan and widow crisis. In Africa, violence, poverty and the AIDS epidemic have overwhelmed the capacity of many communities to care for the orphans and widows in their midst. In Latin America, patterns of addiction and abuse separate children from their families. In Asia, discrimination against girls or single mothers leaves many families in a desperate situation.

While these are generalizations and every vulnerable family is in a unique situation, there is a crisis. And the Bible calls us to go and do something about it.

James 1:27 teaches that we should visit orphans and widows in their distress. In Chapter 3, we discussed how STM trips sometimes harm the churches and communities they visit. In particular, trips to visit orphanages have the potential to hurt the vulnerable children we want to help.

We believe that despite the potential for harm, Christians are called to go and serve vulnerable children and families. Moreover, we believe it is possible for short-term missions to make a long-term difference.

To do this, we must first define where we want to go. Our vision is to see children growing up in safe, loving families. We want short-term mission trips to support this long-term goal. As a result, our focus in visiting orphans should be like the doctor visiting a patient. First, do no harm. Second, diagnose the problem. Third, make a lasting impact towards healing and wholeness. This chapter will empower you to engage in cross-cultural ministry differently.

The Way Forward

Now that we've defined where we want to go, let's look in more detail at how to get there. What can we as American or European Christians do to minimize harm and maximize the positive impact on the children, families and communities we go to serve?

Plan the Right Team

> After this the Lord appointed seventy-two others and sent them on ahead of him, two by two, into every town and place where he himself was about to go. And he said to them, 'The harvest is plentiful, but the laborers are few. Therefore pray earnestly to the Lord of the harvest to send out laborers into his harvest.' (Luke 10:1-2)

In Luke 9 and 10, Jesus sent His followers on a mission to 'proclaim the kingdom of God and to heal,' (Luke 9:2). Jesus calls His disciples to share the good news: God's kingdom is coming and God's kingdom is good news. These passages describe the first short-term mission trips – and we believe Christians today should follow the example of Jesus and His disciples.

When Jesus sent out His twelve disciples and then His seventy-two followers – the first short-term missionaries – He sent them out in pairs. Jamie Wright is a blogger and former missionary to Costa Rica. In a blog describing what is wrong with how many Christians go on short-term mission trips today, Jamie writes:

> Basically, we do it, like, exactly opposite to the way Jesus did. Where Jesus appointed, we take volunteers. Where Jesus sent pairs, we send herds.[7]

---

7   Wright, Jamie. 'Healthy Short Term Missions? Do it like Jesus.' Jamie The Very Worst Missionary. 10 April 2012. Web. 12 June 2014.

We believe planning the right short-term mission team is critically important to having a long-term positive impact. Christians should go on a mission trip for one reason: because they are appointed by God. Going to serve cross-culturally in ministry is not the same thing as going on a vacation. Desiring an adventure or a life-changing experience is not a good enough reason to go.

Churches and ministries that send STM teams must develop an application process to determine who should go and serve in cross-cultural ministry. The primary purpose of the application process for a mission trip should be discerning who is called. The application process should also require references and background checks to ensure that the people who are going to serve, especially with vulnerable children and families, have no history of violence or abuse.

This application process must include prayer. In Luke 10, Jesus commands His disciples to 'pray earnestly' for God to send laborers for the harvest. Having the desire to serve orphans and vulnerable children is a good place to start. Prayer offers us an opportunity to consult with God about how best to respond to this desire. As Christians, we believe that God speaks to us in prayer and can shape our plans into His plans. As Jesus commands, pray for laborers and tell God that you want to be sent. Ask Him to appoint you.

We believe that the primary purpose of cross-cultural ministry is to build relationships with local believers. This means it is vitally important for churches to send teams that are diverse. It also means teams need to be small enough to actually build relationships. Short-term mission trips should not be used to give high school and college students a learning experience at the expense of vulnerable children. When teams represent the whole church body – from teenagers to families to grandparents – they can better minister to the diverse needs of the community they visit. Women and men in their fifties, sixties and beyond have an especially important role to play.

His Hands His Feet welcomes families to bring their school-age children along on their mission trips. Jenni is a mom of three, and has invited her sons to serve alongside her in El Salvador and Guatemala. Jenni is passionate that 'every trip is life-changing and has the potential to help young people form an international worldview that will carry through the rest of their lives.' But the fact that the trip makes a profound impact on the child's life is not the main point. Jenni believes that children who go on STMs have a unique ability to connect with the children they serve:

> The children we serve are so overwhelmed and thrilled when our teams bring children. Although they love spending time with visiting adults from North America, they especially enjoy spending time with other kids. Love is truly an international language and children are able to connect, laugh and enjoy one another despite language barriers.[8]

Prepare Well

Churches and organizations that send teams to do cross-cultural ministry need to prepare team members to focus first on how they will impact the people they visit. Educate the team that the primary purpose of the mission trip is to learn, observe and build relationships, not to get a lot done. Preparation should include a careful analysis of the goal of the trip, including the potential positive and negative impacts.[9]

Jesus' instructions to His followers in Luke 9 and 10 are relevant to STMs today. Jesus called His followers to pray earnestly, to enter quietly with an offer of peace, to live communally, and to take nothing except the Good News.[10] Prayer is an essential part of preparation for a mission trip. Praying together strengthens relationships and aligns us with God's plans.

Teams should prepare by learning about the place where they are going. Instead of focusing on logistics like what to pack, focus on understanding the culture you are entering. It is important for team leaders to set clear expectations for how to dress, eat and communicate with people. Teams must be equipped to travel simply, respect people's dignity, and to protect vulnerable children.

- **What to wear:** Dress modestly and simply in a way that respects the local culture. Be aware that wearing t-shirts with slogans about orphans may be perceived as discriminatory and hurtful.

---

8   Ramsey, Jenni. 'Kids are Welcome.' His Hands His Feet Orphan Outreach Trips – A Ministry of All Blessings International Adoptions. All Blessings International Adoptions. N.d. Web. 10 September 2014.

9   Thegospelcoalition.org. 'A Philosophy of Short-Term Missions at Cornerstone Church.' Cornerstone Church, 2012. Web. 10 September 2014.

10   Wright, Jamie. 'Healthy Short Term Missions? Do it like Jesus.' Jamie The Very Worst Missionary. 10 April 2012. Web. 12 June 2014.

- **What to eat:** Prepare to be flexible about eating and drinking. Remember you are a guest in the culture you are visiting. Don't eat or drink anything in front of the people you are serving unless you have enough to share. At the same time, it's important for teams to eat, drink and sleep enough that they can serve well.

- **Welcome and thank people:** Learn about the local customs and a few words in the language. Heartfelt greetings in the local language honor the people you are visiting.

- **Travel simply and humbly:** Do not wear expensive clothes or jewelry and put away your technology. Be careful not to create comparative poverty.[11]

- **Respect people's dignity:** Mission trips should not be about poverty tourism. It is never okay to take pictures of other people's homes or children without asking permission. It may be helpful to have one team member who is responsible for taking photos and to ask everyone else to leave their cameras at home.[12]

- **Protect vulnerable children:** Learn best practices for how to interact with children who come from difficult places.[13] Team members should never be alone with children.

For many people, a short-term mission trip to Africa, Asia or Latin America is their first experience of poverty in the developing world. Indeed many people want to go on a mission trip in order to gain perspective on poverty and to see how the majority of the world's people live. Traveling in a developing country for the first time can be overwhelming. Visiting missionaries must be prepared for a roller-coaster of emotions. Seeing conditions that people live in may elicit feelings of sadness, hopelessness or guilt.[14] Therefore, it is very important to equip teams with a Biblical understanding of poverty. Poverty is about more than a lack of resources, and it is dangerous to see poverty solely in a material way.[15]

11   Saint, Steve. 'Projecting Poverty Where It Doesn't Exist'. Mission Frontiers 2011. Web. 4 Sep. 2012.

12   Ramsey, Jenni. Personal Interview. 2014.

13   Styffe, Elizabeth. 'How to- help- without-hurting'. Christian Alliance for Orphans. 2 Jul. 2012. Webinar.

14   'Module 3: Coping with Culture Shock and Emotions.' Cultural Competency Online Course. Unite for Sight. 2010-2013. Web. 10 September 2014.

15   Corbett, Steve, and Brian Fikkert. *When Helping Hurts*. 1st ed. Chicago, IL: Moody Publishers, 2009. Print.

Likewise, teams need to learn about the legacy of colonialism and the impact of aid in the developing world. The racist policies of the colonial powers are at the root of much of the injustice and violence experienced today by the poor in countries such as India and Rwanda. Over the last fifty years, developed countries have poured $2.3 trillion of aid into the developing world. Approximately $1 trillion of this has gone to countries in Africa. There is little evidence, however, that this massive influx of aid has stimulated economic development.[16]

What is clear, however, is that colonialism and aid have created a culture of dependency where some people believe that only rich white people can solve their problems. As Americans and Europeans, we may unintentionally feed into that belief with our attitudes and actions. We have resources, education and technology, and as a result we may believe we have something to offer those who are living in poverty. While there may be some truth to the idea that our resources can make a difference in the developing world, assuming that we're in the best position to help 'may produce a "god-complex" in the helper, while ensuring perpetual shame in the one who is always being helped.'[17]

We are called to offer mercy and to fight for justice for those who are in need. We must offer the 'right kind of help in the right kind of way, otherwise we may actually hurt both us and the ones we are seeking to help.'[18] STM teams need to learn how to come alongside local believers in order to equip them to be the answer to the problems in their own communities.

Build Partnerships

We believe that building partnerships is the key to successful cross-cultural ministry. By building partnerships with local churches and ministries, we can have a long-term impact on a short-term trip. By building relationships, we can encourage the people who are on the ground making disciples and caring for orphans and widows. Through thoughtful partnership, we can protect vulnerable children and families from harm.

It is important to build partnerships with both long-term missionaries and indigenous churches. Successful long-term

---

16   'Foreign Aid as Government Assistance.' Foreign Aid. Poverty Cure. N.d. Web. 14 June 2014.

17   Thegospelcoalition.org. 'A Philosophy of Short-Term Missions at Cornerstone Church.' Cornerstone Church, 2012. Web. 10 September 2014.

18   ibid.

missionaries build relationships with local leaders, aiming over time to work themselves out of a job. One goal of cross-cultural ministry should always be local ownership. While they can learn the language and study the culture, Western missionaries will never be Ugandan, Rwandan, or Ethiopian. The best way to make disciples from a different culture is to build relationships with the believers who understand this culture.

Focus on people not projects.

Many STM trips focus on a project, such as building a house or painting an orphanage. While supporting a project may be helpful if this is at the request of the local church or ministry, we believe STMs should place a high value on building and strengthening relationships with people.

Mission is about making disciples. To make disciples, we must build relationships. When we have just a few days or weeks to make a difference, it is easy to focus on accomplishing something tangible rather than spending time with people. We all know relationships take time and commitment. If we want to make a lasting difference in the communities we serve, we need to build strong relationships with people who will remain there when we go home.

Instead of thinking about cross-cultural ministry as a chance to do something – to accomplish our plans or our programs – we can think about cross-cultural ministry as an opportunity to see the needs of the community we are visiting. Why not go on a vision trip where the primary aim is to understand how to pray for the indigenous church leaders and long-term missionaries we visit?

Encourage long-term missionaries.

There's no doubt that churches and ministries serving in difficult places need support. Instead of having teams put together to accomplish a project, put teams together to encourage missionaries working with orphans and vulnerable families. The burnout rate for people doing this work is incredibly high. Go and show them they are important, loved and not forgotten by their brothers and sisters. Trips should be about being with people and building them up spiritually.[19]

Several years ago, my husband and I (Amanda) went with a group to visit and serve long-term missionaries working in Baja, Mexico.

19   Wright, Jamie. 'Love People Not Projects.' Jamie The Very Worst Missionary. 10 April 2012. Web. 12 June 2014.

We provided child-care for the missionary families and prepared all their meals while they attended a week-long conference. When we decided to go on the trip, we initially lamented that we weren't planning to do hands-on work. We would not be doing construction, providing medical care, or visiting orphans - things that sounded more exciting and life-changing.

And yet our lives were changed by serving those who were called to be long-term missionaries. We were blessed to stand shoulder-to-shoulder with people who had left family, home and comfort to minister to a community in another culture. We witnessed their exhaustion and their joy. We went home wanting to be like them. More importantly, I believe they left the conference feeling encouraged, prayed for, supported, and pampered. Our hope is that they were rejuvenated to go back into the field to do the hard work God has called them to do.

One of the most powerful things we can do on a short-term trip is to encourage long-term missionaries. Bring supplies they need to do their work, or bring things that may remind them of home. Come and give them respite as we did in Mexico. Go and pray for and with them, taking photos and stories back to your home church to profile the amazing work that they do. Don't create more work for them by asking them to organize projects and excursions. Go to serve, not to be served.

Long-term missionaries need support: spiritual, financial and physical. Small groups of people who are able to travel and bless missionaries can be hugely important to those who are unable to regularly see family and familiar faces from home.[20] Even Paul himself, one of the world's greatest long-term missionaries, found great encouragement from local churches when they sent people like Epaphroditus to minister to his needs.[21]

Listen to the experts.
We should not plan to go on an STM trip unless we have been invited. Cross-cultural ministry trips should be initiated by the churches or ministries with whom we will serve. We need to be intentional in listening to indigenous church leaders and long-term missionaries. These people are the experts who understand

---

20   Lull, Ramon. 'There's Nothing Short About Short-Term Missions.' Desiring God. 24 February 2014. Web. 12 June 2014.

21   Philippians 2:25-29.

the deep needs of the vulnerable families in their communities. We cannot assume that we understand their needs or the solutions to their problems. We must listen to the experts.[22]

For instance, if the local church determines that the children of its community need a social worker to really address the root causes of children living on the streets, the STM team should be comprised of social workers with experience in dealing with broken families to train the local social workers.

STM teams should respect the ideas of the local believers and long-term missionaries.[23] Teams should be encouraged to ask questions instead of offering solutions. Define what the expertise is of the team, but remain flexible on the process, accounting for cultural differences.[24] Realize that many cultures in the developing world place a dangerous trust in foreigners, deferring to their authority and judgment even when they might know a better solution.

Equip the local community.

Many people don't realize that volunteering actually can result in jobs being lost locally. Why pay a local construction team to build the new school when a team of Americans will pay to come and do it? That might seem like a good thing, but jobs are often one of the most important things in a developing country.

Don't do anything that could be done by local community members. Come alongside to build capacity, provide training or develop resources. Pass on skills not available locally. But do not do for others what they can do for themselves. We can use our resources and skills to empower Christians to make a difference in their local communities.

Empower the local church.

Be there with someone who is going to be there when you are not!
Elizabeth Styffe[25]

Christianity is the fastest growing religion in the world, and most of this growth is happening in Africa, Asia and Latin America. As

---

22 The Gospel Coalition. 'A Philosophy of Short-Term Missions at Cornerstone Church.' Cornerstone Church. N.d. Web. 10 September 2014.

23 Kleis, Judy. Personal Interview. 2012.

24 Jenkins, Jana. Personal Interview. 2012.

25 Styffe, Elizabeth. 'How to Help Without Hurting.' Christian Alliance for Orphans. 30 June 2010. Webinar.

we prepare to serve cross-culturally in the developing world, we need to understand that many of the communities we serve are more reached than our neighborhoods in America or Europe. The *Philosophy of Short-Term Missions at Cornerstone Church* describes the new reality:

> As missionaries...we need to keep in perspective the fact that many of the places where we are sending our STMs are more 'reached' than the West! Churches have been established, missionaries...are being sent out...We *need* to learn from them and see ourselves as learners, servants, and partners as we *come alongside* the global church in *its* mission.[26]

Truly, if we want to make a difference in the global orphan and widow crisis, we need to partner with indigenous churches that are in nearly every community in the world. When we go on a short-term mission trip, we have a unique opportunity to come alongside local believers. We can encourage our brothers and sisters in Christ to see that God wants them to be the answer to the problems in their communities. We can then equip and empower them to help solve these problems. Discipleship is about planting churches full of people who care for orphans and widows in response to and as a demonstration of God's mercy.

So how do we empower local churches? Start by forming a partnership with a church in a community where you feel called to make a difference. Send teams, when requested, to serve alongside these local believers in order to strengthen the relationship and to understand the needs of the local community.[27] Many local churches are doing incredible work on tiny budgets. As local community members, they understand the culture and the needs of the people.[28] We should aim to see what the local church is doing well and how we can support churches' goals.[29]

Once you understand the needs of the church and community, identify how you can come alongside to make a difference without disempowering the local church. For example, instead of sending

26 Thegospelcoalition.org. 'A Philosophy of Short-Term Missions at Cornerstone Church.' Cornerstone Church, 2012. Web. 10 September 2014.

27 'The Seven Standards.' Standards of Excellence in Short-Term Missions. 2003-2014. Web. 12 June 2014.

28 Carlson, Darren. 'Toward Better Short-Term Missions.' The Gospel Coalition. 27 June 2012. Web. 10 September 2014.

29 Corbett, Steve, and Brian Fikkert. *When Helping Hurts.* 1st ed. Chicago, IL: Moody Publishers, 2009. Print.

an STM team to build a house for a widow in the community, empower the local church to build the house! Consider providing matching funds for a capital campaign. Do not depend on resources from overseas; instead use local materials, design and labor. Listen to the ideas of the local church and support their efforts side by side, or even behind the scenes.

Let the local church be the hero and give the gifts.[30] We are not seeking our own glory so let the local church give the glory to God while we anonymously support them.

Make a lasting difference

If we want to make a long-term difference on a short-term trip, we must focus on relationships. Kurt Ver Beek, a sociology professor at Calvin College, reviewed twenty years of studies into the impact of short-term mission trips and concluded that:

> STM groups need to do everything possible to ensure that they are partnering with organizations, missionaries, churches...who are involved in excellent, life-changing, long-term work with those they serve...long-term excellent relationships are the ones which will most contribute to creating positive change.[31]

Christian economists Steve Corbett and Brian Fikkert, the authors of the excellent book *When Helping Hurts,* conclude 'that building relationships is the single most important thing we can do to alleviate poverty!'[32] We often see poverty as a lack of stuff; however poverty is not about stuff. Poverty is about broken relationships with God, others and creation. Giving material resources may be essential in situations where immediate relief is needed, such as in the aftermath of a natural disaster, but resources alone cannot create lasting change.

It's not about stuff.

You might be surprised to know that we can get a lot of stuff in Kigali, Rwanda! We can get clothes, shoes, medicine, diapers, and formula. Don't bring donations on trips unless the items cannot

---

30   Styffe, Elizabeth. 'How to Help Without Hurting.' Christian Alliance for Orphans. 30 June 2010. Webinar.

31   Ver Beek, Kurt Alan. 'Lessons from the Sapling: Review of Quantitative Research on Short-Term Missions.' N.p. July 2007. Web. 19 April 2014.

32   'A Philosophy of Short-Term Missions at Cornerstone Church.' Cornerstone Church. The Gospel Coalition. N.d. Web. 10 September 2014.

be bought locally – and the items are truly needed. If you want to provide diapers to a family who is fostering or adopting a child, support the local economy by buying them when you arrive. But first, make sure they want disposable diapers. Cloth diapers might be culturally appropriate and a much more sustainable gift. Rather than buying formula for new mothers, it might be appropriate to encourage extended breastfeeding. This is why supporting local leaders is so important. They have a better perspective to be able to identify the community's real needs.

Teams should bring only those donations that are requested by the local church or local missionaries and respect their guidance on what not to bring. For instance, it can be difficult to get good, up-to-date Christian books, which many long-term missionaries or local church leaders might really cherish. Remember to bring books in a language the missionaries or church leaders can understand. Only bring gifts that meet a real need.

Meet a real need.
More than the material items, use your actual skills to meet a need. Your short-term trip should extend your local ministry.[33] Use the expertise that team members have gained through their work locally to minister cross-culturally.

For example, gather a team of dentists to provide services and to train local dentists. Bring child psychologists who can train new foster-parents on parenting children from hard places. Or invite teachers from low-income schools districts who know how to teach at-risk children to the school you are supporting abroad.

We should also think about who can meet the needs of the community when we go home. Instead of going solely to provide vaccinations, why not work on how to make vaccinations available locally so that teams don't need to go every year?

In the last chapter, we introduced you to Ekisa Ministries International which operates a residential care facility and community care program for families of children with disabilities in Jinja, Uganda. The facility houses about twenty children with the goal of reuniting them with their families, or if that's not possible, finding the child an adoptive family in Uganda. The staff is made up of social workers and occupational therapists who work with

---

33   Carlson, Darren. 'Toward Better Short-Term Missions.' The Gospel Coalition. 27 June 2012. Web. 10 September 2014.

the children and train families on how to care for their children's special needs.

Last summer, Ekisa hosted a small STM team with great success. Founder and Director of Ekisa, Emily Worrall describes, 'before forming the team, the leaders asked us what we needed, and that made a difference.' As a result, the team was made up of nurses, speech therapists, physical therapists, and a child psychologist. Before arriving, the team sent a film crew to Uganda to produce a documentary that Ekisa could use for fundraising. The video has been essential in spreading the word about what Ekisa is doing.

The medical team came specifically to work with Ekisa. By not splitting time with other ministries and organizations, the team was able to focus on building relationships with the staff, children and families. Emily describes the impact of the team of experts:

> Our staff especially benefitted from the presence of the child psychologist. There are only a few child psychologists in all of Uganda, and their fees are prohibitively expensive. Our children have all been through trauma, and the psychologist was able to train us on how to help them. We continue to use the tools they left us and hope they come again.

From Visiting Orphans to Empowering Families

Planning, preparation and partnership are all essential to making a lasting difference when we serve in cross-cultural ministry. This is true whether you are going to serve alongside a church or to equip business leaders or to train medical professionals. But what about visiting orphans?

Throughout this book, we've learned that children need families, not orphanages. We've seen that mission trips to visit orphanages often support a broken system that separates children from their families and communities. At the same time, we know that there are up to 8 million children living in institutional care, and we believe that we are called to go and do something about it.

If we want to make a lasting difference, we need to focus on getting children out of orphanages and into families. We also need to improve orphanages to make them better for children who cannot be reunited with their families or placed for adoption. So how do we make a lasting difference by visiting orphans?

The most significant difference we can make in the life of a child living in an institution is to find him a safe, loving, permanent family. But to visit orphans doesn't necessarily mean to save, to rescue or to fix all the problems. We may be called simply to pray, love and walk alongside others.

A simple first step might be to educate ourselves and raise awareness. Through writing this book, we've had countless opportunities to both learn and educate others about orphan care. Each conversation is a blessing to us as we see people get excited about what they can do to support vulnerable families and children.

Protect vulnerable children.

If the team will be serving at an orphanage or with vulnerable children, it is extremely important to ensure the protection of children. Many of the ways we would naturally show love to children, including giving gifts, sharing candy, or providing affection can be harmful to children living in institutions.

When we see a baby crying or a small child tugging on our arms and legs at an orphanage, every part of us wants to pick him up and tell him that he is loved and wanted. But we must remember what the child needs to thrive and to grow into an adult capable of love and trust. Children living in orphanages have experienced trauma including the loss of their first families. They are vulnerable to abuse and neglect. They have a critical need for connection with safe, loving caregivers.

We must remember that on a short-term trip, we are not in the best position to meet this need. With good intentions, visiting missionaries have hurt the children they want to help by failing to understand the children's developmental and psychological needs. Just as we wouldn't send a team untrained in medical care to perform surgery, teams that work with vulnerable children need to be trained on best practices.[34] According to orphan care expert Elizabeth Styffe:

> If our help is not based on best practices for children there is potential harm developmentally, psychologically, relationally – and the most alarming part is there's a potential for harm for a lifetime.[35]

Remember the first goal of visiting orphans: first, do no harm. If we want to help a child living in an orphanage, we must remember

---

34   Styffe, Elizabeth. 'How to Help Without Hurting.' Christian Alliance for Orphans. 30 June 2010. Webinar.

35   ibid.

that she needs to connect with her caregivers. We are not in the best position to offer the love and security she needs, but we are able to make a difference. While it goes against our instincts not to hold that baby in the orphanage, it is far better to empower her caregivers to meet her needs.

God calls Himself the Father of the fatherless, the Protector of widows, and the Defender of the weak. Jesus takes child protection seriously. And we are called to protect vulnerable children from harm:

> At that time the disciples came to Jesus, saying, 'Who is the greatest in the kingdom of heaven?' And calling to him a child, he put him in the midst of them and said, 'Truly, I say to you, unless you turn and become like children, you will never enter the kingdom of heaven. Whoever humbles himself like this child is the greatest in the kingdom of heaven. Whoever receives one such child in my name receives me, but whoever causes one of these little ones who believe in me to sin, it would be better for him to have a great millstone fastened around his neck and to be drowned in the depth of the sea.' (Matt. 18:1-6)

When I (Amanda) volunteered for children's ministry at my church in Chicago, I had to undergo an interview and background check. I had to agree to the child protection policy with rules about never being alone with a child. These restrictions are necessary to protect children from abuse. It's the reality of the world we live in that millions of children are victims of abuse. A simple Internet search will tell you that these perpetrators are not strangers to our churches or homes.

Institutionalized children are particularly vulnerable because they have no consistent caregiver to protect them and no place to go that is safe. Many orphanages do not have child protection policies that protect children from abusers. The devastating truth is that some pedophiles volunteer in orphanages in order to gain access to vulnerable children.

We must take the calling to protect children seriously. Anyone who wants to visit an orphanage or volunteer with vulnerable children must undergo a background check. Volunteers also need training. We need to hold the same high standards for those who care for the children overseas as we would for children in our communities. If we are visiting an orphanage that does not have a child protection policy, it may be helpful to come alongside the leaders of the orphanage to develop one.[36] The risk is great, and we must do everything in our power to protect children from abuse.

Care for the Caregivers

In 2002, Kimberly and her husband David[37] made the decision to adopt a child from China. After five years of infertility, Kimberly felt God was calling her to trust 'His vision for our family, not my vision.'[38] Kimberly and David began to learn and pray about adoption. They lived and worshiped in an ethnically diverse city and David spoke Mandarin, and so they decided to adopt from China.

Kimberly and David adopted Lily four days before her first birthday. For the first year of her life, Lily was neglected and left alone. When Kimberly first held Lily, she was unable to sit up, hold her head up, or roll over. 'We were told on the adoption form that her favorite place to play at the orphanage was in her crib,' Kimberly remembers. 'We truly believe she laid there all the time.'

When Kimberly and David adopted Lily, they didn't know that they should have 'held her, treated her like a newborn.' Lily seemed like a good, quiet baby, and they let her sleep in her own crib. Kimberly remembers, 'We learned the lessons the hard way.'

When Lily was about four years old, she became extremely defiant and the parents were at their wit's end. Kimberly and David read *The Connected Child* by Karyn Purvis and attended a two-week camp for kids who come from hard places. The camp was life-giving for the family:

> We learned that when children like Lily aren't held or picked up when they cry and when they don't attach to one person, they begin to control things for themselves. Their sympathetic nervous system literally doesn't develop correctly. The neurotransmitters that produce dopamine and serotonin never form properly – all because they were neglected and left alone.

Lily is now a beautiful ten year old girl. But getting to a place where Lily feels more secure has been a long process. Kimberly and David have done attachment therapy with Lily, helping her to express her feelings about being abandoned by her birth mother and left alone at the orphanage. Kimberly has worked closely with Lily's teachers

---

36   For more information on child protection policies, see defenseofthefatherless.com.

37   Names changed for security.

38   Personal Interview. 1 July 2014.

to help her learn how to control her emotions and her stress at school. Through therapy, diet and spiritual healing, and with the love of a family and support of a community, Lily has come very far.

Adoption changed Kimberly and David's life. After adopting Lily, the family adopted one more child from China. Soon after they travelled on a vision trip to Uganda with a sense that the trip would help them discern what was next. While on this trip, they felt God call them to move to Rwanda to start a business that would empower the poor. Within six months, Kimberly and David had moved to Rwanda.

Kimberly began to volunteer twice a week at an orphanage in Kigali. 'I was quite angry at first when I realized the implications of my daughter's orphanage experience,' Kimberly remembers. 'I have since visited and volunteered in many orphanages...when [children] are denied care at the beginning of their lives, it is so important that we meet them where they are at and try to restore that which was lost.'

At the orphanage in Kigali, many of the volunteers caring for children were the poorest of the poor, many of whom are orphans themselves. Kimberly realized that the caregivers were just as needy for care as the children: 'If they had never received care, then how could they give care?'

At the time, Holly, an American adoptive mother, was living in Eastern DRC and working closely with a local orphanage called Kaziba. Kaziba provides care to babies and toddlers who have experienced the death of their mother during childbirth. In the rural community where the orphanage is located, it is nearly impossible for widowed fathers to feed and care for their children after the death of the child's mother. The orphanage aims to provide lifesaving care to the babies and to ultimately reunite them with their families. While this orphanage is meeting a real need in its community, the work is not easy.

Kimberly began to talk with Holly about the work she was doing in Kigali. Kimberly understood how important it was to empower the caregivers at the orphanage to meet the children's developmental needs. Kimberly has seen how simple things – such as a child being held several hours a day – can make a significant difference for a child living in an orphanage.

Holly invited Kimberly to lead a mission trip to the orphanage in DRC in order to equip the caregivers to meet the babies' physical and emotional needs. In preparation for the trip, Kimberly hired

Rwandan women to make weighted blankets, which are like 'a huge hug that triggers the sympathetic nervous system in positive ways.'

On the mission trip, Kimberly led an overnight training that was focused on encouraging the caregivers themselves. They taught the staff about attachment, sensory play, and the story of the Good Shepherd. Holly remembers the impact the trip had on the orphanage:

> The team brought weighted blankets made for all the kids, and instead of having us give them to the children she had all the mamas find one child and give them the gift so it came from the mamas instead of us. This actually profoundly changed how we did any kind of gift giving after that. Now we always give the mamas the gifts or food we bring to give to the children, so the act of love and kindness is given from the hands of the caregivers and not from the hands of the foreigners.
>
> The team then spoke to the women and men who cared for the children about the love of the Good Shepherd for them and how it was so important that they know this deep and profound love in their own hearts so that they can then show this love to the children. It was very moving. Many of the staff were crying, which is not exactly culturally appropriate, during her sessions with them. Any training or work done with the children was only done with the staff interacting with the kids, not us as foreigners.[39]

We believe this is an excellent example of how to do short-term, cross-cultural ministry at an orphanage. The trip met a real need. The trip focused on improving the orphanage by coming alongside the local people. The trip focused on building relationships rather than accomplishing something tangible. The trip ministered to the women who are caring for the children in the orphanage, helping them to feel loved and not forgotten so that they could give love to the children.

As we've seen throughout this book, children have a critical need for connection. While many STMs to visit orphans aim to connect with children, visitors are not in the best position to meet this need. The caregivers in the orphanage are in the best position to provide children with a sense of love, security and belonging. This trip empowered the caregivers to love and connect with the babies living in the orphanage.

---

39   Mulford, Holly. Personal Interview. 2014.

Visit families and churches instead of institutions.

Throughout this book, we have seen that it is possible to care for orphans without orphanages. While many short-term missionaries visit orphanages in order to care for children, we believe this is often not the best approach. Many orphanages welcome visitors and volunteers for financial reasons. After caring for children and seeing the conditions in an orphanage, many visitors donate funds. Some orphanages keep children living in horrible conditions to elicit more generous donations. Orphanages that welcome volunteers for financial reasons are taking advantage of children.

If you want to make a lasting difference in a child's life on a mission trip, consider partnering with a church or ministry that is supporting children in families. If we do visit an orphanage on a mission trip, we should do this with the local church. By building relationships and doing ministry together, we can encourage local believers to care for orphans in their communities. We can use our resources to come alongside and strengthen these efforts. While orphanages are sometimes necessary, we know families are best, so let's not settle for anything less.[40] Instead of building orphanages to care for orphans, we can empty them.[41] That may mean partnering with an orphanage to develop alternative care solutions or train social workers on how to rehabilitate families. There are endless possibilities if we keep the ultimate goal of children in families in mind.

What happens when we go home

> We hope to impact the lives of each team member so that they return home with broken and renewed hearts for the people who have been forgotten in their own communities. Our dream is that each team member has a life changing experience which affects their future careers and decisions in how they spend money, live, serve and give away their lives for others.
>
> His Hands His Feet Mission Statement

There is no question that STMs *can* be life-changing for participants. Yet if we look at the statistics, it is not clear that short-term mission trips *are* life-changing for everyone who goes.

---

40   Styffe, Elizabeth. 'How to Help Without Hurting.' Christian Alliance for Orphans. 30 June 2010. Webinar.

41   Ibid.

In 1998 Hurricane Mitch dropped historic amounts of rainfall on Honduras and other countries in Central America, causing catastrophic flooding that left more than 2.7 million people homeless. In the aftermath of the storm, many STM teams traveled to Honduras to assist in the construction of houses. Kurt Ver Beek, a sociology professor at Calvin College, did research to explore the long-term impact of some of these short-term missions on the participants. He began his study assuming that participants would 'pray more, study more, give more',[42] however, he found that the experience made little difference in the participants' lives. The participants were asked to rate how much of an impact the short-term mission trip had on their lives. Sixteen per cent reported a significant positive impact, 45 per cent reported a slight positive impact, and 40 per cent reported no change. When he compared these results with the participants' actual behavior, however, the amount they gave was unchanged by the trip.

This surprising result challenged Kurt Ver Beek to do a review of other studies into the impact of short-term mission trips on participants. The other studies measured factors including attitude towards missions, concern about poverty, time spent in prayer or reading the Bible, and charitable giving. The results of the studies were remarkably similar. While most people who go on a mission trip have a positive experience and report significant changes, few people actually change.[43]

But we want mission trips to be a life-changing experience. If we want STMs to make a lasting difference not just in the communities where they serve, but also in the lives of the people who go, we need to do more to help participants integrate their STM experience with their everyday life.

Jenni, the Director of His Hands His Feet, sees re-entry training as the most critical part of the short-term mission experience. His Hands His Feet requires participants to participate in significant training before they go on a mission trip. Participants attend meetings, read books and articles about missions, and often spend months preparing for the trip. Participants learn how to submit to and learn from the local believers alongside whom they will serve. They learn the importance of respecting the local culture. While all

---

42   Ver Beek, Kurt Alan. 'Lessons from the Sapling: Review of Quantitative Research on Short-Term Missions.' N.p. July 2007. Web. 19 April 2014.

43   ibid.

of this is important, Jenni believes that what happens on the last day of the trip makes a big difference:

> The whole short-term mission journey is a process of discipleship. I require teams to participate in training before we go, but the most important aspect of the training is what happens as we go home. On the last day of the trip, we spend a day processing what the team has experienced. Often participants are in emotional turmoil. It is vital for team members to have the space and time to process all that they have experienced before arriving home. Our desire is that our team members return home with a different view of their lives - how they spend their money, time, passions, and talents.

His Hands His Feet teams spend the last day of the mission trip sharing, praying and processing their experiences. They meet again after the trip to talk about their emotions and challenges. This process prepares participants to answer questions or to deal with the lack of interest about their trips from friends and family at home.

There's nothing short-term about mission

Ever since sin separated Adam and Eve from their Creator, God has been on a rescue mission to create a people who will be His people. Mission is not something we go and do. Mission is a part of who we are.

For those of us who believe in the gospel, God is our Father, our Redeemer, and our King. We are the adopted children of God. We are disciples who live with God as our King. And we are missionaries who have been sent by God.

The Gospel is the foundation for mission. We are called to reflect the heart of our Father – and to be His hands to a broken world. We are called to protect and provide for the fatherless in response to what we have received and to demonstrate God's heart. We are called to be people of mercy and justice in a broken world.

So while God may call us to go and serve in cross-cultural ministry for a few weeks or months, we are all called missionaries from the moment we receive the Holy Spirit. Short-term missions are a part of God's long-term mission.

QUESTIONS FOR DISCUSSION AND REFLECTION

1. Have you ever gone on a short-term mission trip? What was the purpose of the trip?

2. Describe how your experience serving cross-culturally challenged your values or perspective. Did the STM trip change your life?

3. Have you ever participated in a mission trip that had a negative impact? What would you do differently next time?

4. How can churches and ministries that send STM teams plan and prepare to make a lasting difference?

5. Why is building relationships the most important part of STM?

6. How can short-term trips to visit orphans make a long-term difference?

Redeeming International Adoption

After I (Sara) left the Christian Alliance for Orphans Summit in 2012, I was flying to Kigali, Rwanda to work with a women's sewing cooperative and to continue research for this book. As I drove to the Los Angeles International Airport, I got an email from my friend Kate[1] asking for prayer and saying simply:

> I think God is calling me to adopt a three year old boy from Russia.

What Kate didn't know was that I had on my phone the picture of Anton, a three year old boy who desperately needed a family through international adoption. The little boy was Russian by ethnicity and Latvian by nationality. He was living with a special need that meant he was unlikely be placed with an adoptive family in Latvia. I had been praying for a family to step up and adopt Anton.

Latvia is a Hague Convention country with a stable, ethical adoption program. Latvia supports vulnerable families and reunification when possible while also encouraging domestic foster care and adoption. When Latvian families cannot be found

---

1   Names have been changed for security.

for orphaned or abandoned children, Latvia places children for international adoption. Most Latvian children who are adopted internationally are older, have special needs or are a part of a sibling group.

I replied to Kate's email and told her about Anton, and then said a quick prayer as I boarded my flight to Amsterdam. Nine hours later when the plane landed and I checked my email at Amsterdam Schiphol Airport, Kate had responded:

> My husband Daniel and I have prayed about it. We believe God is calling us to adopt Anton.

Over the next eighteen months, Daniel and Kate went through the heart-wrenching, expensive and difficult adoption process. A few months in, the family discovered that Anton had a younger brother named Ivan who also needed adoption. Daniel and Kate said yes to both boys. In the fall of 2013, Daniel and Kate travelled to Latvia to meet their sons – and to ultimately bring them home.

'When we first met the boys, they were scared, confused and traumatized,' Kate remembers as she describes the first few months after the boys left the orphanage. 'The first few months home were terrible.' Anton, who was now four years old, did a lot of spitting, punching, screaming and kicking. Kate was worried the behaviors wouldn't stop and this would be the 'new emotional reality' for their family. They found support from their community, began to meet with therapists weekly, and prayed for God to heal Anton and Ivan. Kate describes what happened next as God answered their prayers for healing:

> Three months after bringing the boys home from their orphanages, we saw radical changes. Speaking and understanding our language was the biggest help. Anton and Ivan began to relax and to attach to us. Violence was replaced by sweet words. Rages were replaced by emotional self-regulation. We were in awe of their transformation.

> Yes, we were committed to giving them emotional skills for coping and healing. We developed a love strategy that included play therapy, holding them as they raged, and learning new ways to discipline unlike we had with our biological children.

> However, we believe that God reached into their hearts and minds to show them love. We believe He uses the love of patient, adopting parents to heal broken hearts of children who have been forsaken

by their parents. It's a dramatic story of redemption where we are the main characters and Jesus is the hero. And power for change is Jesus' love.[2]

There are few things more beautiful than seeing a child who was an orphan thrive in the love and security of a family. As an adoptive parent and as friends of many adoptive parents, we support international adoption as one of the responses to the orphan crisis. We believe it is absolutely necessary. While the current system of international adoption is inherently flawed and lends itself to corruption, we believe there is hope.

As Christians, we must defend the right of every child to grow up with their birth family - and when this is not possible with a loving family through domestic or international adoption. If we want to defend and protect this right, we must both fight corruption in international adoption to protect vulnerable families *and* make it easier for orphans who are truly without the love of a family to be adopted. This chapter will empower Christians to make wise decisions in the adoption process and to advocate for reform in international adoption.

When Adoption is the Answer

As we've discovered throughout this book, 'orphan' does not equal 'adoptable.' Though there are an estimated 151 million children who could be considered orphans because of the death of one or both of their parents, relatively few of these children need new families. Most of the world's orphans live with their families and do not need to be adopted. At the same time, there may be millions of children who are not technically orphans but who are growing up without the love of a family.

We live in a broken world where children are sometimes orphaned, abandoned or abused. There are situations where a child is separated from their biological families and where reunification is not possible – or not in the best interests of the child. While strengthening vulnerable families is important, international adoption is an important part of the response to the orphan crisis.

Throughout this book, we have discussed how the current system of international adoption is broken. It is not working for vulnerable families, orphaned children, or adoptive parents. The

---

2   Personal interview. 2014.

current system of international adoption does little to prevent corruption and trafficking. The entire process lacks transparency. Adoption agencies and their representatives who are most often responsible for corruption are not held legally accountable. Meanwhile, the poor and marginalized families who lose their children to adoption have no voice.

Adoption is expensive. The cost of adoption prevents good families from adopting children who truly need new families. At the same time, greed corrupts the system, as those who should be responsible for protecting the rights of children have incentives to do the opposite.

Adoption takes too long. Children who desperately need families are stuck in orphanages. Government bureaucracy makes the adoption process longer than it needs to be. Yet even as American families wait months or years to bring home the children they have adopted, families in the developing world wait far longer for justice.

The current system of international adoption finds children for families, not families for children. The children who need families the most – those who are older or have special needs – are typically the least likely to be adopted.

So when is international adoption in the best interests of a child? When a child cannot grow up with their family of origin, it is generally in the child's best interest to have a new family through adoption. Broadly speaking, there are four reasons why children may need to be adopted.

Termination of parental rights

When a child experiences neglect or abuse, often as a consequence of a parent's addiction or mental illness, the responsible authority may permanently terminate the parent's right to care for the child. In some cases, it may be possible for the child to be cared for by a family member, such as a grandparent or aunt. When this is not possible, the child needs a new family.

Abandonment

There are situations where children are abandoned by their parents as a result of poverty, discrimination, or other issues. If the family cannot be found after a careful investigation, or if reunification is not in the child's best interests, then the child needs a new family.

Orphanhood

When a child experiences the death of both parents and there is no one else in the family who is willing or able to care for the child, the child needs a new family. Under the law in the United States, a child is legally an orphan if they have experienced the death of just one parent. As we've learned throughout this book, however, many children who fit this definition have a parent or extended family members who love and want them.

Relinquishment

This is where the decision of whether or not a child needs a new family through adoption becomes complicated both legally and ethically. There are countries, such as Rwanda, where relinquishment is illegal. On the other hand, there are other countries, including Uganda and Ethiopia, where it may be legal for a child's birth parents to relinquish the child for adoption.

It is fairly common for birth parents in the United States who do not feel prepared to raise a child to place their child for adoption. We must remember that in the United States, there are laws and social services in place to help birth mothers and fathers freely choose what is best for their child.[3] In countries like Uganda and Ethiopia, however, desperately poor parents who feel they have no choice at all may relinquish children for adoption. As we've learned throughout this book, relinquishment is sometimes the result of coercion, including bribes, lies or even threats of violence.[4]

We believe children should grow up in families where they are wanted and loved. In a broken world, there will be situations when relinquishment is in the best interest of a child and a family. When this is the case and the relinquishment is legal under the laws of both the sending and receiving countries, then the child may need a new family through adoption. But if poverty is the primary reason why a child is relinquished for adoption, then the child

---

3   We are aware that even in the United States, the issue of whether a birth parent can make an empowered and informed choice to place his or her child for adoption is unclear. We are in no way suggesting that the domestic adoption system in America is without its ethical problems, but it is important to distinguish the ways in which parents in America have more choices than parents in the developing world.

4   Another distinction between American domestic and foreign international adoption is that under United States immigration law, a child who has two living and known birthparents is not eligible to receive a visa to immigrate as an orphan. In other words, that child, by law, is not an orphan and not adoptable.

does not need a new family. Instead, the child's family needs to be empowered to have a path out of poverty.

Even when a child needs a new family through adoption, international adoption may not be in the best interest of the child. Whenever possible, children should have the opportunity to grow up with a family in the country and culture of their birth. We believe domestic adoption should generally be prioritized over international adoption, allowing for exceptions when a child's specific needs may be more easily met through international adoption.

At the same time, there are situations where international adoption may not be in the best interest of a child and where the child's specific needs may be better met through foster care or institutional care. However, we believe long-term institutional care should always be the last resort.

We should see international adoption as the answer only when a child truly needs a new family and cannot be adopted locally, and when international adoption meets the needs of the specific child. As Christians, we should fight for the rights of children who need adoption to be adopted. In the following sections, we will explore the principles that should guide a system of international adoption.

Our Ideal International Adoption System

As Christians, we are called to both protect and provide for the vulnerable widows and orphans. First, we have a responsibility to support vulnerable families – to prevent children from becoming orphans. Second, we have a responsibility to support churches and families around the world to care for the orphans in their communities. Third, we have a responsibility to provide for and protect orphans who cannot be adopted domestically through international adoption.

Instead of accepting the status quo, let's explore what an ethical, transparent international adoption system might look like.

Encourage Family-Based Care

To care for vulnerable children, the system must begin with the fundamental belief that children need families. Whenever possible, children should grow up in their first families. We begin with supporting vulnerable families to keep children in their homes.

When this is not possible as a result of sin or brokenness, children should have the opportunity to grow up in a family in their community and culture. An ethical adoption system prioritizes and supports local solutions, including foster care and domestic adoption. International adoption should be considered only when an adoptive family cannot be found in a child's community or country. Our ultimate goal is for every child to grow up with a family who loves and protects them.

Prioritize Domestic Adoption

It is a good thing for a child to grow up with a family who shares his culture and heritage. While family is more important than culture, internationally adopted children often struggle with issues around cultural or racial identity. Without laws in place that favor domestic adoption, many people in developing countries would favor international over domestic adoption for financial reasons. International adoption can be highly profitable for adoption attorneys, orphanages and government officials, as well as for the tourism industry. Laws that favor domestic adoption must be in place to protect the interest of families in developing countries who want to be able to adopt.

Likewise, international adoption is only a possibility for a tiny fraction of a percent of the world's orphans. Most of the world's orphans live in countries where international adoption is closed or extremely limited. If we take steps to encourage domestic adoption around the world, many more children will have the opportunity to grow up in families rather than institutions.

We do not believe domestic and international adoption compete with one another or are mutually exclusive. Children need families. As Christians, we believe we're called to care for orphans through both domestic and international adoption. As long as policies are in place to support vulnerable families and prioritize domestic adoption in developing countries, international adoption can actually encourage domestic adoption by creating a culture where orphans are welcomed into families, rather than hidden in institutions.

Find Families for Waiting Children

If there truly is an orphan crisis for which international adoption is the answer, there should be no waiting parents, only waiting children. An international adoption system needs to find families for the world's waiting children, who typically are older or have special needs. This is where the resources of developed countries are really needed. Churches and communities need to be equipped to support the families who adopt older and special needs children.

Require Transparency

A careful investigation is necessary in determining whether international adoption is in the best interests of the child. Accurate information is also essential for authorities to match the needs of the adopted child with the strengths of the adoptive family. Adoptive parents should accept nothing less, and agencies must be prohibited from giving referrals for children without complete and accurate investigations into their stories and families.

Place Children Quickly

When safeguards are in place to ensure that international adoption is in the best interests of the child, the international adoption system should work quickly to place children in families, recognizing that children grow up quickly and suffer permanent damage when the process takes longer than needed. An orphanage is no place for a child to spend his time when there is a family waiting for him. In an ideal world, children who need alternative care would be placed with a permanent, loving, safe family within six months to one year.

Limit the Influence of Money

While people should be paid for services rendered in the adoption process and certain government fees will always be required, the financial incentives surrounding international adoption must be analyzed and revised. It should be against the law for adoption agencies to operate as for-profit businesses. Fees paid to government officials, adoption attorneys, orphanages and others responsible for the well-being of children must be transparent, itemized and in line with the cost of living in the country where the adoption takes place. No one who makes money from adoption services should have any contact with birth families or orphanages. Bribes should never be paid. The buying and selling of children for the purpose of international adoption should be illegal.

Accountability

Adoption agencies must be held accountable for their actions *and* for the actions of their representatives overseas. Every country that sends or receives children through international adoption should have a central authority responsible for overseeing the process and regulating adoption agencies. Adoption agencies that are involved in corrupt, unethical practices must face real consequences, including the loss of accreditation, financial restitution, and criminal penalties. Trafficking children for the purpose of international adoption must be criminalized.

Justice
As Christians who believe in a God of justice, we must fight for justice within the international adoption system for birth families, children and adoptive parents. We should oppose all forms of corruption and the injustices that incentivize poor families to place their children in orphanages. We must stop advocating for international adoption for the world's poor families. Poor and marginalized parents must have a voice.

How to Defend the Fatherless
We are not the first to criticize the current system of international adoption. Many adoption advocates are outraged by the decline in international adoption. They criticize governments for red tape and lobby to make adoption easier. At the same time, those who oppose international adoption advocate for local solutions and pressure governments to end international adoption altogether.

In writing this book, we have listened to the stories of adoptive families and adult adoptees. We've studied the ideas of adoption advocates and critics. What we have found is that most people who are passionate about orphans live somewhere in the middle. We want international adoption to be an option for children who truly need it, but we also want the corruption to end.

While much ink has been spilled about what's wrong with international adoption, few people have proposed solutions that meet both of these goals. In this book, we hope to provide a way forward. While much change is needed, we believe it is possible to make adoption easier for children who need it while also protecting vulnerable families. We believe that corruption and adoption do not have to go hand in hand. We can imagine an international adoption system that is ethical and transparent, respecting the rights of children and families.

Children Have Rights
Under international law, nations from around the world have agreed that children have rights. These rights are spelled out primarily in

the United Nations Convention on the Rights of the Child and also in the Hague Convention on Inter-country Adoption.[5] Experts agree, 'Since human rights issues are at the core of current debates on inter-country adoption, international children's rights law is central to the discussion.'[6]

The most basic right children have is the right to grow up with a family. Children need the protection and provision offered by a family to thrive. When a child cannot grow up with his biological family, he has a right to grow up with another family. In other words, a child who has been orphaned or abandoned has a right to be adopted. Christians who believe that God created children to grow up in families agree with this principle.

Governments Have a Responsibility

Governments of countries that either send or receive children for international adoption have a responsibility to protect the rights of children. To defend children's rights to grow up with a family, governments must protect children from abuse and neglect. Governments have a duty to decide who needs to be adopted and who can adopt. It is the government's responsibility to make sure the process is transparent, requiring careful investigations to gather accurate information. Governments also have an obligation to make it easier for children who need new families to be adopted – this applies to both domestic and international adoption.

At the same time, governments also have a responsibility to protect vulnerable families from corruption. It is the government's duty to ensure that the adoption process is free from coercion, including bribes, lies and threats, and to hold those who take advantage of the process for selfish gain legally accountable. Governments are responsible for enforcing the rule of law, ensuring that the poor and marginalized are not the victims of injustice.

What about the Hague Convention?

The Hague Convention on Intercountry Adoption is an international treaty that was developed to prevent corruption in international adoption. The treaty serves two purposes: to create

---

5   While the United States has signed the United Nations Convention on the Rights of the Child, it is the only developed country and soon will be the only member of the United Nations that has not ratified the Convention.

6   'Intercountry Adoption: An African Perspective.' African Child Policy Forum. 2012. Web. 15 June 2014.

a set of safeguards providing legal accountability and protecting the best interests of children, and to develop a system of cooperation, communication and common ethical standards between sending and receiving countries.

Consider the Hague Convention a minimum set of standards. To be considered a part of the Hague Convention, a country must sign the treaty and implement adoption laws and procedures that meet the requirements of the treaty. This means that while all Hague countries meet the same minimum standards, the adoption process still varies from country to country.

Under the Convention, all adoptions should consider what is best for the child. The Convention offers a three-part definition of a child's best interests. First, authorities must take steps to ensure a child is adoptable. This protects children and prevents the abduction, sale and trafficking of children for the purpose of adoption. Second, authorities must preserve the child's background information. Third, governments must match the child with a suitable adoptive family. The prospective adoptive parents must be thoroughly assessed. The matching is not done by parents, but by professionals matching the needs of the child with the qualities of the parent.[7]

The Hague Convention relies on the principle of *double subsidiarity* to guide decisions about what is in the best interests of a child who has been orphaned or abandoned. Whenever possible, it is in the best interests of the child to grow up with their biological family. Vulnerable families have a right to receive support in order to parent their children. When a child is separated from their parents, the first step should be considering reunification with the family. If this is not possible, the child has the right to a new family through adoption. For children who do need adoption, domestic adoption is prioritized over international adoption. Whenever possible, children should be placed with adoptive families in their own communities, cultures and countries.

In principle, the decision of what is in the best interests of a child should be based on actual alternatives. It is not fair to make children wait for years in orphanages while countries develop a system of alternative care. Governments have a responsibility to

---

7   Hague Convention on Private International Law. 'The Implementation and Operation of the 1993 Hague Intercountry Adoption Convention: Hague Guide to Good Practice'. *Bristol: Family Law*, 2008. Guide No 1. Print.

find a balance between preserving the child's culture and placing the child in a permanent family as soon as possible.

How is the Convention being implemented?
A growing number of countries, including many in the developing world, are ratifying and implementing the Convention. The process takes years and involves significant development.

Guatemala closed to international adoption in 2008. Since then, Guatemala has signed the Hague Convention; however, 'the [United States] Department of State has determined that Guatemala has not yet fully implemented legislation that would create a Convention-compliant adoption process.'[8] Likewise, Rwanda closed to international adoption in 2010 and then became a party to the Hague Convention in July 2012. Rwanda is continuing the suspension of all intercountry adoption until 'the country has a fully functional Hague Adoption Convention process in place.'[9]

Some countries are further down the road to implementing the Hague Convention. After suspending adoptions in 2008, Vietnam has since worked to ratify and implement the Convention. In 2011 the Convention was ratified and in July 2013 Vietnam's Central Adoption Authority announced it would be accepting applications for accredited adoption service providers 'to operate a limited inter-country adoption program only for children with special needs, as defined by Vietnamese law.'[10]

In April 2014, Haiti made a switch from processing adoptions under non-Hague procedures to processing adoptions under the Hague Convention. As a result, the number of licensed adoption service providers authorized to process adoptions in Haiti has decreased.[11] Many are hopeful that this will decrease corruption in adoptions from Haiti. South Africa has also ratified and implemented the Hague Convention. Since June 2012, two licensed and accredited adoption service providers have been processing international adoptions to the United States from South Africa under the Hague Convention.[12]

---

8 'Hague Convention Information.' Country Information – Guatemala. Bureau of Consular Affairs. Intercountry Adoption. US Department of State. N.d. Web. 16 June 2014.

9 ibid., – Rwanda.

10 ibid., – Vietnam.

11 ibid., – Haiti.

12 ibid., – South Africa.

Why does the Convention have a bad reputation?

Within the Christian adoption and orphan care movement, the Hague Convention often has a bad reputation. There are three areas of concern. Does the Convention create unnecessary barriers to international adoption that increase the cost or difficulty of adoption? Is it right for the Convention to favor domestic adoption over international adoption? Is the Convention so difficult to implement that it essentially closes developing countries to international adoption?

Does the Hague Convention make international adoption too difficult?

It is true that the Hague Convention adds some additional requirements for adoptive parents, adoption agencies and governments. Under the Convention, adoptive families in the United States are required to use accredited adoption agencies and to go through more thorough background checks in the home study process. Adoption agencies are held to a higher standard in Hague countries. The Convention requires governments to designate a central authority to oversee international adoptions. The central authority is responsible for regulating the adoption process and adoption service providers and determining who can adopt and be adopted. Governments are also required to implement safeguards to prevent solicitation of birth families and trafficking of children for the purpose of international adoption.

While these requirements do make certain aspects of the adoption process more difficult, they also serve to protect children and families from harm in the adoption process. While the Hague Convention may make the wait to adopt a healthy, young child from overseas longer, it typically expedites the process of adopting children who have special needs.

Likewise, while the Convention requires families to use an adoption agency and this can increase the cost compared to independent adoption, it also requires transparency in the fees charged by adoption agencies. As a result, most countries that have signed the Hague Convention, such as China, Colombia and Latvia, have moderate adoption fees compared to countries like Democratic Republic of Congo where fees are unregulated. A typical adoption from China may cost approximately $25,000, whereas some adoption agencies in Congo charge over $50,000.

Is it right to favor domestic over international adoption? In order to implement the Hague Convention, a country must create an adoption system that prioritizes domestic over international adoption. One responsibility of the central authority is to create a registry of all children available for international adoption. Children can only be placed for international adoption after authorities have determined that the child cannot be placed with their biological family or for domestic adoption. Children who are difficult to place for domestic adoption, such as children who are older or have special needs, may be considered for international adoption more quickly than children who are young and healthy.

In 2003, American families adopted nearly 7,000 children from China. Most were healthy baby girls who allegedly were abandoned because of China's restrictive one-child policy. Since China implemented the Hague Convention in 2005, there has been a significant increase in domestic adoption in China.[13] The increase is likely due to a combination of factors, but certainly the Convention's prioritizing of domestic adoption is one of those factors.

Today most domestic adoptions in China are of healthy babies. There remains a significant need for families open to adopting older or special needs children. Americans who seek to adopt healthy infants from China may wait up to seven years to complete an adoption. However since 2005, the majority of children adopted from China to America have special needs or are older.[14] Adoptions of children with special needs can be completed in as little as six months.[15] While the implementation of the Hague Convention has not eliminated corruption in Chinese adoptions, it has made a difference. China is widely considered to have one of the most stable, ethical adoption programs that effectively prioritizes domestic adoption and places special needs children with loving families internationally.

Is the Hague convention too difficult to implement?

Some adoption advocates argue that the Hague Convention is so difficult to implement in a developing country that it effectively

---

13   Cote, Simone. 'International and Domestic Adoption in China'. CRIEnglish, 2013. Web. 16 June 2014.

14   Reyes, Emily Alpert. 'International adoptions' shift to special-needs kids tests adopters'. *LA Times*, 29 October 2013. Web. 6 June 2014. *See also* Jayson, Sharon. 'International Adoption Special Needs'. *USA Today*, 30 September 2013. Web. 16 June 2014.

15   'China Overview'. West Sands Adoptions. 2001. Web. 16 June 2014.

closes the country to international adoption. This is perhaps the most significant objection to the Hague Convention. The critics are right that the Convention is hard to implement. As we have seen, it takes time, money and political will – three things lacking in many developing nations with large populations of orphans.

Haiti has just implemented the Hague Convention in 2014 – but it's too early to tell whether the new process will be free from corruption or will make the adoption process easier. Vietnam is in the last stage of implementation, authorizing adoption service providers. Vietnam is scheduled to reopen its international adoption program as early as the end of 2014.[16] Time will tell whether the Convention will make a difference in Vietnam.

The Hague doesn't go far enough

There are also those who recognize the limits of the Hague Convention. While we believe the Convention is a step in the right direction, corruption is still present in countries like Colombia and China. A minority of opponents to the Hague Convention believes all international adoption is trafficking, and see the Hague Convention itself as a violation of the Convention on the Rights of the Child.

While the Hague Convention is a good start, we believe it does not go far enough to protect vulnerable families, fight trafficking, or encourage the adoption of the children with special needs. The most significant flaw in how the United States has implemented the convention is that our country continues to allow international adoptions from non-Hague countries. Two-thirds of international adoptions are from non-Hague countries, including countries such as Ethiopia, Uganda, and DRC, where corruption is widespread. Likewise, the Convention does not go far enough in holding adoption agencies accountable or in regulating adoption fees.

Ultimately, we believe Christian families should be supportive of the Hague Convention, as it takes important steps to protect vulnerable children and families from harmful adoption practices. Likewise, we believe Christians should support the idea of double subsidiarity, favoring domestic adoption over international adoption.

---

16   'Hague Convention Information.' Country Information – Vietnam. Bureau of Consular Affairs. Intercountry Adoption. US Department of State. N.d. Web. 16 June 2014.

Responsibilities of Receiving Countries

Receiving countries have a responsibility to protect the rights of children – including the right of an orphaned child to be adopted – and to ensure that the adoption process is free from corruption. We are Americans, and we believe it's time for the United States to take responsibility for the role our country has played in the cycle of corruption in adoption. If we want international adoption to remain an option for children for whom this is their only shot of having a family, our government needs to do far more.

While red tape can prevent good families from adopting children who need families, appropriate regulation is absolutely necessary. So what is missing from current law?

Adoption agencies must be held accountable.

Current United States law regulates how adoption agencies do business within our borders. For example, there are detailed standards for the home study and post-placement process. In principle, there are regulations requiring adoption agencies to work in an ethical and transparent manner overseas. In practice, however, these regulations have failed to hold adoption agencies and their representatives overseas accountable.[17]

We hear time and again in speaking with adoptive families who have experienced corrupt adoption practices that when something goes wrong, they feel powerless to make it right. The adoption process lacks transparency and families rely solely on information from adoption agencies. When adoptive families question the information they receive, language, distance, and culture are barriers to seeking the truth. By the time adoptive families see red flags or raise serious questions, they have spent thousands of dollars and hundreds of hours on the adoption process.

Most adoption agencies are resistant to any claims or questions by parents about the ethics of the adoption. By remaining evasive or silent, agencies can maintain deniability and manipulate vulnerable parents into continuing with their adoptions.

When Charlotte (from Chapter 7) approached her adoption agency about working towards resettlement of the children with their mother instead of adoption, the agency director and her lawyer responded by accusing Charlotte of coercing the mother into taking her children back. When I (Amanda) questioned our

---

17   Want more details? See defenseofthefatherless.com

agency about red flags, our caseworker told me that the stories I was hearing from other families were nothing more than 'spiritual persecution' of the agency director who sought only to help orphaned children.

We believe these experiences are not rare. In Kathryn Joyce's book, *The Child Catchers*, she recounts retaliation against adoptive parents by agencies such as threatening lawsuits and reporting parents to child protection services. Investigators in Ethiopia who asked hard questions have been imprisoned at the request of orphanage and agency staff.[18] Social workers and friends of adoptive parents who have helped them research cases in DRC have received threats of death.

So what happens when an adoptive family suspects their adoption agency is involved in corrupt, unethical or illegal practices?

At this time the only recourse available to adoptive parents is to file a complaint with the Council on Accreditation (COA), the body that works with the US Department of State to oversee the Hague accreditation process.[19] As of July 2014, all adoption service providers must be accredited or approved by the COA. Before filing a complaint with the COA, adoptive families are required to file a formal complaint with the adoption agency. If the complaint is not resolved directly, the family may then file a complaint with the COA. Only then does the COA investigate the complaint to see if the agency is in violation of the standards. Finally, when adoption agencies are found to be out of compliance with the standards, the only penalty, if they do not take corrective action, is the loss of accreditation.[20] Sometimes the loss of accreditation is enough to put a corrupt adoption agency out of business.[21]

We believe this system does not go far enough. While under the Convention the US Department of State and the Council on Accreditation are charged with ensuring that international

---

18   Joyce, Kathryn. *The Child Catchers: Rescue, Trafficking, and the New Gospel of Adoption.* New York: PublicAffairs, 2013. Print.

19   'Hague Accreditation and Approval.' Council on Accreditation. N.d. Web. 15 June 2014.

20   'Hague Accreditation and Approval: Monitoring and Oversight.' Council on Accreditation. N.d. Web. 15 June 2014.

21   As of July 2014, the adoption agency that Charlotte (from Chapter 7) and I (Amanda) used for our adoptions from DRC has just had their accreditation suspended for ninety days due to substantiated violations of the Convention. As a result, the agency filed bankruptcy and is closing.

adoptions take place in the best interests of children and are free from corruption, this system fails to truly hold adoption agencies accountable. While the worst adoption agencies should be shut down, they should also face legal penalties for destroying families and trafficking children.

Trafficking children for the purpose of international adoption must be illegal.

It should be illegal to buy and sell children for the purpose of international adoption. It should likewise be illegal to coerce, threaten or lie to birth families to find adoptable children. When adoption agency employees have faced legal action for their involvement in corrupt adoption practices – and very few have – they have been charged with conspiracy to commit fraud[22] or money laundering.[23]

Why aren't the people who are responsible for buying and selling children charged with human trafficking?

Richard Cross is a United States Department of Justice criminal investigator who traveled to Cambodia to find out whether any United States citizens were involved in corrupt adoption practices. Cross documented how Lauryn Galindo found more than 800 children for adoption, as described in Chapter 4. When people asked Cross why he didn't charge Galindo with human trafficking, he explained the limits of the law:

> She couldn't be charged with human trafficking, human trafficking only deals with sex or forced labor. You can get away with buying babies around the world as a United States citizen, it's not a crime, and most people don't understand that.[24]

If we want international adoption to be an option for children who truly need new families and have no alternative, we believe this must change. The United States government must hold adoption agencies accountable for their actions and the actions of their representatives overseas. Most importantly, the United States must make trafficking children for the purpose of international adoption illegal.

---

22 'Four Employees of Adoption Service Provider Charged with Conspiracy to Defraud the United States in Connection with Ethiopia Operations.' Office of Public Affairs, US Department of Justice. 11 February 2014. Web. 15 June 2014.

23 Samford University, Cumberland School of Law. Interview with Richard Cross. 15 April 2005. Web. 15 June 2014.

24 ibid.

Under current law, human trafficking is the act of recruiting, harboring, transporting, providing, or obtaining a person for forced labor or sex slavery through the use of force, fraud, or coercion.[25] While most adopted children are not exploited in their adoptive families, the means by which some of these children are found for adoption are the same. It should be illegal to use force, fraud, or coercion to find a child for international adoption – and all who are involved in trafficking should face criminal penalties.

What about the Children in Families First Act?

To address the decrease in international adoptions in the United States, adoption advocates have lobbied for the Children in Families First Act (CHIFF), a bill introduced by Senator Mary Landrieu in 2013. The main goal of CHIFF is to increase the number of international adoptions by making the process quicker and easier for adoptive parents.

CHIFF seeks to establish a bureau in the Department of State that oversees foreign policy on international child welfare. CHIFF also proposes to consolidate responsibility for processing international adoptions to the United States Citizen and Immigration Services (USCIS). This would include transferring the accreditation of adoption service providers from the Department of State to USCIS.[26]

The legislation claims to strengthen child protection and to make adoptions more ethical and transparent; however it is not clear that CHIFF goes far enough. If CHIFF were to establish a centralized bureau where adoptive parents can report fraud or corruption, this would be an excellent improvement. To make a difference, however, this bureau needs real power to monitor and evaluate adoption agencies, with the ability to close and prosecute agencies involved in corruption.

Before we streamline the adoption process in the United States – which would be good – we must stop the exploitation of poor families that results in children being placed for international adoption. CHIFF doesn't make trafficking for the purpose of international adoption against the law. It also fails to address the reality on the ground in developing nations, where there is little

---

25   'Trafficking in Persons Report.' U.S. Department of State. 2013. Web. 15 June 2014.

26   'Legislation: What CHIFF Does.' Children in Families First. The CHIFF Working Group. N.d. Web.

to no protection for birth families. For instance, in DRC, there are thousands of children who need international adoption, but the government is corrupt. We should not pressure our government to make it easier to adopt without addressing widespread poverty and injustice in sending countries.

Sending Countries' Responsibility

Countries that send children for international adoption also have a responsibility to protect the rights of vulnerable children and families.

We believe that every country has a responsibility to protect the rights of its people – and most importantly its children. The UN Convention on the Rights of the Child says that every child has the right to be protected from harm, to receive an education, to be healthy (including having clean water, nutritious food and medical care), to be treated fairly, and to be heard.[27] The Convention also says that children have a right to grow up with their families and that children should not be separated from their families. Furthermore, the Convention says that governments are responsible for ensuring that decisions made for children who are deprived of a family – including the decision to place a child for adoption – are made in the child's best interests.[28]

Practically, the Alternative Care Guidelines we explained in Chapter 7 are designed to give countries the tools to protect the rights of children who have been separated from their families. Vulnerable families need support to avoid placing their children in orphanages. Countries should aim to reunite institutionalized or abandoned children with families. Countries should develop foster care and domestic adoption programs as alternatives to institutional care. When this is not possible, the government has a responsibility to decide who needs international adoption and to ensure that this process is free from corruption.

We've seen that many of the countries that are popular for international adoption lack the resources or political will to protect the rights of children. The very fact that there are many orphaned or institutionalized children in a country usually means that poverty, corruption, violence, or conflict is widespread. Many poor

---

27   'A Summary of the United Nations Convention on the Rights of the Child.' UNICEF. N.d. Web. 15 June 2014.

28   ibid.

countries have neither the resources to support vulnerable families nor safeguards to prevent against corruption in adoption.

DRC is a country where many children may need adoption, but where there is little to no infrastructure to protect vulnerable families. Widely considered a failed state by foreign policy experts, DRC has no law on international adoption, no centralized authority to review files and little cooperation between the branches of government.

In 2013, the DRC immigration authorities stopped issuing exit letters – a crucial and final part of the adoption process that allows the child to actually leave the country – while the Congolese courts continue to process adoption cases. This broken system victimizes the children and families it is intended to serve: birth families who place children in orphanages hoping they will be adopted, adoptive families who are stuck not knowing if the children they have adopted will ever come home, and the children caught in the middle.

As of the writing of this book, American adoptive parents are flying to our nation's capital to beg the United States government to intervene in DRC. While this situation is heartbreaking, we believe this effort is misguided.

Frequently when a sending country closes to international adoption, adoption advocates call on the United States government to put pressure on the sending country to keep adoptions open. But making adoption easier in countries where there is widespread poverty and no safeguards against corruption will inevitably result in vulnerable families being destroyed to find children for adoption.

So how do we respond to this? How do we defend the fatherless in a situation where making adoption easier will only make things worse?

We believe that Christians should support the work of UNICEF and other NGOs that partner with governments to implement the Alternative Care Guidelines and the Hague Convention. We should likewise support efforts to develop justice systems that protect children from trafficking and exploitation, including corrupt adoption practices.

The Africa Child Policy Forum

In May 2012, leaders from dozens of African countries, human rights advocates, and organizations caring for orphaned and vulnerable children gathered together in Ethiopia. The Africa Child Policy Forum (ACPF) is an organization that exists to improve the wellbeing of children in Africa through policy and dialogue. The purpose of the forum was to discuss the future of international adoption in Africa. Many leaders were concerned that international adoption had increased 300 per cent from 2003 to 2010 even as most African countries were ill-equipped to safeguard vulnerable children.[29] Following the forum, the ACPF published a position paper offering an African perspective on the explosion of international adoption in Africa. While this Forum went largely unnoticed by the Christian adoption and orphan care movement in the United States, we are hopeful it represents the beginning of an important shift.

Let's look back at the events that led to the closure of international adoption in Vietnam. By the time the United States made the decision to stop adoptions from Vietnam, there was widespread corruption that resulted in the trafficking of children. Some Vietnamese government officials were profiting through the buying and selling of children. The Vietnamese authorities objected to the American government investigating the corruption in the adoption system, shifting the blame to the American adoption agencies. While adoption agencies and the United States government all share responsibility for what happened, ultimately it was a failure of the Vietnamese government to protect Vietnamese children that allowed the corruption.

Was the ACPF gathering the beginning of a shift where more African leaders step up to the responsibility of protecting African families and children? We hope so – and we are optimistic that this is beginning to happen. The leaders of many African countries, including Ghana and Rwanda, have made the decision to close to international adoption in order to implement the Hague Convention. A few countries, such as South Africa, have successfully implemented the Convention and are now open to international adoption. While in Vietnam it was primarily American officials who objected to the corruption in international adoption, more and more in Uganda, Ethiopia and DRC it is African officials who are saying enough is enough.

Be committed to ethical adoption

Ultimately if we are called to adopt, we must be committed to

---

29   'Intercountry Adoption: An African Perspective.' *African Child Policy Forum.* 2012. Web. 15 June 2014.

ethical adoption. We must decide how we will respond if we discover that the children we love and feel called to adopt are not orphans who need new families.

In July 2014, Amy and John were preparing to fly to Uganda. They were adopting a little girl named Hope. The night before they were scheduled to leave, Amy woke up after midnight and decided to check her email. The private investigator had located Hope's family, and had emailed Amy with chilling news.

'The family felt hopeless,' Amy shared, 'but they want their daughter, if only they could support her financially.' Initially Amy and John wrestled with what this would mean for Hope. If her family was too poor to support her, was international adoption in her best interests?

As Amy and John thought about it, however, they realized that poverty alone should never be the reason to adopt:

> It's not right, it's not ethical, and it's certainly not biblical. We said from the beginning, we wanted to commit ourselves to an ethical adoption...to adopt this little girl, after knowing this, would go against everything we believe in.

Amy describes the decision to walk away from the adoption as 'undoubtedly the hardest decision we have ever had to make.' The couple had imagined their adoption journey would have a happy ending with a beautiful little girl joining their family. Instead, they have made the courageous decision to support the reunification of Hope's biological family. While this is not an easy road, they have faith it is best for Hope: 'in my eyes, this is a happy ending.'

In researching this book, we've heard stories from many families who have found themselves in this position. They discovered that the children they hoped to adopt had families who loved and wanted to parent them, but who were desperately poor and felt they had no other choice. They realized the child's birth parents had been lied to and taken advantage of. By the time families discover the truth, they have typically invested years and thousands of dollars in the adoption process. The family must then make a decision. Will they fight to bring the child 'home' to America? Or will they fight to reunite the child with their first family?

While some families like Amy and John make the heartbreaking – and brave – decision to stop the adoption process, other families gather prayer and financial support and fight legal battles to bring these children home. They usually win: legal systems favor the rich, the educated, and the powerful. The poor families who have been destroyed by a corrupt system of international adoption have no voice.

Think back to the words of Isaiah and Ezekiel from Chapter 6. The people of Israel were condemned for oppressing the poor and needy, wronging the fatherless and the widow, dealing corruptly, loving bribes and 'destroying lives to get dishonest gain.'[30] In many international adoptions, nearly everyone who should be responsible for justice for children exploits the process for selfish gain. And sadly, many of the people who are involved in this corruption claim to be Christians. This should not be.

As Christians, we know that the world is full of brokenness. As holders of the truth of the gospel of Jesus Christ, we can go forward with boldness to fight for the cause of the poor, the vulnerable, and the orphan. But we must also never forget our own propensity to sin.

As former prospective adoptive parents, we know what it is like to look at a photo and pray for a child for months. We are familiar with the very real love we feel for a child we hope to adopt long before she is placed in our arms. It's nearly impossible to remain objective through the adoption process. We know how hard it is to walk away from an adoption, even when it's the right thing to do.

Nevertheless, we believe that with support, adoptive parents can remain committed to ethical adoptions. So what practical steps can adoptive parents take to avoid corruption?

Take Responsibility.

The past has taught us that relying on the government and adoption agencies is not enough to ensure an ethical adoption. As adoptive parents, we must be vigilant and hold ourselves to a higher standard. We cannot outsource the care of the most vulnerable. When we suspect things are not right, we need to speak out for those who cannot speak for themselves. It is very hard to see the red flags when we are emotionally invested in the process.

Commit.

We must commit to only adopting a child who truly needs a new family through adoption. We should refuse to get on a waiting list to

---

30   Isaiah 1 and Ezekiel 22.

adopt a healthy baby, and should instead be willing to adopt a child who is waiting for a family. Being committed to ethical adoption means refusing to pay bribes or accepting false documents. We must be prepared to walk away from an adoption if we discover corruption. We need to be aware of the problems and refuse to be part of them.

Seek the truth.

We must seek accurate information about a child's story and needs. We should demand transparency from everyone who is involved in our adoptions. We recommend always obtaining an independent investigation, especially in countries where corruption is common.

We live in an age where information is accessible like never before. Of the world's seven billion people, over six billion – including most of the world's poor – have access to a cellphone.[31] When we ask for answers from adoption agencies or lawyers, we must not accept excuses that the information is not available. Countless adoptive parents have located birth families and found accurate information after their adopted children are home in the United States. We should accept nothing less than the truth.

Listen.

As adoptive parents, we need to listen to experienced adoptive families and adult adoptees. By listening to the stories of those who have gone before us, we can gain perspective. It may be difficult to listen to the truth, but we must not turn a blind eye to the very real stories of adult adoptees and families who have been hurt by unethical adoption practices.

Advocate.

Even as we take responsibility for our own adoptions, we need to advocate for change. We need to speak the truth in love. If we want international adoption to be an option for children who truly need it, we need to demand better from our own government.

In this chapter, we have outlined the many ways that prospective adoptive parents and churches can support ethical adoptions. Unless we make a commitment to being above reproach when it comes to the ethics of our adoptions, we will continue to see the

---

31   Worstall, Tim. 'More people have mobile phones than toilets'. Forbes, 2013. Web. 14 September 2014.

corruption cycle repeated. In the next three chapters, we'll talk about addressing the poverty, injustice and brokenness at the root of the orphan crisis.

Questions for Discussion and Reflection

1. When is international adoption in the best interests of a child? Describe your own experience or the experience of someone you know where adoption was the best choice for a child.

2. Is there too much 'red tape' in the adoption process? Why or why not?

3. Do you believe it should be illegal to traffic children for the purpose of international adoption? Should those who are responsible for corruption in adoption face criminal penalties?How can we advocate for the rights of children to be adopted while also protecting vulnerable families from injustice?

4. What steps can adoptive families take to ensure that their own adoptions are free from corruption?

First Families First

Visiting orphans and widows

Imagine you are walking through the Kimihurura neighborhood in Kigali, Rwanda. Large homes surrounded by walled gates and lush gardens line the main road. On one side of the road, a muddy path takes you down a steep hill where poor families live in tiny houses. You are visiting the home of Asha, a widow who is struggling to care for four young children. She was a child when nearly one million people were slaughtered in the Rwandan genocide. She was just eighteen years old when her husband died from complications of diabetes and she became a widow. When her husband died, her daughter Zahara was a toddler and she was pregnant with her son Eli. One year later, Asha's sister died, leaving her with two more children to care for, Sarah and Clementine. Not even twenty years old, Asha was a widowed mother caring for four children.

After her husband and sister's death, Asha went to her husband's brother for help, but he refused. A friend of her husband's provided her with a small sum of money to start a business to provide for her children. She began to sell jewelry on the side of the road, but she could not afford to obtain a business license. When the police discovered her business lacked the proper documentation, they took away her goods and put her in jail for five days. While she was in jail, they shaved her head, took her jewelry and the money she had saved, and then 'forgave' her. When this young mother was released from jail, she had no way to provide for her children. Every day, she had to decide which of her children would eat – or which of her children would go to school.

What would you tell Asha? Would you offer her the opportunity to give her children a brighter future through international adoption? Would you place her children in an orphanage where they would have food to eat and could go to school? Placing the children in an orphanage would meet their physical needs, but it would deprive them of the most important thing in the world: the love of a family.

By visiting Asha, you are living out James 1:27: 'Religion that is pure and undefiled before God, the Father, is this: to visit orphans and widows in their affliction.' Asha is a widow who is caring for orphans. And she is certainly afflicted. The Greek word 'to visit' means to go see and is commonly used for visiting the sick. Here it refers to the Christian's gracious care for orphans and widows, much like a doctor visiting a patient. Elsewhere in the Bible, the same word describes God's gracious care for man. God sees our needs and responds to them with mercy. In the same way, we are called to see Asha's needs and to respond to them with compassion. Asha's story represents the stories of millions of widows who are struggling to care for orphans in the world today.

Poverty is at the root of the orphan crisis

Christians are uniting around the powerful vision of ending the orphan crisis. We cannot end the orphan crisis, however, without giving vulnerable families a path out of poverty, which remains the primary reason why children are abandoned or orphaned. At the Orphan Summit in 2012, Peter Greer was like a voice in the wilderness pointing out the connection between poverty and the orphan crisis. Peter Greer is the President and CEO of Hope International and the author of *The Poor Will Be Glad*. An expert in international development and microfinance, Peter made the case that adoption wasn't the answer to the orphan crisis:

When we say millions of orphans and that we can solve this problem through adoption, we are wrong. The majority of the world's orphans have families. 80-90 per cent of the children living in orphanages have parents. Orphanages create orphans. Why? Poverty.[1]

While many American and European Christians focus on adoption and orphan care as the response to the orphan crisis, African leaders recognize poverty is at the root of the crisis:

> Poverty is often one of the main reasons why parents abandon or voluntarily relinquish their children. In addition, many children taken away from their original families come from homes where parental neglect is sometimes barely distinguishable from the effects of dire poverty. This reality is arguably more acute in Africa than in any other region in the world.[2]

Cycle of poverty

Throughout this book, we've seen the connection between poverty and the orphan crisis. But what is it about poverty that leaves the poor vulnerable to exploitation and hopelessness?

Consider Ethiopia. Ethiopia is a country in East Africa where there are approximately 4.6 million orphans. Over the last ten years, over 13,000 Ethiopian children have been adopted by families in the United States. There is an orphan crisis in Ethiopia – but the orphan crisis is a symptom of a much deeper problem.

While most of the orphans in Ethiopia continue to live with their families, approximately 80 per cent of Ethiopians live on less than $2 a day.[3] More than four out of five live in rural areas where they struggle to access services including health care.[4] Approximately 15 per cent of these children have been orphaned by HIV/AIDS and may face discrimination as a result.[5]

Six out of ten women in Ethiopia are married before the age of 18. Many of these marriages are forced.[6] When women in their early

1   Greer, Peter. 'Microfinance and Orphan Care.' Orphan Summit, Saddleback Church, Lake Forest, California. 2012. Breakout Session.

2   'Intercountry Adoption: An African Perspective.' African Child Policy Forum. 2012. Web. 15 June 2014.

3   Borgenproject.org. '10 Facts About Poverty in Ethiopia.' The Borgen Project, 11 June 2013. Web. 30 June 2014.

4   KidmiaFoundation.org. 'Programs.' Kidmia Foundation, 2014. Web. 19 June 2014.

5   Younglives.org.uk. 'Beyond Orphanhood: Rethinking Vulnerability In Ethiopia.' Young Lives, 2014. Web. 19 June 2014.

6   Girl Effect.org. 'Family Planning 2012 Getting it Right for Girls.' The Girl Effect, 23 November 2013. Web. 30 June 2014.

teens get pregnant, they are far more likely to experience pregnancy complications. This is especially true for women who have been malnourished. In Ethiopia, two thirds of children grow up hungry.[7]

While 80 per cent of Ethiopian girls start primary school, few are able to finish. Less than one in five Ethiopian women can read and write.[8] When girls do not go to school, they tend to have more children and are less likely to give birth in a hospital. The same families that cannot – or choose not – to educate their daughters may be unable – or unwilling – to seek medical care should something go wrong during pregnancy or birth.

When something goes wrong during birth, it is incredibly difficult for poor, rural women to get to a hospital with a doctor or midwife who can save her life – or the life of her child. Across Africa, there are very few doctors and nurses in rural areas where 'relentless hours, lack of supplies, and difficult conditions'[9] make practicing medicine nearly impossible. In Ethiopia, a woman would have to walk an average of sixty miles while in labor in order to reach a medical clinic.[10] Women in Ethiopia have a 1 in 50 chance of dying during childbirth, compared to one in 6,900 women in the United Kingdom.[11]

In Ethiopia 1 in 68 children die before they turn five years old. When families don't know if their children will survive and when mothers are not educated, they tend to have large families. Sometimes families have more children than they can provide for. Most Ethiopian children live in extreme poverty, many of these children will grow up hungry and illiterate, and so the cycle will continue.

So what do we do to end the cycle of poverty? Is it enough to train more doctors and build more schools? Over the last fifty years, billions in international aid has poured into Ethiopia. While Ethiopia has one of the fastest growing economies in the world, the benefits of this growth are not equally distributed. Eighty per cent

7   Wfp.org. '10 Things Everyone Should Know About Hunger in Ethiopia.' World Food Pro-
     gramme, 24 June 2013. Web. 11 September 2014.

8   Unesco.org. 'UNESCO Global Partnership for Girls' and Women's Education – One Year On:
     Ethiopia.' UNESCO, 2012. Web. 11 September 2014.

9   Kristof, Nicholas D, and Sheryl WuDunn. *Half The Sky*. 1st ed. New York: Alfred A. Knopf,
     2009. Print.

10   Halftheskymovement.org. 'Issues: Maternal Mortality.' Half the Sky Movement, 2014. Web. 26
     Mar. 2014.

11   Data.worldbank.org. 'Data: Lifetime Risk of Maternal Death.' The World Bank, 2014. Web. 20
     June 2014.

of families still live on $2 per day – and these families are highly vulnerable to injustice. When something goes wrong, the poor live with no margin and are more vulnerable.

Over time, this cycle of poverty can lead to desperation – a loss of hope. Families living in poverty may make dangerous choices, selling themselves or their children into prostitution or slavery, abusing drugs or alcohol, or getting involved in crime. Extreme poverty leads to children being abandoned. Poverty is also a reason why many communities struggle to provide for the orphans in their midst.

Poverty is not just about money.
To think about addressing the poverty at the root of the orphan crisis, we must first understand poverty from a holistic perspective. Poverty is more than a lack of resources. Poverty is a brokenness that affects every area of life. When we study the Biblical story of creation, fall and redemption, we see that poverty is about broken relationships. If we were designed to live in relationship with God, with ourselves, with others, and with creation, poverty is about these four relationships being broken.[12]

In a fallen world, we experience poverty in our relationship with God. We struggle with sin that separates us from God who is our Father and our Creator. Apart from Jesus' death on the cross, we have a broken relationship with God.

Likewise, we experience poverty in our relationship with ourselves. We do not see ourselves as God created us. Our identity is distorted by shame or pride. We may struggle with depression or anxiety. Apart from God renewing us with His Spirit, we have a broken relationship with ourselves.

We experience poverty in broken relationships with others. We are designed to live in loving community; however many people feel alone in the world. Sin destroys relationships, tearing apart families, communities and nations. From child abuse and divorce to trafficking and war, much of the evil and pain in the world is rooted in broken relationships.

We also experience poverty in our relationship with creation. God designed us to steward creation in order to provide for our families and to worship Him. Our broken relationship with creation can look like a lack of resources – or an abundance of resources.

---

12   See Corbett, Steve, and Brian Fikkert. *When Helping Hurts*. 1st ed. Chicago, IL: Moody Publishers, 2009. Print.

God created us in His image to work, but in a fallen world this work may fail to produce fruit or may become an idol.

All poverty is the result of sin, but not all poverty is the result of our own sin. Poverty can be caused by harmful or sinful choices, such as addiction or laziness. But poverty is also a result of the fall. Poverty is often caused by things that are not a choice: injustice, violence, natural disasters, and so on. Many of the world's poor are hardworking but are kept poor by forces beyond their control.

We are called to protect and provide for the vulnerable.

Throughout this book, we have described how God calls His people to protect and provide for orphans, widows, foreigners, and the poor. We've seen how these four groups of people were vulnerable in the ancient world, and how God calls us to offer justice and mercy to those who are vulnerable in the world today. While we all experience poverty in broken relationships with God, ourselves, others, and creation, we believe God calls us to have a special concern for people who are materially poor.

So how do we provide for the poor? We aim to provide not simply a hand out, but a means for people to provide for their own families. Our goal is that families would be able to work to provide for their needs. By supporting and empowering vulnerable families, we can prevent children from being orphaned or abandoned.

If we want to make a lasting difference, we must remember the difference between relief and development. While relief is a temporary response to a crisis, development aims to create lasting, sustainable change. In the short term, we may provide a family assistance with the cost of school fees to prevent a child from being abandoned to an orphanage. But in the long term, we should aim for the family to find a path out of poverty – so that they can pay their own school fees!

For our efforts to be sustainable, they must empower a community and not depend on outside resources. In many developing countries such as Uganda, the legacy of colonialism and aid is dependency. Some Ugandans fall into the trap of believing that only 'muzungus' – or comparatively rich white people – can solve their problems. This is not sustainable. We want to empower Ugandans to solve their own problems. We want Ugandans to see that God created them to work and provide for their families.

Poverty is not about us and them.
A deeper understanding of poverty should bring us to a place of humility. We all experience poverty in one way or another. If we want to make a difference in the lives of the materially poor, we must start by reflecting on how we are poor. Living in a big city like London, I may not have to worry about where my next meal will come from, but I do struggle with loneliness. When we reflect on our own poverty, we realize it's not about *'us and them'* – but rather *'us and God'*. We all have the same problem. We all live under the same curse. We all sin and we have all been sinned against. And in one way or another, we all experience the effects of this brokenness. None of us chose to be born in London or Los Angeles – or Kigali or Karachi.

If our goal is to empower people to experience restored relationships with God, others and creation, we must stop seeing ourselves as somehow better than the people we serve. Instead of us helping them, we serve alongside one another. In *When Helping Hurts*, authors Steve Corbett and Brian Fikkert explain why this is so important:

> It all goes back to the definition of poverty alleviation. Remember, the goal is to restore people to experiencing humanness in the way that God intended. The crucial thing is to help people to understand their identity as image bearers, to love their neighbors as themselves, to be stewards over God's creation, and to bring glory to God in all things...people exercise dominion over their individual lives and communities, constantly seeking better ways to solve problems and create bounty in service to God and others.[13]

What does poverty alleviation look like?
In Uganda, over two million children have experienced the death of at least one parent. At the same time, one in four households in Uganda fosters at least one orphan. These families are often vulnerable as the result of poverty and injustice.

Action for Children is a Ugandan NGO that aims to empower these extended families to care for children in their communities.[14] Action for Children aims to empower families and measures the

---

13   Corbett, Steve, and Brian Fikkert. *When Helping Hurts*. 1st ed. Chicago, IL: Moody Publishers, 2009. Print.

14   Holtinternational.org. 'Uganda Adoption.' Holt International Adoption Agency, 2014. Web. 19 June 2014.

effectiveness of their efforts in eight key areas: housing, food security, education for children, income generation, health and hygiene, psychosocial wellbeing, community participation, and opportunity to mentor other families.[15]

These standards are a great starting point for identifying what families need, or for measuring the impact of poverty alleviation efforts. Do families have safe housing? Do they have enough to eat? Do their children go to school? Are the adults able to work to provide for their needs? Is the family able to access medical care?

Yet as Christians, we know this list is not complete. Mercy is a kingdom endeavor. Our goal is not simply restoring a family financially. We want people to experience restored relationships. We want people to experience restored dignity, believing that work is valuable and as God's image bearers we are created to work. We also want people to experience renewed hope, discovering that not all is out of their control. We want people to experience the kingdom of God.

In the Old Testament, God's people were called to provide for orphans and widows by letting them glean in their fields, sharing their food through the tithe, inviting them to join in feasts, lending freely and forgiving debts. They were called to leave a margin in their lives to care for the poor. God's people were called to be generous because they had received grace. To put it simply, the poor were invited to worship and to work in community with God's people.

What does this look like in a world today where few of us have fields where we could let the poor glean? We are called to be generous – to leave a margin for the needs of orphans and widows. We are invited to be open-handed with our wealth. Everything we have is a gift from God, and we are simply stewards of His resources. Furthermore, we must consider how our efforts to provide for orphans and widows offer a path out of poverty. Vulnerable families should be invited to work and worship in community with God's people.

Grace demands change.

When my family (Sara) travelled to Uganda to adopt our daughter Gabrielle, we spent several days at the orphanage where she had been living. One day when we were sitting outside playing with

---

15   Roby, Jini L., and Stacy A. Shaw. 'Evaluation Of A Community-Based Orphan Care Program In Uganda.' 1st ed. Alliance for Children and Families, 2008. Web. 19 June 2014.

children, a father with a disabled child showed up at the gate begging for help. The child's mother, ashamed that she had given birth to a child with disabilities, had abandoned the family. The father was unable to both care for his daughter and to hold down a job, and so he wanted to place the child at the orphanage. He saw no alternative.

This particular orphanage was not equipped to care for children with special needs, and so suggested that the father take his daughter to Ekisa. A few days later, I sat with Emily Henderson, one of the Founders of Ekisa, and this desperate father. Although Ekisa provides institutional care for children with disabilities, they see this as a last resort and endeavor to keep children with their families whenever possible. Emily was adamant that this father care for his daughter, rather than place her in an orphanage. Emily reminded the father that the child was his responsibility and that she was a gift from God, without shaming the man for having a child with special needs. He loved her and was able to work; he simply needed an alternative. Ekisa agreed to provide childcare and therapy during the day so that the father could both work and care for his child.

For a family who is poor, placing a child in an orphanage is sometimes the easy way out. It is much easier to place a child in an institution than to deal with the whole life. Broken relationships, poverty and injustice may leave a family feeling desperate, as if they have no choice. With this in mind, we can see how allowing a father to abandon a child to an orphanage is allowing him to abdicate his responsibility. Sometimes our efforts to help can enable a person to continue in sin that is at the root of their poverty.

When we want to help someone who is struggling with poverty, we must remember that sometimes helping hurts. Tim Keller, author and Pastor of Redeemer Presbyterian Church in New York, suggests that when helping the poor, we should 'let mercy limit mercy.'[16] When helping someone would enable them to act irresponsibly and protect them from the consequences of their sin, it is not really help. Likewise, doing something for someone that he can do for himself is a form of victimization.

We who believe in Jesus have received undeserved grace from God. We don't have to do anything to receive God's mercy. And yet God's grace demands change. According to Keller:

16   Keller, Timothy J. *Ministries Of Mercy*. 1st ed. Phillipsburg, N.J.: P&R Pub., 1997. Print.

Grace does not come to the deserving (there is no such person), and it does not discriminate. Rather initially it comes to us freely. But once it enters our lives, God's grace demands changes; it holds us accountable.[17]

We must remember that change is a process, not a project. The broken relationships at the root of poverty cannot be restored in a few weeks or months. Lasting change requires a deep commitment and local ownership over years or decades. We must extend mercy with patience.

The rest of the story

Do you want to know what happened to Asha? Her story has a happy ending.

Jennifer and Dano Jukanovich's family moved to Rwanda in 2009. Jennifer's husband Dano partnered with two other men to start a social business working with Rwandan enterprises. The family intentionally moved into an economically diverse neighborhood in Kigali, Rwanda. In addition to facilitating adoptions from Rwanda when the country was open for international adoption, Jennifer spent her time in Rwanda getting to know her neighbors.

The women living in Jennifer's neighborhood would approach her to ask for emergency help with school fees or medical care. Over time, Jennifer's neighbors became her friends, and she longed to do more to empower these women to provide for their own families.

In September 2010, Jessica Honegger held the first Noonday Collection trunk show. Noonday Collection is a start-up social enterprise selling jewelry and accessories made by artisans in the developing world. Noonday Collection uses fashion and design to create economic opportunity for the vulnerable by creating a market for their goods. When Jessica started Noonday Collection, she and her husband were in the process of adopting from Rwanda. In 2011, Jessica and Joe traveled to Rwanda to adopt a little boy named Jack. Jennifer helped Jessica and Joe through their adoption process. Together, Jessica and Jennifer began to dream of how they could create a path out of poverty for Jennifer's neighbors.

Over the next year, Jennifer partnered with Jessica and Noonday Collection to start a sewing cooperative. When Jennifer met Charlotte, she was doing hair in Kimihurura, Jennifer's neighborhood. Charlotte is one of Asha's relatives. Jennifer invited

---

17   ibid.

both Asha and Charlotte to join the cooperative. In partnership with Noonday Collection, the women were able to go to sewing school for six months and to set up a sewing cooperative called Umucyo. In 2012, I (Sara) travelled to Rwanda to meet Charlotte, Asha and the other women of Umucyo to help them design their first collection for Noonday Collection.

Two years later, Umucyo is thriving – and so is Asha. Umucyo continues to produce gorgeous accessories for Noonday Collection, paying the artisans a fair price for their skilled work. Asha is able to care for all four of her children with her earnings from Umucyo. She is able to pay her rent, to buy food, and to provide them with a good education. Asha says that she experiences 'much happiness working here' and is thankful that she no longer needs to beg to provide for her children.[18]

Asha is now able to dream of a brighter future for her children, who are now teenagers. She encourages them to study and to do well in school. She wants her daughter Zahara to be a doctor and her son Eli to be a lawyer. She wants her niece Clementine to be an electrician and Sarah to be a businesswoman.

Living out James 1:27

> A central priority for the church should be family preservation to the fullest extent possible, from micro finance projects to health initiatives to community development. Although those efforts are rarely measured as investments in orphan care, they certainly are a vital part of living out James 1:27.
>
> Jedd Medefind, President of the Christian Alliance for Orphans[19]

Sometimes living out James 1:27 doesn't mean building orphanages or encouraging adoption. If we want to end the orphan crisis, we need to empower families, churches and communities to escape the poverty at the root of the orphan crisis. We have a tremendous opportunity – as well as a Biblical responsibility – to support widows and orphans *together*.

So how do we get to the root of poverty? We've seen there are hundreds of millions of widows and orphans living in extreme poverty. How do we begin to make a difference when the problem is this huge? It is easy to be overwhelmed.

---

18   Asha. Personal Interview. 26 March 2014.

19   Medefind, Jedd. 'Ethics in adoption and orphan care.' Personal interview by phone. April 2012.

Let's go back to something we said at the beginning of this book. Of all of the numbers we have talked about in this book, *one* is the most important. It only takes one to change the life of one. Each one of us can make all the difference in the world to one.

We know that international adoption is not efficient. It is time-consuming, difficult and expensive. And yet we believe it is worth it because through adoption we can change the world for one child. Those of us who have a heart for adoption get that making a difference one child at a time is worth it. So while the statistics about global poverty are overwhelming, we can fight poverty one child, one family, or one community at a time.

This chapter is just an introduction to poverty alleviation. Writing in great detail about relief and development, social business, or microfinance is beyond the scope of this book. If you want to learn more, there are many fantastic books and websites that will give you the information and tools you need. Our aim in this chapter is simply to inspire and empower you to begin to make a difference.

Ending Hunger

> For I was hungry and you gave me food, I was thirsty and you gave me drink, I was a stranger and you welcomed me, I was naked and you clothed me, I was sick and you visited me, I was in prison and you came to me. (Matt. 25:35-36)

Throughout this book, we've shared stories of mothers and fathers who struggle to feed their children. For the hundreds of millions of orphans and widows living in extreme poverty, hunger is a daily battle. Roughly five million children die each year as a result of hunger and malnutrition.[20] If we want to fight the poverty at the root of the orphan crisis, this is a good place to start.

There are many approaches to alleviating hunger. Sometimes hunger is a response to a crisis, such as a natural disaster or violent conflict. In the aftermath of a crisis, many governments and NGOs offer emergency food relief.

Some organizations use child sponsorship or feeding programs to fill in the gaps in a vulnerable child's diet. Other organizations prevent or treat malnutrition in children, providing lifesaving care to children and families in crisis.

---

20   Worldhunger.org. '2013 World Hunger and Poverty Facts and Statistics.' World Hunger Education Service, 27 July 2013. Web. 30 June 2014.

While relief is the right response to an emergency, reducing hunger is ultimately about development. Approaches that depend on outside resources are not sustainable. Imagine you have an orphanage full of children who are hungry. One approach would be to fill a shipping container with food in the United States and to send it to the children. While this would temporarily give the children food to eat, it would not be sustainable – and it might unintentionally hurt the local economy. A better approach would be to buy food locally, providing income to the people who grow and sell food. The best approach would be to empower the local community to fight hunger and to strengthen vulnerable families.

There is enough food in the world for everyone to eat, yet one in eight people in the world struggle with hunger. The primary reasons the poor struggle with hunger is that they do not have land to grow food or money to buy food. The poor may be more vulnerable to hunger as a result of conflict or climate change. Likewise, across much of the developing world, hunger is closely related to inequality between women and men.

Women comprise nearly half of the agricultural labor force, but women who are unpaid or who work on family farms or home gardens, or who cook or care for children are seldom counted in these figures.[21] When we include them, women do up to 80 per cent of the food production[22] and up to 90 per cent of household food preparation.[23] According to the World Food Programme:

> In many countries, there are more women farmers than men. Most often, they are the ones who prepare food for the whole family. Women are the key to improving household security and nutritional wellbeing.[24]

Yet in the developing world, women own only 1 per cent of agricultural land. Women are more likely to go hungry than men – and this has devastating consequences for children. Vulnerable women and their children are unfairly affected by poverty and hunger.

21 Actionaid.org 'What Works for Women: Proven Approaches for Empowering Women Small-holders and Achieving Food Security.' ActionAid International, March 2012. Web. 30 June 2014.

22 Fao.org. 'A Synthesis Report of the Africa Region – Women, Agriculture and Rural Development.' Food and Agriculture Organization of the United Nations, 1995. Web. 30 June 2014.

23 Wfp.org. 'Women and WFP: Helping Women Help Themselves.' World Food Programme, March 2011. Web. 30 June 2014.

24 ibid.

Research suggests that empowering women may be the secret weapon to fighting hunger. Giving women equal access to resources and opportunities could reduce the number of hungry people in the world by 100 to 150 million.[25] Research indicates that putting more income in the hands of women helps health, education and child nutrition.

According to ActionAid, a global human rights and development organization, women need access to 'knowledge, information and productive assets including land, livestock, and credit.'[26] They need training, access to technology and markets. Women tend to cultivate crops to feed their families and sell locally, while men tend to grow cash crops to sell to regional and international markets. To earn more, women need access to markets and fair financing. They also need support. Cooperative groups can help farmers negotiate for better prices, access services, and have a voice. They can also create a safe environment for women to meet and tackle social problems.

For farmers producing crops for regional or international markets, Fair Trade can be critically important. Fair Trade is about fair prices, good working conditions, and sustainability for farmers and producers in the developing world. Fair Trade is also about gender equality. Fair Trade means a higher price for farmers, and this can benefit the whole community. Fair Trade premiums often fund projects like wells for clean drinking water, medical clinics, or building schools.

The majority of poor children who drop out of school are girls, but an amazing thing happens when girls have enough to eat.

When girls have enough to eat, they are more likely to stay in school. When girls reach puberty, they are far more likely to suffer from anemia, which makes it difficult for girls to concentrate. Good nutrition can prevent anemia and help girls stay in school. School feeding programs and other low cost initiatives to improve children's nutrition can increase school attendance and performance – especially for girls.

If girls stay in school, they tend to delay marriage and have fewer children. They are less likely to die in childbirth. Development experts agree that promoting gender equality is crucial to fighting global poverty. According to the United Nations World Food

---

25 Actionaid.org 'What Works for Women: Proven Approaches for Empowering Women Small-holders and Achieving Food Security.' ActionAid International, March 2012. Web. 30 June 2014.

26 ibid.

Programme, empowering women with education is crucial: 'educated mothers have healthier families. Their children are better nourished, are less likely to die in infancy and more likely to attend school.'[27] Likewise, when parents are well educated and earn a good income, they value educating their daughters.[28]

According to Lawrence Summers, former chief economist at the World Bank, 'investment in girls' education may well be the highest-return investment available in the world. The question is not whether countries can afford this investment, but whether countries can afford not to educate more girls.'

But what happens when a family must decide which child should go to school? When poor families in Africa and Asia are forced to decide whom to send to school, they often choose their sons.

In Uganda, just 26 per cent of the students who start primary school at age four are girls. By the time children reach Primary 7 – when girls are 13 years old – they represent just 6 per cent of the students.[29] In Uganda, 85 per cent of girls leave school early.[30]

Girls drop out because of cultural expectations, early marriages and pregnancies, and the cost of school fees. Particularly in rural areas in Uganda, parents have different cultural expectations for boys and girls. While parents value education for their sons as preparation for supporting the whole family, they may discourage girls from studying. Ultimately girls are expected to marry, cook and care for their households, and produce children.[31]

Early sexual activity and pregnancies are a serious problem in Uganda. As a result of the HIV and AIDS epidemic, older men may view school age girls as a risk-free alternative. Once a girl is pregnant, she is often kicked out of school. Likewise once a girl is married, it is culturally forbidden for the girl to leave her new family to continue her education.[32]

The cost of school fees is the most significant reason why girls leave school. During times of economic hardship, when families

27   Wfp.org. 'Women and WFP: Helping Women Help Themselves.' World Food Programme, March 2011. Web. 30 June 2014.

28   Atekyereza, Peter R. 'The Education Of Girls And Women In Uganda.' *Journal of Social Development in Africa.* 2001. Print.

29   ibid.

30   Girleffect.org. 'The Simple Case for Investing in Girls.' The Girl Effect, n.d. Wed. 30 June 2014.

31   Atekyereza, Peter R. 'The Education Of Girls And Women In Uganda.' *Journal of Social Development in Africa,* 2001. Print.

32   ibid.

have to decide which child should go to school, preference is given to boys. Some parents prioritize spending on essentials like medical care and food, while others squander income on alcohol, sugar and prostitutes.[33] In turn, to try to make enough money to pay for school fees, girls may turn to prostitution.[34]

A Path Out of Poverty

We've seen that keeping girls in school is crucial to fighting poverty, but how do we empower families to make an investment in their daughters' education?

When I met Jalia in 2011, she was homeschooling her five year old daughter Zoe. Jalia grew up in a large family in Uganda, but was fortunate to be able to complete her education. Trained as a jewelry designer, Jalia had a passion to use her skills to provide a path out of poverty for women living in her community. Though she was ambitious, the truth is Jalia and her husband Daniel were struggling to care for their children. They were homeschooling because they could not afford school fees.

Three years later, Jalia and Daniel are the owners of a quickly growing social business, African Style, which produces handmade jewelry for Noonday Collection. Over just a few years, African Style has grown from two artisans to more than 300. The artisans receive regular paychecks, a daily hot meal, emergency assistance, and scholarship opportunities.[35] Jalia and Daniel have been able to enroll both their son and their daughter in good schools. The artisans who work for African Style can also afford the cost of school fees. As this social business empowers hundreds of families to keep their girls in school, it will impact generations as the cycle of poverty is broken.

Business is a powerful tool to fight the poverty at the root of the orphan and widow crisis. The billions of people living in poverty in the world today need economic opportunity. If we look at the last twenty years, nearly one billion people have risen out of extreme poverty. This is largely as a result of rapid economic development in China and other emerging markets.[36]

33   Kristof, Nicholas D, and Sheryl WuDunn. *Half The Sky*. 1st ed. New York: Alfred A. Knopf, 2009. Print.

34   Atekyereza, Peter R. 'The Education Of Girls And Women In Uganda.' *Journal of Social Development in Africa*, 2001. Print.

35   Noondaycollection.com. 'A Glimpse Inside Uganda.' Noonday Collection, 2014. Web. 30 June 2014.

36   Economist.com. 'Towards the End of Poverty.' The Economist, 1 June 2013. Web. 30 June 2014.

And yet it is clear that growth in a country's economy does not always benefit the poorest of the poor. Indeed, in many countries around the world, the gap between rich and the poor has only grown wider over the last thirty years.[37] The poor are being left behind in a global race to the top – and the bottom.

This is why social enterprise is so powerful. Social entrepreneurs see business as a tool to create social change. Many social businesses are designed to generate income, strengthen community, and provide opportunity for the poor and marginalized.

Sometimes the best business opportunities in developing countries are simple: raising chickens and pigs or growing cash crops like coffee and tea. Many developing countries have quickly growing economies and populations, which together mean a growing local demand for goods and services.

Many social enterprises create a bridge between people living in Africa, Asia or Latin America and people living in North America or Europe, giving small-scale artisans, farmers and producers access to international markets. Other socially responsible enterprises aim to reform industries that typically exploit the poor.

Consider the growth of the ethical fashion industry. The recent history of the garment industry has been filled with stories of dangerous factories and slave wages. Yet at the same time, the growth of the garment industry in countries like Bangladesh has created economic opportunity for millions of women. The authors of *Half the Sky* note that the factories that produce the goods that fill America's shopping malls have created economic growth driving the world's most effective antipoverty program. According to *The Guardian*:

> The textile and clothing industry is the second largest employer after agriculture in the developing world, and a large percentage of this workforce are women. Research shows that empowering and investing in women has a cumulative bonus: women are likely to spend their income on their children and families, on education, health and nutrition, bringing long term positive change and prosperity to communities.[38]

Socially responsible fashion businesses aim to transform the textile industry, to provide better working conditions and wages and to protect workers from exploitation.

37 Oxfam.org. 'The Cost of Inequality: How Wealth and Income Extremes Hurt Us All.' Oxfam Media Briefing, 18 January 2013. Web. 30 June 2014.

38 Mustafa, Ayesha. 'The Fashion Brands Empowering Women in Developing Countries.' The Guardian, 18 June 2014. Web. 30 June 2014.

In this chapter, we've introduced you to Noonday Collection. Noonday Collection is a social enterprise that uses fashion and design to empower the poor. We have seen first-hand how Noonday has transformed families and communities in Rwanda, Uganda and beyond. But Noonday Collection is not alone.

In recent years, we've been inspired by the growth of dozens of ethical fashion businesses that come alongside communities in the developing world. Nisolo is a footwear brand that gives Peruvian shoemakers access to international markets. Nisolo pays fair prices for shoes, empowering its artisans to invest in education and to save for the future.

FashionABLE is a social enterprise in Ethiopia that aims to alleviate poverty by creating opportunities for vulnerable women. FashionABLE produces lovely scarves and leather goods hand made by artisans. Many of the women who work in small business cooperatives with FashionABLE were once trapped in prostitution – the only means the women had to support their families. FashionABLE gives women an alternative to the sex industry, restoring their dignity.

People Tree is an ethical fashion brand that makes clothing with organic, recycled and hand crafted materials. For more than twenty years, People Tree has partnered with farmers, artisans and textile producers in the developing world to pioneer a new way of doing fashion. In 2013, People Tree was certified by the World Fair Trade Organization as the world's first Fair Trade fashion brand. People Tree provides jobs for more than 7,000 people in the developing world. People Tree has served as an example to the fashion industry, proving that it is possible to make garments without exploiting the poor.

A Vision for the Future

In 2001 when my then fiancé Mark and I (Sara) were planning our wedding, we made the decision to give our guests an unusual gift. In lieu of personalized mints, chocolates or wine, we made a donation to World Concern to fund a rice bank in a poor community in South East Asia. Both Mark and I had traveled in South East Asia and our hearts were broken for children living in poverty. We hoped our marriage would last – and we wanted to offer our guests a gift that would make a lasting difference.

Rice banks are one of the simplest forms of microcredit. Rice banks offer families a way to borrow rice in order to have enough to eat while they wait for the next harvest. After harvest, the family restores the rice borrowed from their crops, so another family can have it. Rice banks bridge the gap between relief and development. Over time, with agricultural training, support and tools, families no longer need the rice bank. The rice they grow and sell provides enough food and income that they can make it from harvest to harvest.

As I was writing this chapter, I reached out to World Concern to find out what had happened. Did the seed capital for the rice bank make a difference? I discovered that World Concern used our gift to set up a rice bank in a village in Southeast Asia.

World Concern partners with communities, building respectful and empowering relationships with local leaders. While rice banks are vital, 'they are just one piece of the picture that makes holistic community development work.' Cathy Herholdt, Communications Officer at World Concern explained, 'the goal is always to equip communities to stand on their own.' World Concern believes that lasting change comes from within and aims to be the 'catalyst to change, but not the change-maker.' While World Concern makes a long-term commitment to the communities where they work, they aim to work themselves out of a job by equipping poor communities to be their own solutions to poverty.

By the time a village is ready to graduate from a community development program, you can see the transformation. The community learns to work together to solve problems and meet needs. There are 'wells supplying clean water...the fields surrounding the village are producing abundant rice, and crops are thriving.' People care about their environment. Cathy explains that the real difference is 'the confidence on people's faces.' Perhaps the most tangible evidence of the transformation is simple, according to one grandma in a village in Myanmar: 'children are not dying.'

It is nearly impossible for the world's poor to access fair banking services. To start or grow a business, the poor need a loan. Yet traditional banks are not interested in lending to people who survive on less than $2 a day. To get a loan, the poor often have no choice other than to borrow from money lenders who charge exorbitantly high interest rates – as much as 300 per cent. Likewise the poor need a safe place to save money, but few banks will allow the poor to open bank accounts.[39] Likewise there are no banks in many rural communities.

39   Marotta, David John and Megan Russell. 'Microfinance: Loans that Change Lives.' Marottaonmoney.com, 4 May 2014. Web. 30 June 2014.

From India to Uganda to Brazil, microfinance is giving the poor a path out of poverty. Microfinance is about giving the poor access to fair banking services, including savings and loans. Microcredit is about providing small business loans at moderate interest rates. A loan can help a woman start or expand a business, creating a sustainable source income for her family. Some microfinance banks also lend to growing businesses in the developing world that also struggle to access loans at fair rates.

Likewise, savings circles are a simple and effective model for empowering vulnerable families. Savings can allow families to start a business, pay school fees, or survive a crisis. In a savings circle, members meet regularly and contribute tiny sums of money. At each meeting, one member of the circle receives a lump sum. Unlike microcredit, savings circles require no external capital. They are effective because they build community and accountability within the savings circle. When people are able to save to invest in future goals, they develop a different outlook on life.

Giving families access to fair banking services is an essential part of sustainable development. Without the ability to safely save for the future, many families remain trapped in poverty. While microfinance is not without its challenges, it is one of the most powerful strategies for addressing the poverty at the root of the orphan crisis.

Nicholas Kristof and Sheryl WuDunn, authors of *Half the Sky*, describe markets and microlending as a 'revolution sweeping the developing world' and a 'powerful system to help people help themselves.' From Bangladesh to Brazil, microfinance is improving the status of women and protecting them from abuse. In Kristof and WuDunn's words, 'Capitalism...can achieve what charity and good intentions sometimes cannot.'[40]

Embracing Hope Ethiopia

Embracing Hope Ethiopia (EHE) is an organization that puts all of these principles into practice. EHE is a ministry that comes alongside vulnerable families in Ethiopia offering a range of holistic services that empower families to stay together.[41]

---

40   Kristof, Nicholas D, and Sheryl WuDunn. *Half The Sky*. 1st ed. New York: Alfred A. Knopf, 2009. Print.

41   Shannon, Jerry. 'Embracing Hope Ethiopia.' Personal interview completed by email. 30 June 2014.

Offering a Day Care for the poorest and most vulnerable families is at the heart of EHE's work in the Kore slum in Addis Ababa. EHE relies on staff, community leaders and government officials to identify and serve the poorest of the poor. Preference is given to women who are unemployed or underemployed, who are sole breadwinners for their family, and who earn less than $22 USD a month upon entry to the project. EHE aims to come alongside mothers who are 'orphan vulnerable,' meaning they are at risk of abandoning children to an orphanage. According to Jerry Shannon, the Founder of EHE:

> Our aim here is to come alongside families who are living on the edge and face the stark reality that they may have to relinquish their children and 'orphan' them because of their current inability to provide basic needs for the child.

In 2008, Jerry and Christy Shannon adopted one of their daughters, Hanna, from Ethiopia. Through the adoption experience they realized, 'that while adoption was a beautiful option for children who did not have any parents,' poor families in Ethiopia needed more options to stay together. A year later, the family moved to Ethiopia with a deep desire to come alongside the poor, orphans, and widows. Once they arrived in Ethiopia, they studied the needs in their new community to discern how God was calling them to get involved. As they looked around, they became aware of a need for something like a Day Care:

> As we looked around we began to see thousands of mothers who would be faced with giving their child up for adoption because they had no one to care for their young child. These moms were begging, doing labor, doing whatever it took to keep their child because they loved them.

They asked themselves if it would be possible to care for children while their moms went to work. They saw a way for a child to be nurtured, a mother to be empowered, and a family to stay together. They realized that without support, moms were one crisis away from facing the painful decision of placing a child in an orphanage or for adoption.

When Jerry and Christy started Embracing Hope Ethiopia, there were few organizations serving families with babies and toddlers. Though they faced many obstacles, the Shannons were passionate about providing women with a way to work and to raise their children. The first Day Care began with twenty children in their living room, giving children a safe place to go while their mothers went to work during the day.

Embracing Hope Ethiopia now runs a day care and school serving 188 babies, toddlers and children with plans of adding 40 new children every year. They employ over 50 Ethiopians. During the day, the children play, eat, learn, and grow in a loving, safe environment while their parents are free to find work in the community. At the Day Care, children are fed nutritious meals, clothed, provided health care and early childhood education, while at the school they receive daily formal education.

The Day Care serves as a hub providing holistic services to children and families through the generosity of local and international partners. These services aim to empower families, giving them a path out of poverty. Social workers build relationships with the families, helping them to identify each family's specific needs. EHE then offers a range of services to strengthen families:

- Financial assistance to help families afford food and shelter

- Supplemental food, hygiene materials and clothing

- Free health care for children and moms

- Special assistance for those who are HIV+ or have special medical or nutritional requirements

- Micro grants and income generation opportunities to help moms start a business and build savings

- Training for moms in literacy, job skills, health, and hygiene

Embracing Hope Ethiopia aims to restore families to the fullness of life that God intended. EHE partners with every family in the program to tailor a 'phase out strategy' that combats dependency. They recognize that poverty is not just about resources and opportunity. Poverty is also about broken relationships. EHE partners with moms to build community, helping the women to embrace hope in all areas of their lives. EHE offers opportunities for moms to use their gifts and abilities to help their communities.

Rather than sponsoring children in orphanages, EHE offers churches and individuals a way to sponsor children in families. Sponsorship covers the cost of the Day Care and family support.

While some forms of child sponsorship are not sustainable, the EHE program aims to empower families over time to be able to provide for their own needs.

As Embracing Hope Ethiopia has grown, the vision has expanded to identify and meet more needs in the community. Working in partnership with the local community, EHE has identified a need for a children's library and literacy center where moms can learn to read and write. In 2013, EHE opened a Kindergarten to serve children who have graduated from the Day Care. Each year, they aim to add an additional grade at the school. This will allow EHE to continue to provide Day Care and holistic support to more families.

Embracing Hope Ethiopia has also started an after-school program for children who are school age. The program is a place where children can eat nutritious food, learn English, be tutored, play and grow in character. EHE recognizes that over time, a family's needs change. When moms and babies enter the Day Care program, they are struggling to survive day by day and the family needs an intensive amount of support. As the mom finds work or starts a business, she discovers her strengths and develops new skills. The after-school program offers EHE a way to walk alongside the family in a less intensive way.

Within Ethiopia, spiritual and development activities must remain separate. This can make it difficult to address the spiritual side of poverty. To meet this ongoing need, EHE has started a separate ministry that can disciple moms who want to grow in their relationship with God.

What impact does Embracing Hope Ethiopia have on the families they serve?

Mothers and children have their dignity restored. They have family, means to provide, and a safe place where they know people care about them. While dignity is hard to quantify, Jerry describes dignity as something that 'shows up in every mom's face after they are with us for a while. They no longer have to beg. They no longer have to sell themselves through prostitution. They describe themselves as having found a kind of freedom.'

Through nutrition, healthcare and hygiene, Embracing Hope Ethiopia makes a significant difference in the health of children and moms. Social workers provide assistance and education to improve the health and wellbeing of families. For example, social workers help moms get started on antiretroviral therapy for HIV if needed, and they demonstrate relationship and parenting skills. The social workers provide community to moms so they do not feel alone anymore.

Most children start at the Day Care having sat with their mothers all day everyday begging by the roadside. These children would have never had the opportunity to attend a good school. Now, the children receive an excellent early childhood education that allows them to get a head start on their peers. Through partnership and cooperation, EHE has been able to build a strong relationship with the local government.

Moms who are in the program are encouraged to save so that they have the means to survive a future crisis. Most women are able to save the equivalent of one month's salary within the first six months with a little assistance. Other women are able to start small businesses that will sustain their families:

> One of the biggest factors for orphans being created is when sickness or disaster hits – such as when rainy season means that there is no work or a mom is not able to get the medicine that she needs. We have been able to cooperate with Moms during these times. The crises are overcome and families stay together. We believe that God has placed children into families and our end aim is to do all we can to make sure that child can stay there.[42]

Over the last three years, Embracing Hope Ethiopia has empowered 110 families to stay together who would otherwise not be together. While EHE is not able to share God's love in word, they aim to share God's love in deed. Jerry and Christy believe this changes moms and children from the inside out.

Embracing Hope Ethiopia is passionate about 'providing opportunities where [vulnerable families] can be reconciled to God, to self, to others and to creation, and are trained in becoming fully devoted followers of Jesus who bring change to their generation and the ones to come.' EHE aims to address the root causes of poverty, including sin and broken relationships. EHE demonstrates and proclaims the Gospel throughout their ministry. Jerry sees the ministry as 'an opportunity to demonstrate Jesus' love in a very practical way which has the potential to transform life for a family.' EHE wants the poor families and children they come alongside to discover their true identity as children of God with a gift to share.

Shannon, Jerry. 'Embracing Hope Ethiopia.' Personal interview completed by email. 30 June 2014.

We believe this is an excellent model for how to provide for orphans and widows in response to and as a demonstration of the Gospel. We asked Jerry to share a story of how one family has been transformed through the work of Embracing Hope Ethiopia.

I think one story that shares the heartbeat of what we do is the story of Ruth and her son Yonas.[43] Ruth came to us three years ago while begging on the street with her small child. We welcomed her into the project on the condition that she would need to go to work. She agreed. A couple of weeks after coming into the project, however, our staff discovered her begging during one of the large religious festivals on a Saturday. She had chosen to beg outside of an Ethiopian Orthodox Church where she could easily make enough to live for a week in one day. Our staff located her and asked her to come and talk with them on Monday.

She arrived on Monday, afraid that she was going to be expelled from the project because she had gone back to begging. We tell moms they are not permitted to beg nor are they permitted to prostitute any longer, because our aim is that they have dignity restored as a step out of poverty and toward The Gospel. If they continue to beg, they will not discover this dignity that they are made in God's image.

Our staff told Ruth that they would take care of her child's needs and some of her needs. She now was free to go to work - so she must go to work. Ruth was afraid to work because she came from generations of only begging. We told her that the type of work was not important. Rather, her working was the first step. She should do whatever she could find. Ruth started working a day labor job [that] paid about $1.20 per day. She was working 10 hour days carrying rock, debris, sand, and dirt on construction sites. It was back-breaking labor for very little. But it was work.

Three months later we asked Ruth what had changed for her. Her reply was, 'I am free. I never saw that begging was like a cancer that was destroying my soul, but now I am free.' Ten hours a day of back-breaking labor for $1.20 and she describes a freedom. She was experiencing dignity.

Fast forward a year. Ruth was working and was finding better work. She was making great headway. And then she got pregnant.

She knew that we discouraged moms from getting pregnant

---

because it would mean a much longer road for them to try to move toward sustainability. So out of fear, she hid her pregnancy. Then as she started to progress, she decided to get an abortion, unknown to our staff.

While on her way to the abortion clinic where she could get a free abortion, a broker convinced her that she should instead have an abortion in this back-alley, horrific room. She had the abortion, but they botched the surgery. She started having issues of bleeding and pain soon after this abortion.

This left Ruth in a difficult situation. Courageously she came to our staff and confessed about her abortion. She did this out of fear that she would be rejected. It required our staff to prayerfully consider a response. We are Pro-Life. We do not believe in abortion. If she had asked our opinion, we would have discouraged the abortion and have sought other solutions. But how would Jesus respond toward this outcast woman with a bleeding issue who had already had the abortion?

I was so stinkin' proud of our staff that day. We prayed and thought through the theological issues and were left with a response of compassion. We needed to reach out to this mom and care for her in this time. She needed to be comforted and consoled, while we looked for a medical response for her bleeding. Our staff wrapped their arms around this Mom on that day.

A couple of months later this Mom came to our staff and said, 'Guess what I did? I gave my life to Jesus.' She then went on to share that the reason was that she had seen the compassion and mercy of Jesus through our staff during her time of need. She came expecting rejection, but what she received was a care and compassion. Even while our staff did not agree with her decision, she could see a depth of love that resembled Jesus' love. So, she became a Jesus follower.

What stands out to me about Ruth's story is what is true of the stories of so many of our moms. It took generations for the family to end up in this depth of poverty – there is no quick way out. Many moms will do whatever it takes to keep their children, even hours of back-breaking labor for next to nothing.

If a mom can get a glimpse of dignity and understand that she is made in God's image, it is a huge game changer. If we can show the mercy and compassion of Jesus to the widow, the outcast and the orphan, they will respond to His love.

Ministry among moms and children is a long-term solution, with many twists and turns along the way. God sovereignly uses those twists and turns to bring Himself Glory. There is nothing sexy about ministry among these moms and children. It requires difficult choices, empowering of mothers, not being too soft and not being too hard - and being committed to touching them and building relationship with them every single day. Without that, gutting it out in the trenches alongside these mothers, a solution will not have lasting effects.

QUESTIONS FOR DISCUSSION AND REFLECTION

1. Describe the link between poverty and the global widow and orphan crisis. Why is poverty often the reason why children are abandoned?

2. Is poverty about more than just resources? Explain how poverty is about broken relationships.

3. How is empowering a family to care for their child better than placing a child in an orphanage or for adoption?

4. What are some of the most effective ways to alleviate poverty?

5. What is one thing you can do differently in order to help one family have a path out of poverty?

Defending the Fatherless

*He defends the cause of the fatherless and the
widow, and loves the foreigner residing among you,
giving them food and clothing.*
(Deut. 10:18, NIV)

Angelique's Story

Angelique lived in a small village in Rwanda with her mother until
her mother died giving birth. She travelled to Kigali, the capital
city of Rwanda, to look for her father. When Angelique arrived in
Kigali, however, she discovered her father was dead and she had no
living relatives. Angelique was just fifteen years old when she found
herself orphaned and alone in Kigali.

Angelique took a job as a housekeeper living with a family,
but the opportunity soon became a nightmare. Not long after she
started her job, Angelique's boss began to rape her when his wife
was out of the house. Angelique discovered she was pregnant as
a result of the abuse. When her pregnancy became apparent, the
man's wife kicked her out. She was terrified.

A modern-day Hagar, Angelique was left alone with no one
to help her. Even though she was pregnant, she worked carrying
water for neighbors earning just enough to barely survive. A kind

neighbor saw her in labor on the side of the road and took her to the hospital. Angelique gave birth to a baby boy named Felicien at the age of sixteen. As an orphaned teenage mother living in a big city, she was desperately poor and extremely vulnerable to injustice.

Unfortunately Angelique's story is not unique. As an extremely poor orphan living in Rwanda, she was vulnerable to exploitation. Abandoning a child is illegal in Rwanda, but in her desperate situation she might have thought to abandon her son with the hope that he might find a better life at an orphanage. If it had been an option at the time in Rwanda, she might have thought to give her son up for international adoption.

Would anyone intervene to help Angelique and Felicien? Would anyone take up her cause and hold her rapist accountable for his violent crime?

Nothing else would do.

In 1994, Gary Haugen was a human rights attorney working for the United States Department of Justice when the United Nations sent him to investigate the Rwandan genocide. Over the course of 100 days from April to July that year, nearly one million people were slaughtered and half a million women were raped.[1] Haugen's experience in Rwanda would become a defining moment. As he investigated mass graves and listened to survivors, he realized the Rwandan victims 'did not need someone to bring them a sermon, or food, or a doctor, or a teacher, or a microloan. They needed someone to restrain the hand with the machete—and nothing else would do.'[2]

Gary Haugen founded International Justice Mission (IJM) in 1997 along with a small team of lawyers, investigators, and human rights advocates. IJM uses the skills of criminal justice professionals to protect the poor from violent oppression. IJM is now a global organization working in nearly twenty countries across Asia, Africa and Latin America. While the organization is best known for its work fighting sexual violence and trafficking, IJM also protects the poor from slavery, property grabbing, illegal detention, and police abuse of power. In Rwanda, IJM walks alongside children and teenagers who are victims of sexual violence, intervening to help girls who have been raped and abused.

---

1   Survivors-fund.org.uk. 'Statistics'. *Survivors Fund*, 2014. Web. 7 Jul. 2014.

2   IJM.org. 'Get to know us'. *International Justice Mission*, 2014. Web. 7 Jul. 2014.

Amanda's Story: How I ended up serving in Kigali, Rwanda

In 2005, I (Amanda) decided to go to law school because I wanted to make a lot of money, and corporate lawyers in America generally have very high starting salaries. I transferred law schools after my first year to a 'Top 20' school to make my job prospects even better. After graduation I was hired by a large corporate law firm and worked there for four years. I enjoyed my colleagues and received training from top lawyers. The work was challenging if not fulfilling, and it felt good to be compensated well.

Then we started the adoption process – and suddenly the Scriptures came alive. Jesus spoke against the dangers of trusting in and hoarding wealth. He was speaking to me and about me. In calling me to care for widows and orphans, I couldn't (and still can't) reconcile my wealth with their need. As we began to pray for these children we were adopting, we learned a lot. We read books on DRC history, global poverty and racism. We went on a tour of the American South, learning the history of Civil Rights in our own country.

When we went to DRC to investigate our adoption and began to see the extent and effects of corruption in international adoption, we knew we couldn't stay still any longer.

As a lawyer, I wanted to use my skills to fight the injustice that we had witnessed. I wanted to use my privilege and wealth on behalf of the vulnerable, instead of myself. When I returned from DRC, I quit my job with no real plan in place. We talked about foster care, but we still felt led to serve internationally.

I applied for a volunteer legal fellowship with IJM. A week before I gave birth to my son, I accepted a position in Kigali, Rwanda. We sold almost everything we owned and put the rest in our parents' basements. My husband quit his job, and we hopped on a plane with our six month old son.

The rest of Angelique's Story

Soon after her baby was born, Angelique met social workers from IJM Rwanda. She was living in a dirty room and sleeping on a dirt floor. She had no clothes for the baby and nothing to eat. Felicien was sick. I was volunteering at the IJM office that day, and I remember when the social worker came back to the IJM office after meeting with Angelique. She was heartbroken for the orphaned girl and her son, who were living in a critical situation. As a poor, young mother, she was extremely vulnerable to exploitation.

But this day was a turning point in Angelique's life. IJM Rwanda came alongside Angelique, helping her to find a safer place to live and giving her proper food and clothing. They helped Angelique register Felicien for a government insurance card so he could receive medical care. At the same time, IJM's attorneys supported Angelique in court, advocating for justice on her behalf. After meeting with Angelique and learning her story, the IJM team knew that the most important evidence for the criminal action would be the DNA of her baby to prove that the accused was the father. IJM provided this evidence to the government attorneys, which was key to getting a conviction.

I will never forget rocking Angelique's baby to sleep while his father sat on trial for rape. On November 29, 2013, the Rwandan judge found Angelique's rapist guilty, sentencing him to prison and requiring that he pay civil damages to the court that will help to support the family's healing and future. Angelique wept with pain and relief at the trial.

Today, Angelique's perpetrator is in prison. Meanwhile, Angelique and Felicien have been able to start a new life together. Angelique has a home and a job selling second-hand clothes at a large market in Kigali. She absolutely adores and dotes on Felicien, who is an active boy now walking and learning to talk. Every day he rides on his mother's back to the market where she works. His face lights up when he sees her, and she smiles bashfully when we praise him.

While much of Angelique's life has been filled with injustice, some of her story has been redeemed. Angelique is turning her pain into a future for her son – and she is no longer alone. Angelique and Felicien have moved in with another young mother, who has also been a client of IJM. Together they move forward in community and hope.

Angelique is not alone.

Had Angelique been a woman in America, the fact that her rapist was arrested and charged with a crime would not be unusual. In the United States, we can more or less trust the police and the judicial system to hold violent criminals accountable.

In Rwanda, however, the fact that Angelique's rapist was arrested and charged with a crime is remarkable. The fact that he was ultimately convicted of rape and sentenced to ten years in prison is nothing short of a miracle.

Angelique's story is not unique. In Rwanda, young girls who are poor are especially vulnerable to sexual abuse and rape. Despite tremendous progress over the last twenty years, the judicial system in Rwanda still lacks the resources needed to successfully protect these girls. In 2011, IJM began a project to address the widespread issue of sexual violence against children in Rwanda.

IJM partners with Rwandan authorities to help individual victims of a rape or abuse and to bring criminals to justice. IJM intervenes to help clients in three ways: investigation, legal casework, and aftercare. IJM assists local government attorneys in investigating and building legal cases against perpetrators. IJM's Rwandan attorneys represent clients and their families in court. IJM aftercare professionals conduct needs assessments to determine the social, psychological, and economic needs of clients.

Because IJM Rwanda is active in the community, the organization receives referrals of cases from hospitals, health centers, community health workers, and churches. Since the project began in 2011, IJM Rwanda has served 72 girls, successfully advocating for convictions in 45 cases. As IJM takes on individual cases, the organization also works to identify weaknesses in the justice system that leave the poor vulnerable to violence.

Injustice at the root of the orphan crisis

As we have seen throughout this book, widows and orphans are particularly vulnerable to injustice. This is especially true for widows and orphans living in poverty. We've learned there are 115 million widows who live in extreme poverty. These mothers, aunties, and grandmothers are caring for roughly half a million children. A typical widow in Africa is a young mother who is alone in providing food, shelter, education, and protection for her children. Many of the world's poorest widows live in countries where they face discrimination because of their gender and marital status.[3]

Of course, widows and orphans are not the only people in the world today who suffer injustice. Throughout the Bible,

---

3   Ondimba, Sylvia Bongo. 'The World Must Support Its Widows'. *The Guardian*, 2011. Web. 22 Mar. 2014.

we see God's compassion not only for widows and orphans but for all who are oppressed. In ancient Jewish culture, orphans, widows, immigrants, and the poor would have been vulnerable to exploitation. God defends the vulnerable from oppression – and calls His people to do the same.

So who are the marginalized and the oppressed in our communities and around the world today? This certainly includes widows and orphans, but it also includes billions of people who live in extreme poverty. It includes victims of trafficking, forced labor and sexual slavery. It includes people living in countries devastated by war, political oppression and violence. It includes women and girls who live in countries where they are considered less valuable than men and boys. It includes children living in orphanages or on the streets.

What does injustice look like for widows and orphans?

Injustice comes in many forms. Injustice comes in the form of widespread conflict and war and government oppression. Injustice is often spoken about as the everyday violence the poor suffer in developing countries where they lack protection of the law.[4] Women and minorities face injustice in the form of discrimination and oppression. Global poverty is a form of injustice, where the poor can work from sunrise to sunset and remain poor while others become rich at their expense.

If we want to end the orphan crisis, we have to address the injustice that causes children to be orphaned or abandoned. What injustice causes children to be orphaned, abandoned or separated from their families?

Violence and Discrimination against Women and Girls

In many countries of the world, women are oppressed because of their gender. Across much of the developing world, women lack equal rights and protection under the law. Women are forced to marry. Women and girls are denied education, food and medical care. Nearly 350,000 women die every year in childbirth.[5] We believe that maternal mortality is primarily an issue of injustice, not poverty. When a mother dies in childbirth, her children are orphaned.

---

4   Haugen, Gary A, and Victor Boutros. *The Locust Effect*. USA:OUP 2014. Print.

5   TheGuardian.com. 'Maternal Mortality: How Many Women Die In Childbirth In Your Country?' *The Guardian*, 2010. Web. 7 Jul. 2014.

In Africa, Asia and Latin America, women are frequently denied the right to own property. For poor families, a house and a small plot of land provide 'shelter, food and desperately needed income.'[6] An estimated 1.5 billion people in the world live in urban slums without any secure right to their homes. Likewise, 90 per cent of people who live in rural Sub-Saharan Africa have no proof that they own their homes or land. Without secure property rights, the poor are vulnerable to having their homes and land stolen. This is especially true for widows, who may become the victims of violent property grabbing after the death of a husband. When a mother is thrown out of her home and off her land, she may have no way to provide for her children and may have to abandon them.

It's not too much to call violence against women a global epidemic. Like Angelique, millions of women experience rape, abuse and violence. Other forms of violence against women in the world today include female genital mutilation and honor killings. According to the Half the Sky Movement, 'women aged 15-45 are more likely to be maimed or die from male violence than from cancer, malaria, traffic accidents and war combined.'[7]

One out of three women around the world has been beaten, forced into sex, or otherwise abused in her lifetime.[8] Around the world, hundreds of millions of children have been victims of physical or sexual abuse.[9] But many countries fail to protect vulnerable children and women from abuse. Even when cases do go to trial, perpetrators are unlikely to be held accountable. Weak, corrupt legal systems fail to protect women and children from abuse and exploitation. What happens when a woman is violently raped or killed? Her children are often left behind and remain vulnerable to further abuse.

Trafficking and Slavery
Even though Christians are becoming more aware of modern day slavery, it is hard to believe that there are nearly 30 million slaves in the world today. Trafficking generates more than 32 billion dollars

---

6   IJM.org. 'Casework: Property Grabbing'. *International Justice Mission*, 2014. Web. 12 Jul. 2014.

7   Halftheskymovement.org. 'Gender Based Violence'. *Half the Sky Movement*, 2014. Web. 26 Jun. 2014.

8   'Fact Sheet: Violence Against Women Worldwide'. New York: *United Nations Development Fund for Women*, 2009. Print.

9   Krug, Etienne G. et al. 'World Report On Violence And Health.' Geneva: *World Health Organization*, 2002. Print.

in profit each year for those who sell men, women and children into slavery.[10] The total market for slave labor and sex is an estimated $150 billion a year.[11] Every year, more than 1.2 million children are trafficked and forced into various forms of slavery. Broadly speaking, there are two types of slavery: forced prostitution and forced labor.

What is forced labor? According to International Justice Mission:

> Forced labor slavery uses deception, threats or violence to coerce someone to work for little to no pay. Although slavery has been outlawed in nearly every country, millions of men, women and children are working as slaves in brick kilns, rice mills, garment factories, fishing operations, and many other industries.[12]

When parents are held captive as slaves, their children are extremely vulnerable to exploitation. One out of four people who are enslaved in forced labor is a child.[13] Children of desperately poor families are often at risk of being coerced or sold into slavery.

There are an estimated two million children around the world who are enslaved in the sex industry.[14] There are many ways in which women and girls are forced into lives of prostitution. While some women enter the industry willingly, most are forced by threat of violence or coerced by desperate circumstances. One study suggests that nearly nine out of ten people working in the sex industry want to escape. Many women who are enslaved in prostitution face the threat of violence. Women may lose hope and 'resign themselves to selling sex because they perceive themselves to have no other options.'[15]

This issue is inextricably linked with the orphan crisis. Children who grow up in orphanages are particularly vulnerable to being forced into slavery. Often the children of prostitutes are forced into the industry. For example, some studies show that 90 per cent of

---

10   IJM.org. 'Injustice Today'. *International Justice Mission*, 2014. Web. 22 Mar. 2014.
11   IJM.org. 'Casework: Human Trafficking'. *International Justice Mission*, 2014. Web. 22 Mar. 2014.
12   IJM.org. 'Casework: Forced Labor Slavery'. *International Justice Mission*, 2014. Web. 22 Mar. 2014.
13   ibid.
14   IJM.org. 'Casework: Sex Trafficking'. *International Justice Mission*, 2014. Web. 22 Mar. 2014.
15   Halftheskymovement.org. 'Forced Prostitution'. *Half the Sky Movement*, 2014. Web. 29 Jun. 2014.

the daughters of sex workers in India end up working in brothels.[16] Parents in desperate circumstances may face a choice between selling themselves or their children into slavery simply to survive. Trafficking and slavery leave millions of children in desperate situations without the love and protection of a family.

Broken Justice Systems

Violence against women, trafficking and slavery are illegal in almost every country, yet most of the world's poor live outside the protection of the law.

When a poor child in Bolivia is raped by a wealthy man, her family cannot afford a lawyer and so the wealthy man goes free. When a widow in Uganda is thrown off her land by her husband's family, the local leaders ignore her pleas for justice. When a young mother in Vietnam is coerced into placing her baby for international adoption, she has nowhere to turn.

In developed countries, we enjoy relative safety because our justice systems restrain violence. In developing countries, wealthy people can hire lawyers or security guards and can pay bribes in order to stay safe. The poor, however, do not have these options. The world's poor live under the constant threat of violence.

Though many development initiatives fail to address this insecurity, poverty and injustice are inseparable. We can dig a well to provide clean water to a village; but if a girl gets raped on her way to fetch the water and we do nothing to stop this violent crime, are we really helping her?

Gary Haugen argues that 'the end of poverty requires the end of violence.'[17] Haugen authored *The Locust Effect*, a groundbreaking book that describes in great detail how violence is an everyday threat for the poor who live in the developing world. After nearly twenty years of experience working to protect the poor from rape, slavery, trafficking, property grabbing, and police brutality, the leaders of IJM believe that these have one underlying issue in common: everyday violence.

Across the developing world, justice systems are broken. According to Haugen, 3.5 billion of the world's poorest people live 'with a constant threat of being raped, robbed, assaulted and

---

16   ibid.

17   Haugen, Gary A. 'Why the end of poverty requires the end of violence'. *Huffington Post*, 2014. Web. 2 July 2014.

exploited.[18] The justice systems that should protect people from violence leave the poorest people desperately vulnerable, with 'no defense whatsoever from those who seek to rape, abuse, exploit and assault them.'[19]

Not only do justice systems across the developing world fail to protect the poor, in some cases the systems take advantage of the poor. According to *The Locust Effect*, 'the most pervasive criminal and predatory presence for the global poor is frequently their own police force.'[20] In some countries, the police can detain and hold suspects indefinitely without any evidence. For example, the average length of pre-trial detention in Nigeria is 3.7 years.[21] When a father is arbitrarily detained or abused by the police such that he is forced to flee, he leaves behind his wife and children.

Sustainable development is impossible without security. The United Nations Office on Drugs and Crime has found that 'restraining violence is a precondition to poverty alleviation and economic development.'[22]

Conflict

Justice is not simply about the absence of violence – it is about the presence of peace. We live in a world torn by violent conflict, where 25 million people have been forced to flee their homes. The World Bank estimates that 1.5 billion people live in countries affected by violent conflict.[23] As of the writing of this book, there are violent conflicts in twenty-four countries, including Syria, South Sudan and DRC.

The civil war in Syria that began in 2011 has pulled apart families and communities, forcing nearly three million people to flee their homes and seek safety outside the country. Most of the refugees are women and children, many of whom have experienced the death of a husband or father in the conflict. Women are the sole providers for one in four Syrian refugee families. These widows face discrimination and a constant struggle to provide for their families.[24]

---

18   ibid.

19   ibid.

20   Haugen, Gary A, and Victor Boutros. *The Locust Effect*. USA:OUP 2014. Print.

21   ibid.

22   ibid.

23   World Bank World Development Report, 2011.

24   Sherwood, Harriet. 'Women Head Quarter Syrian Refugee Families'. *The Guardian*, 2014. Web. 8 July 2014.

South Sudan became an independent nation in July 2011. Just two and a half years later, however, the country was engulfed by violence. By July 2014, more than 1.4 million people have fled their homes, many into neighboring Uganda and Ethiopia.[25] Experts now believe that nearly 4 million people are in critical need of humanitarian assistance. Ongoing violence has prevented the United Nations and other international organizations from delivering desperately needed food and supplies.[26]

The communities along Lake Kivu in Eastern DRC have been devastated by twenty years of violent conflict. After two decades of war, the families in the region live in extreme poverty. One million children are struggling with severe malnutrition. Hundreds of thousands of children in Eastern DRC live under the constant threat of violent attack by a multitude of armed groups.[27] Both the army and the rebels are involved in human rights abuses, including widespread rape and violence against women.

Experts believe 2.7 million people have fled their homes looking for safety, leaving many children separated from their families. A World Vision report describes eastern DRC as one of the 'toughest places in the world to be a child.'[28] In the region, atrocities like rape and abuse are committed so frequently that children believe they are inevitable and normal. The report describes how children have been devastated by the loss of their parents and families:

> The impact of this is devastating. Feelings of grief and pain are most acutely expressed when children talk of losing their parents or family members. They talk of lying awake in fear of attack and feel they have no one to turn to for help. Their experiences tell of a devastating reality, not just for children directly affected, but also for the hopes for the country and region. The long-term impact of children being exposed to violence for so long and so often is difficult to overstate. It typically has intensely disturbing and far-reaching effects on children's social, emotional, cognitive and spiritual well-being and development. It interferes with children's educational performance, ability to form social relationships and lead healthy lives.[29]

---

25 Anderson, Mark and Achilleas Galatsidas. 'South Sudan Interactive Timeline Crisis Conflict'. *The Guardian*, 2014. Web. 9 July 2014.

26 Jones, Sam. 'South Sudan food security crisis could spiral into famine, agencies warn'. *The Guardian*, 2014. Web. 12 May 2014.

27 Ridout, Anna. 'No One To Turn To: Life for children in Eastern DRC'. *World Vision International*, 2014. Print.

28 ibid.

29 ibid.

Women and children are the most vulnerable victims of war. In the past, wars were fought primarily by national armies and women and children were protected. Over the last fifty years, there has been a shift. The majority of the world's conflicts now take place within countries – and families are no longer spared.

Children living in war-torn countries may be orphaned, abandoned or separated from their families. Desperate parents who are unable to protect or provide for their families may leave children in orphanages, fearing they have no other way to ensure their survival. Many of the countries that have been popular for international adoption in recent years, including Guatemala, Nepal and DRC, have recently emerged from a civil war. The combination of poverty and violent conflict leaves families with few choices.

We have seen that we cannot end the orphan crisis without alleviating poverty. Likewise, we cannot alleviate poverty without fighting injustice. If we want to end the orphan crisis, we must see how poverty and injustice leave vulnerable families in desperate circumstances.

In a perfectly just world, women would not be raped, abused or killed because of their gender. They would receive the same access to medical care and education as men and boys. Women would not be forced by violence or poverty to sell their bodies. Widows or orphans would not have their property stolen from them after the death of a husband or father. In a perfectly just world, poor families would not live in fear of the police. Families would not be torn apart by conflict or disease. Mothers and fathers would be able to provide for their children. Families in crisis would have alternatives to placing their children in orphanages or for adoption.

As Christians seeking to care for orphans and widows, we must care about widespread injustice. Unless we fight the injustice that leaves families vulnerable, we cannot stop children from being abandoned and orphaned. We have seen that poverty is at the root of the orphan crisis and that we cannot end the orphan crisis without giving families a path out of poverty. Yet empowering families with skills and resources to meet their own needs isn't enough. We've learned that there are 1.4 billion people who live in extreme poverty, and that 26,000 children die every day because they lack food, clean water, shelter or medical care. And yet the reasons poor people do not have enough to eat or cannot access medical care are deeply rooted in injustice. Vulnerable families and children need protection from violence. Alleviating poverty and fighting injustice must go hand in hand.

Our God is a God of Justice

God is the creator and ruler of the universe. God is perfect in love, faithfulness and justice. Indeed justice flows from His very nature:

> He is the Rock, his works are perfect, and all his ways are just. A faithful God who does no wrong, upright and just is he. (Deut. 32:4, NIV)

We live in a broken world where we are surrounded by oppression. Sometimes it is hard to understand how a just God could allow the world He created to be filled with injustice and suffering. It is all too easy to join Job's accusers in asking, 'Does God pervert justice?' (Job 8:3)

And yet from Genesis to Revelation, the Bible describes God as a just and righteous king:

> Righteousness and justice are the foundation of your throne; steadfast love and faithfulness go before you. (Ps. 89:14)

God is passionate about justice. From beginning to end, the Bible reveals the heart of God. When God tell us who He is, He is teaching us what is close to His heart. God calls Himself the 'Father of the fatherless and protector of widows.' (Ps. 68:5) He describes himself as a strong redeemer who vigorously defends the cause of the oppressed.[30] God tells us that He loves justice:

> He loves righteousness and justice; the earth is full of the steadfast love of the Lord. (Ps. 33:5)

God is powerful and strong, and yet He identifies with the weak. God seems to have a special compassion for the oppressed. We live in a world where the poor have no voice, but God is passionate about justice for the poor. God has compassion for the weak. He says their blood is precious in His sight, and He promises to redeem their lives from violence and oppression.[31] God listens to the cries of the weak:

> You, Lord, hear the desire of the afflicted; you encourage them, and you listen to their cry, defending the fatherless and the oppressed,

---

30   Jeremiah 50:34.
31   Psalm 72:13-14.

so that mere earthly mortals will never again strike terror. (Ps. 10:17-18, NIV)

We live in a world where we desperately need God. As the perfect Father, God protects and provides for His children:

> He executes justice for the fatherless and the widow, and loves the sojourner, giving him food and clothing. (Deut. 10:18)

Justice is a part of the Gospel

In the book of John, we discover the story of a woman who is in a desperate situation. It is early in the morning and Jesus is sitting at the temple at the Mount of Olives in Jerusalem, teaching people about God. The Pharisees and religious leaders drag in a woman who has been caught in the act of adultery. Under the law, this woman deserves death. The religious leaders, who want to bring a charge against Jesus, ask Him what He thinks.

What happens next is remarkable. Jesus bends down next to the woman and writes something in the ground with His finger. He then stands up and says, 'Let him who is without sin among you be the first to throw a stone at her.' (John 8:7) Jesus bends down and writes on the ground once more. One by one, the woman's accusers go away. John gives us a glimpse into the conversation between Jesus and the woman:

> Jesus stood up and said to her, 'Woman, where are they? Has no one condemned you?'
>
> She said, 'No one, Lord.'
>
> And Jesus said, 'Neither do I condemn you; go, and from now on sin no more.' (John 8:10-11)

When Jesus kneels down next to the woman caught in adultery, He identifies with her. He takes up her cause and calls her accusers to examine their own lives. His powerful words compel the angry religious leaders to identify with the broken woman. They realize that they too have been caught in sin.

Jesus demonstrates the goodness of God's kingdom. Jesus' life on earth reveals God's heart. When He forgives the woman caught in adultery and then calls her to walk away from her life of sin, we see the mercy of God. When Jesus dies on the cross, we see God's perfect love and perfect justice.

Like the adulterous woman and the proud Pharisees, we have been found guilty of sin. God is a righteous judge and the penalty for sin is death. And yet Jesus identifies with us. He takes up our cause. We stand condemned, but Jesus dies on the cross in our place. The cross satisfies the justice of God and reveals the mercy of God.

Justice in a broken world.

> This is what the Lord Almighty said: 'Administer true justice; show mercy and compassion to one another. Do not oppress the widow or the fatherless, the foreigner or the poor.' (Zech. 7:9-10, NIV)

God calls us to be people of justice. We are created in the image of a God who is passionate about justice. As image bearers, we are called to represent God – to be ambassadors for His Kingdom.

From beginning to end, the Bible teaches us how to fight for justice in a broken world. When we are people who pursue justice, our lives reflect God's heart. God calls His people to 'follow justice and justice alone,' (Deut. 16:20, NIV). In particular, God's people are called to defend the vulnerable:

> Defend the weak and the fatherless; uphold the cause of the poor and the oppressed. Rescue the weak and the needy; deliver them from the hand of the wicked. (Ps. 82:3-4, NIV)

In 1 Kings 10, we read the story of the Queen of Sheba visiting King Solomon. Solomon is described as a wise, prosperous and merciful king. The Queen of Sheba praises King Solomon, saying 'Because the Lord loved Israel forever, he has made you king, that you may execute justice and righteousness' (1 Kings 10:9). God calls leaders to execute justice and righteousness. By defending the weak, we demonstrate that God is a righteous and just King.

The purpose of the Old Testament law was to teach God's people how to live in a way that demonstrated God's goodness to their neighbors. Justice and mercy are at the heart of God's law. Jesus summarizes the law in two commandments:

> You shall love the Lord your God with all your heart and with all your soul and with all your mind. This is the great and first commandment. And the second is like it: You shall love your neighbor as yourself. On these two commandments depend all the Law and the Prophets. (Matt. 22:37-40)

We love because we were first loved by God.[32] According to Jesus, justice is rooted in love. We are designed to love God and to love one another. When we get these two relationships right, the result is justice. A life characterized by justice is the natural outpouring of God's love in us.

As Christians, we are called to pursue justice as an act of worship in response to the cross. We have received justice and mercy from God. We were slaves and God has set us free. We have been rescued by a God who intervened to save us from sin and death. We are called to remember that we have been redeemed – and to respond by protecting and providing for the least of these. We're called to fight for justice for widows, orphans, the poor, and all who are oppressed.

Furthermore, doing justice is an opportunity to understand more deeply the justice God has done for us. When we kneel down next to the broken and identify with the vulnerable, we see more clearly our need for a Redeemer.

Throughout this book, we have seen that injustice is at the root of the orphan crisis. It is not possible to end the orphan crisis without addressing the violence and injustice that destroy families. While the statistics about injustice in the world today are overwhelming, we believe it is possible to make a difference. While this chapter is simply an introduction to a huge issue, we hope it will challenge and empower you to fight the injustice at the root of the orphan crisis.

Justice starts in our hearts

So how do we begin to do justice? The prophet Micah summarizes the kind of life that reflects the character of God:

> He has told you, O man, what is good; and what does the Lord require of you? But to do justice, and to love kindness, and to walk humbly with your God. (Micah 6:8)

At first glance, doing justice and loving kindness sound like two different things. Tim Keller points out that in Hebrew, the word for 'kindness' is *chesedh*, which means God's unconditional grace and compassion. The word for 'justice' is *mishpat*, which means to treat people fairly. According to Keller, the point of Micah 6:8 is, 'To walk with God, then, we must do justice, out of merciful love.'[33]

---

32   1 John 4:19.

33   Keller, Timothy J. *Generous Justice*. 1st ed. New York, N.Y.: Dutton, Penguin Group USA, 2010. Print.

If we want to do justice, we must start by examining our own hearts. Does how we live in daily life reflect God's kindness and justice – especially to the poor? Jesus teaches us that our wallets reveal our hearts: 'For where your treasure is, there your heart will be also' (Matt. 6:21).

Increasingly, Christians are aware that millions of women and girls are exploited in the sex industry. Christians rightly condemn sex trafficking and forced prostitution. We believe that people are made in the image of God – and to rape or abuse a woman or child for profit is to violate something sacred.

And yet many of us would think nothing of buying clothing, chocolate or coffee that may have been produced by slaves. Few of us are even aware that modern-day slavery is used in the supply chains for everything from jewelry to electronics. The truth is millions of people in the world today are held against their will and forced to work for little or no pay to make the clothes we wear, the food we eat and the electronics we love. What does this look like?

Many of the countries that grow cotton and produce clothing for the United States and United Kingdom – including Uzbekistan and Bangladesh – are known to use child or forced labor. Uzbekistan is currently the world's largest exporter of cotton. The Uzbek government forces more than a million people, including children, to pick the crop each year. Schools are closed, and children are forced to work 70 hours a week for little or no pay.[34]

Rana Plaza was a building in Dhaka, Bangladesh that housed dozens of garment factories producing clothes for many of the brands that fill shopping centers in the United States. On the morning of April 24, 2013, the garment workers could see a dangerous crack in the wall of Rana Plaza and were scared to enter, but were beaten and forced to go to work in the building. When the building collapsed later that day, over 1,100 people were killed and 2,500 people were injured. Thousands of children were orphaned when their mothers or fathers were killed in the collapse.[35]

When we purchase cheap clothing for our children in the United States, we seldom consider the true cost. Injustice in the apparel industry means children who should be in school are forced to work. It also means men and women are paid slave

---

34   Notforsalecampaign.org. 'Apparel Industry Trends 2012'. *Not For Sale: End Human Trafficking and Slavery*, 2012. Web. 7 Jul. 2014.

35   ibid.

wages, threatened with violence, and forced to work in dangerous factories. Cheap clothes come at the cost of mothers and fathers being killed and children being orphaned.

Opening our eyes to this injustice is inconvenient – and changing how we shop can be costly. And yet if we are called to be people who do justice, we must start with our own lives. How we spend our money can make a powerful difference.

People are made in the image of God with inherent dignity and worth. Justice is about human rights – and slavery is a violation of these rights – but on a deeper level the reason we believe people have rights is because they are made in the image of God. Tim Keller defines justice as 'giving humans their due as people in the image of God.'[36]

Justice is also about love. We are called to love our neighbors as ourselves. Keller argues that our 'neighbor is anyone in need.'[37] What happens when we realize that cotton pickers in Uzebekestan and garment workers in Bangladesh are our neighbors? We understand that love does not tolerate injustice – and we care enough to change.

Just one at a time

It is hard to comprehend what 30 million modern-day slaves means. It is difficult to imagine 25 million people who have been forced to flee from their homes. It is nearly impossible to grasp the truth that 3.5 billion people live with no protection from violent crime. The statistics about injustice in the world today are overwhelming.

We may not be able to end all of the injustice in the world, but we can do justice for one child, one family or one community at a time.

One woman dies every minute of every day giving birth. Nearly all of these deaths occur in developing countries.[38]

Why do women die in childbirth? Nicholas Kristof and Sheryl WuDunn point to four reasons why women die in childbirth: biology, lack of education, lack of rural health systems, and disregard for women.[39]

We have seen how the cycle of poverty leaves women vulnerable to dying during pregnancy and childbirth. When girls grow up

---

36   Keller, Tim. 'What We Owe The Poor'. ChristianityToday.com, 2014. Web. 2 Jul. 2014.

37   Keller, Timothy J. *Generous Justice*. 1st ed. New York, N.Y.: Dutton, Penguin Group USA, 2010. Print.

38   Kristof, Nicholas D, and Sheryl WuDunn. *Half The Sky*. 1st ed. New York: Alfred A. Knopf, 2009. Print.

39   ibid.

hungry, leave school early, and get pregnant as young teenagers, they are more likely to experience complications in pregnancy and childbirth. When something goes wrong during labor, it can be incredibly difficult for a poor, rural woman to reach a hospital where a doctor or midwife can save her life.

While poverty is a factor, high rates of maternal mortality are not inevitable in poor countries. The United States and Sri Lanka have almost identical rates of maternal mortality, even though Sri Lanka is a developing country that has only recently emerged from civil war. In the United States and Sri Lanka, women have a 28 and 29 in 100,000 chance of dying in childbirth, respectively.[40]

So what is the difference between Sri Lanka and other developing countries where far more women die in childbirth? Sri Lanka has invested in health and education and focuses on gender equality – Sri Lanka values women.

We believe maternal mortality is ultimately an issue of injustice, not simply poverty. In countries where women are marginalized, women are far more likely to die in childbirth. According to the authors of *Half the Sky*, 'maternal mortality is an injustice that is tolerated only because its victims are poor, rural women.'[41]

While the statistics about maternal mortality are overwhelming, we can make a difference one mother and one baby at a time.

Jocelyn Jelsma is a Canadian missionary and a Registered Midwife who lives in Rwanda with her husband and four children. Jocelyn serves vulnerable mothers and babies at the Nyabisindu maternal health clinic. The clinic sits under a tent in an area of Kigali inhabited by families living in extreme poverty, where crime and prostitution threaten the health of the community.

In Rwanda, 320 out of every 100,000 women die from complications during childbirth.[42] Most deaths can be prevented when women have access to prenatal and postnatal care, and when their births are attended by midwives or doctors.

Every Tuesday, about fifty women visit Nyabisindu for free prenatal exams throughout their pregnancies. They learn about

40 'Maternal Mortality in 1990-2013 in Uganda.' WHO, UNICEF, UNFPA, The World Bank, and United Nations Population Division Maternal Mortality Estimation Inter-Agency Group, 2013. Print.

41 Kristof, Nicholas D, and Sheryl WuDunn. *Half The Sky*. 1st ed. New York: Alfred A. Knopf, 2009. Print.

42 'Maternal Mortality in 1990-2013 in Rwanda'. WHO, UNICEF, UNFPA, The World Bank, and United Nations Population Division Maternal Mortality Estimation Inter-Agency Group, 2013. Print.

nutrition and preparing for labor. They listen to the heartbeat of their growing child and sometimes receive ultrasounds. The prenatal team provides prenatal education, weighing the mothers, checking their blood pressure, watching for signs of eclampsia, and sending them to the hospital if there is an emergency.

Then on Thursdays, each new mother comes in every week for six weeks following the birth of her child. This is a crucial time for preventing infant and maternal mortality. The standard of care in Rwanda recommends that postpartum mothers return to see the doctor six weeks after birth, but with one in five children dying before they are five years old, and many dying in the first weeks of their lives, the team at Nyabisindu is essential to the health of these women.

At the postpartum clinic, mothers learn about breastfeeding and family planning. The babies are checked for jaundice, respiratory health, fever, and proper weight gain. Mothers are checked for bleeding, uterus contraction, high blood pressure, and fever. Social workers counsel mothers through postpartum depression and the challenges of having a new baby at home.

Jocelyn's local church is now building a clinic where mothers can give birth. The Iranzi – or 'God knows me' – Clinic will be a place for mothers to go to have well-trained doctors and midwives attend their births. The clinic will open in the fall of 2014.

We first introduced you to Tara Livesay in Chapter 3. Tara is a midwife who serves at Heartline Ministries in Port au Prince, Haiti. Haiti has the highest rate of maternal mortality in the Western Hemisphere. In Haiti, a woman's lifetime risk of dying from complications in childbirth is 1 in 83.[43] Many children are orphaned when their mothers die during or after birth. Heartline Ministries comes alongside poor, vulnerable moms to improve maternal health and stop children from being orphaned.

Heartline provides medical care before, during, and after moms give birth.[44] Heartline has been working in Haiti for more than twenty years. According to Tara, the ministry aims to help women have 'a safe birth in a place where they are treated with love and respect.'[45]

The Haitian nurses and missionary midwives build relationships with the moms. Pregnant moms who join Heartline's program

---

43   'Maternity Center'. *Heartline Ministries*, 2014. Web. 4 July 2014.

44   ibid.

45   Livesay, Tara. '3 Homecomings Madi Nan Ayiti Tuesday in Haiti'. *Livesay Haiti*, 2014. Web. 4 July 2014.

come to the center weekly for monitoring and to receive vitamins, a healthy meal, and education about caring for themselves during pregnancy. The moms typically give birth at the maternity center with help from the nurses and midwives. When necessary, Heartline will provide transport to and support at the hospital.[46]

After moms give birth, they are given time to bond with their new babies, to begin breastfeeding and to recover. Tara is thrilled to be able to offer these women what every woman deserves, a 'unique opportunity to be cared for, pampered, and loved.'[47]

Both Nyabisindu and Heartline demonstrate that it is possible to fight injustice one mom and one baby at a time.

Transforming systems to protect the poor

Doing justice means addressing the broken systems that fail to protect the poor from violence. The justice of a society can be measured on how it treats its most vulnerable. Justice is about protecting human rights. In a just society, the laws, police and courts must protect the weak from the strong, the minority from the majority.

In the Old Testament, God's people were called to set up a legal system that protected vulnerable families from injustice. They were also prohibited from accepting bribes, dealing corruptly, and exploiting the fatherless, the widow, the sojourner, and the poor. Christians today are called to uphold these same principles.

For many families in Uganda, owning a small piece of land is critical to survival. Families grow produce and raise animals on their land, thereby earning a modest income selling vegetables, fruit, eggs, milk, or meat. In Uganda, there are essentially no government services to protect or provide for widows, orphans or vulnerable families. Traditionally, the extended family is the social security network.

But imagine a situation where a husband is unfaithful to his wife. The husband contracts HIV and transmits it to his wife. Soon thereafter, the husband dies of AIDS, leaving his wife who is now in ill health alone with their children. After the father's death, the extended family turns on the widowed mother and her orphaned children. They say 'you're no longer a part of our family' and force her to leave her home and land.

---

46   'Maternity Center'. *Heartline Ministries*, 2014. Web. 4 July 2014.

47   Livesay, Tara. '3 Homecomings Madi Nan Ayiti Tuesday in Haiti'. *Livesay Haiti*, 2014. Web. 4 July 2014.

Under Ugandan law, the widow has the right to inherit the family home, land, and most of the estate. The husband's extended family, however, may disagree. The family may use a variety of tactics to force the widow out of her home, including bribing the local police, stealing the title to the land, or forging the will or other legal documents. Some extended families will go further, destroying the widow's crops or harming her livestock. In extreme cases, the extended family may resort to assault, murder, or involving a witch doctor. As a result, the mother is left with nothing.

This is not a small problem in Uganda. More than one in five widows and orphans is a victim of illegal property seizure after the death of a husband or father.[48] The United Nations reports that as many as 30 per cent of Ugandan widows have been victims of illegal property seizure.[49]

Those of us who live in the developed world have a hard time imagining someone taking our property with impunity, but that is the reality for many poor families living in the developing world. Gary Haugen describes the uncertainty faced by the world's poor:

> Most of the world's poorest people live in circumstances in which they can be summarily thrown out of their homes and off their land because there is no reliable record keeping system for accurately demonstrating who owns the land and the property – and even if there were, there is little willingness or no capacity to actually enforce those rights on behalf of the poor.[50]

A widowed mother caring for orphaned children in Africa is especially vulnerable to having her property rights violated after the death of her husband. Although women who live in the developing world are responsible for up to 80 per cent of food production, they own just 1 per cent of the land. We've seen that empowering women who are farmers is a powerful way to fight hunger – but knowledge, information and credit mean little if women do not have secure title to their homes and land.

In Uganda, land grabbing is illegal. Women who are widowed have a right to inherit their homes and land so that they can have shelter, income and food. Yet land grabbing is widespread because poor women have no voice. Without a home or land, a widowed mother may have no way to provide shelter, food and education to

---

48   IJM.org. 'Injustice Today'. *International Justice Mission*, 2014. Web. 22 Mar. 2012.

49   Csmonitor.com. 'African Widows Left Destitute By Relatives Snatching Property'. *The Christian Science Monitor*, 2003. Web. 5 Jul. 2014.

50   Haugen, Gary A, and Victor Boutros. *The Locust Effect*. USA:OUP 2014. Print.

her children. For many families, this injustice can be the difference between life and death.

In Uganda, IJM focuses on defending the property rights of widows and orphans. The cases IJM takes on are typically complex, involving large extended families. IJM was involved in one case where the extended family literally destroyed the widow's house while she and her children were terrified inside. Often by the time a widow seeks IJM's assistance, she is in a desperate circumstance.[51]

So how does IJM help restore vulnerable families to their homes? As in Rwanda, IJM partners with Ugandan authorities to take on individual cases. IJM provides education through churches and community organizations in order to teach vulnerable widows about their rights. When a case is referred to IJM, the organization assists local authorities with an investigation, facilitates mediation if possible, and represents their client in court when necessary. Since 2008, IJM has helped put over 550 vulnerable families back in homes and has successfully advocated for the conviction and incarceration of over twelve perpetrators.[52]

IJM is launching a structural transformation project in Uganda to equip the justice system in Uganda to more effectively protect the property rights of widows and orphans. As IJM advocates for individual clients, the organization identifies gaps in the legal system that leave poor families at risk of injustice. IJM Uganda has brought hundreds of property rights cases through the Ugandan legal system. Through these cases, they have become aware of the different roadblocks that prevent victims from receiving justice. Structural transformation is about addressing these roadblocks. The goal is to equip the Ugandan justice system to protect the property rights of widows. Structural transformation projects include training police and government officials, developing a 'model courthouse' pilot project, and developing a digital database of property records.[53]

Seeking Shalom

Seek the peace and prosperity of the city to which I have carried you into exile. Pray to the LORD for it, because if it prospers, you, too, will prosper. (Jer. 29:7, NIV)

---

51   Rudy, Jesse. 'Property rights and the work of IJM in Uganda'. Personal interview. 17 May 2012.

52   IJM.org. 'Casework: Property Grabbing'. *International Justice Mission*, 2014. Web. 22 Jun. 2014.

53   Rudy, Jesse. 'Property rights and the work of IJM in Uganda'. Personal interview. 17 May 2012.

Ultimately justice is not about the absence of injustice, but about the presence of peace. The Hebrew word for 'peace' is shalom. God's eternal kingdom will be filled with *shalom*. *Shalom* means physical, emotional, social and spiritual flourishing. *Shalom* is rooted in relationships that are filled with joy.

Doing justice means seeking *shalom*. This means setting up our lives to build a community where people flourish. Justice is not just about a concern for the poor and the oppressed. The Biblical idea of justice includes living with fairness and generosity out of merciful love. It also includes being righteous. The Hebrew word *tzadeqah*, which can be translated 'being just' or 'being righteous', refers to right relationships. As we have seen, poverty is about broken relationships with God, ourselves, others, and creation. So coming full circle, doing justice is about fighting poverty.

We know all too well that the world is not characterized by *shalom*. We have rejected God's rule and His kingdom. War, violence, injustice and oppression are evidence of this fact. When there is poverty, injustice and family breakdown, there is no *shalom*. When children are abandoned, neglected, abused and orphaned, there is no *shalom*.

Though we live in a world that is not characterized by *shalom*, we are called to be people who seek *shalom*. *Shalom* is about complete reconciliation. From Genesis to Revelation, the Bible tells the story of how God is reconciling humanity to Himself. While we live in a world filled with violence and injustice, we know the end of the story:

> And he shall stand and shepherd his flock in the strength of the Lord, in the majesty of the name of the Lord his God. And they shall dwell secure, for now he shall be great to the ends of the earth. And he shall be their peace. (Micah 5:4-5)

Jesus will be our righteous and just King. He will triumph over evil and break the bonds of injustice. He will be our peace – our shalom – and we will be His people. We will flourish in His Kingdom where there will be an end to violence, trafficking, slavery and war. In His Kingdom there will be an end to injustice and poverty. In His Kingdom, there will be an end to the orphan crisis.

QUESTIONS FOR DISCUSSION AND REFLECTION

1. What is the link between injustice and the global widow and orphan crisis?

2. How is justice an integral part of God's character and the gospel? How are we as God's people called to respond to the injustice in the world?

3. How do we defend orphans and widows from injustice? What does justice look like for orphaned children?

4. How can we as Christians work for justice in our own lives? What difference can this make globally?

5. Describe the ultimate end of the orphan and widow crisis. How should this understanding of God's kingdom shape our lives today?

12

Good News
for Broken Families

Sara's Journey

My journey writing this book has spanned three years, two international moves, and many other changes in our lives. I started writing this book in early 2012 after a few posts on my blog went viral. I had started to write about the orphan crisis and how Christians were responding by building orphanages and encouraging adoption. My eyes had been opened to the truth that most children living in orphanages had families. I was struggling to process the fact that a pastor had tried to sell me a child. I was grieving the loss of Grace, the little girl we weren't able to adopt. Like other families who had seen what was happening on the ground in Uganda, I had realized that good intentions weren't enough. Christians, with tremendous love and a sincere desire to help orphans, were destroying vulnerable families in Uganda and beyond.

And so I started to write a book. I read thousands of pages of research. I studied everything the Bible had to say about orphans, poverty and injustice. I prayed. I flew to Africa to learn more. I also began to listen to the stories of families who had experienced corruption in the adoption process.

I first talked to Amanda just a few weeks after she returned home from her first trip to DRC without the three children she and her husband had adopted. Her heart was broken, but she had resolved to tell the truth. She bravely shared her story with me – not knowing the journey we were beginning together.

The writing of this book has been a journey in other ways. Our experiences with orphans and vulnerable families have turned our lives upside down.

When my husband and I began our adoption journey, we enjoyed a comfortable suburban lifestyle. My husband had a great job in the technology industry. We lived in a big house in Seattle, Washington. Our three children attended excellent schools, and I was able to be a stay-at-home mom.

A few years later, we've sold nearly everything we own twice. Six months into writing this book, our family moved to London. Two years later, as we were finishing the manuscript, my family moved to Austin, Texas. My husband left the corporate world, and I've become a social entrepreneur. Our experience adopting our daughter Ella – and witnessing the poverty and injustice in Uganda – challenged our priorities and changed the course of our lives.

Amanda's Journey

As I sit here finalizing this book, I am interrupted by a dear friend. She's been reading articles that I've shared and talking through the book with me, and now she's torn. Her son was adopted years ago, and she wonders whether everything she knows about his story is true.

I'm humbled and awed to think that we can have this conversation as a result of a lonely night in Kinshasa, where my husband and I wept. We sang the hymn *It Is Well With My Soul*, knowing all too well that our adoption journey was over.

I consider it a great privilege to walk through life with friends who have adopted children from all over the world, who serve HIV positive moms in Ethiopia, who reunite children with families in Uganda, who fight for maternal health in Rwanda. I wonder how I got to this place. I can only thank God for taking me on this painful and beautiful journey.

God led us to adoption through infertility. We had our life planned out: my husband and I would pursue our careers in corporate America and we would have a few babies along the way. Our children would go to private school, and someday we would buy a big house in the suburbs. Our life now is a bit different than we planned.

One year after that lonely night in Kinshasa, I returned to DRC. After discovering the children we had adopted were not orphans, my husband and I had decided not to meet them. Over that year we had moved from Chicago to Kigali, and we decided it was time. I scheduled a time to meet the children and their mother one afternoon.

Trembling with anticipation as I waited, I recalled the many sleepless nights while we waited for them to come 'home.' I would lie in bed praying and imagining what it would be like to smell their heads, touch their hands, hear their voices, hold them close, and tell them that their mother loved them.

Despite some twists and turns along the way, the reality of our meeting was even better than I imagined. They walked in holding hands with their mother – the woman who sacrificed her life every day to care for them, nurture them, love them, and serve them. They were not alone. They didn't need to be told that their mother loved them; they already knew it in their bones. What an amazing gift to me it was to see them, an undeserved grace from God. I had prayed that they would know a mother's love – and God had answered my prayer.

When Sara asked me to join her on this journey, I knew it was where God wanted me to take my story and the stories of these mothers. I wanted to use my voice, my resources, and my time to give a voice to the mothers: the mother who walks away from her children in an orphanage believing it's her only option, the mother who gives her life in childbirth, the mother who works her hands to the bone to feed her children.

God has used the winding road of this journey to show me that the heart He gave me was bigger and stronger than I ever imagined. I thought He was stretching me in opening my heart to three children, when instead He was opening my heart for millions more along with their families. When we were making plans for our life years ago, we could have never imagined where God has led us.

Today, we live in Rwanda. We sold our belongings and left our careers behind to pave our own way as social entrepreneurs. Our experience with adoption continues to challenge us to understand what Jesus truly means when He calls us to love our neighbors as ourselves.

A Book that Reflects our Journey

We know this book barely scratches the surface of the issues surrounding adoption and orphan care, poverty and injustice. And we know that this book reflects our unique journey. Most of the stories in this book are of people we know and places we have been. Our experience is largely in Uganda, Rwanda and DRC. We've been fortunate to learn from people working in Ethiopia, India, Haiti and beyond – but still this book is largely shaped by our own stories.

When we first started writing the truth about corruption in adoption, we felt alone. There were very few voices in the Christian adoption and orphan care movement who were brave enough to tell the truth.

Over the last three years, Amanda and I have discovered we are not alone. More and more of us are shining a light in dark places. We are becoming a movement of people who offer mercy and justice to a broken world in response to and as a demonstration of the gospel.

Families and adult adoptees are telling their stories. Journalists are uncovering the truth about corruption in adoption. Bloggers are asking critically important questions. Churches are planting churches engaged in orphan care. Christians are supporting ministries that alleviate poverty and fight injustice. Entrepreneurs are starting businesses to empower the poor.

We are becoming a movement of people who are rearranging our priorities to align our lives with God's priorities. We are becoming people who see our own stories as a part of God's Story. And at the end of the day, we believe this is the part of something that will transform the world – and end the orphan crisis. We believe this is movement is a tiny part of God's kingdom on earth.

Writing this book has been a journey – and much of this book has been written on a journey. In researching this book, we have had the opportunity to travel back and forth to Africa multiple times. When we are on the ground interviewing families or meeting with experts, the stories we hear are often overwhelming. It's only later – sometimes when sitting in the quiet of a long-haul flight – when we can reflect on the significance of what we've heard.

The world needs more daddies

Six months into researching this book, I (Sara) had interviewed the leaders of dozens of organizations serving orphaned children and vulnerable families in Uganda, Rwanda and beyond. Nearly every organization had one thing in common: they were focused on empowering women.

Somewhere above the Atlantic Ocean on a flight from Africa to America, I started to ask a new question. *In our efforts to empower women, are we letting a generation of men abdicate their Biblical responsibility? If one of the root causes of the orphan crisis is men abusing women and abandoning their families, then is the answer to bypass the men and empower the women? Or should we call the men to something more?*

As I was pondering these questions, there was a daddy in the row in front of me holding his son. The tiny boy was smiling and giggling, bouncing up and down in his father's arms. The daddy was tenderly kissing his son's black curls.

It clicked: the world needs more daddies. We cannot solve the crisis of fatherlessness without more fathers. But we have little hope of the men of the world stepping up to be fathers who protect and provide for the vulnerable without the Gospel. The men around the world need to stop abdicating their responsibility to be fathers. Fatherhood is more than passing on genetic material to the next generation.

All of the experts say that empowering women is the most powerful way to fight poverty. Nicholas Kristof and Sheryl WuDunn are the authors of *Half the Sky*, a groundbreaking book about gender inequality in the world today. They write:

> If we're trying to figure out how to get more girls in school, or how to save more women from dying in childbirth, the simplest solution is to reallocate spending. One way to do that is to put more money in the hands of women... when women hold assets or gain incomes, family money is more likely to be spent on nutrition, medicine, and housing, and consequently children are healthier.[1]

The research is overwhelmingly clear. Empowering women and girls is an effective way to alleviate poverty and fight injustice. If we want to end the orphan crisis, we need to empower mothers. As

---

1   Kristof, Nicholas D, and Sheryl WuDunn. *Half The Sky*. 1st ed. New York: Alfred A. Knopf, 2009. Print.

a result of all of this, massive amounts of resources in development are being poured into women. When women earn income, they are more likely to spend it on their families. Empowering women effectively reduces poverty and improves child health. Most of the ministries and organizations we've profiled in this book focus on empowering vulnerable mothers.

So what happens to men when you empower women? What happens to the fathers when we focus our efforts on the mothers?

Sometimes when you empower a woman, she gains more respect from her husband, family or community. But the sad truth is that the women who benefit from these efforts often become victims of violence and abuse. When women start businesses and save small amounts of money, they often become victims of crime. We've heard stories of women in Rwanda who, once they were earning a higher income than their husband, became victims of abuse in their marriages.

Men Behaving Badly

Much of the suffering of orphans and widows in the world today is caused by men behaving badly. Although poverty and injustice contribute to the orphan crisis, alleviating poverty and fighting injustice alone will not end the orphan crisis. The failure of some men to be husbands and fathers who protect and provide for women and children is perhaps the biggest challenge in the developing world.

Across the developing world, 'some of the most wretched suffering is caused not just by low incomes, but also by unwise spending—by men.'[2] When women control spending, families spend more on education, health, food and starting small businesses. But when men control spending, the poorest families in the world tend to spend 20 per cent of their income on a combination of alcohol, sugar and prostitutes – and only 2 per cent on educating their children.[3] According to *Half the Sky*:

> Many African and Indian men now consider beer indispensable and their daughters' education a luxury. The service of a prostitute is deemed essential; a condom is a frill.

Gender inequality and violence often begin at home. Across much of the developing world, it is culturally acceptable for husbands

2   ibid.

3   ibid.

to beat their wives. Research by the World Health Organization has found that 30 to 60 per cent of women experience physical or sexual violence from a husband or boyfriend.[4] Women from age 15 to 44 are more likely to die as a result of violence inflicted by men than from cancer, malaria, traffic accidents and war combined.[5]

In Africa, the woman who is most likely to contract HIV is married. When a man is unfaithful to his wife or has sex with a prostitute, the wife may still be expected to offer sex without a condom. It is overwhelmingly men who buy sex from prostitutes, creating a market for sex trafficking that enslaves millions of women and girls.[6]

What happens when a father believes that his sons are more valuable than his daughters or his wife? In many developing countries, girls are deprived food, education and healthcare simply because they are girls. In India, little girls are 50 per cent more likely to die than little boys. Gender discrimination kills up to two million girls around the world every year.[7] And as we have seen, poor, rural women die in childbirth primarily because they are women.

Empowering women is a powerful way to tackle poverty. Economists and development experts agree that addressing gender inequality is critically important. But we as Christians know that poverty is about more than resources. We know that it is about broken relationships. God has made human beings – both men and women – in His image. We are designed to worship God, to love and serve one another, and to care for creation.

While empowering women may go a long way to address some aspects of poverty and injustice, it's not enough. Fighting poverty is about more than giving the poor access to food, shelter, education, and medical care. Likewise, fighting injustice is about more than protecting the poor from violence. We are called to restore relationships. While the men who neglect their children or abuse their wives certainly contribute to the crisis, we do not believe the solution is to go around the men. If we want to make a lasting difference, we need to change the men. We cannot solve fatherlessness without fathers.

---

4   ibid.

5   ibid.

6   Polarisproject.org. 'Why Trafficking Exists'. *Polaris Project*. N.d. Web. Accessed 27 June 1014.

7   Polarisproject.org. 'Why Trafficking Exists'. *Polaris Project*. N.d. Web. 27 June 1014.

Hearts of the Fathers

And he will turn the hearts of fathers to their children. (Mal. 4:6)

We believe it is possible to call men to be become responsible husbands and fathers. Men who are made in the image of God can demonstrate the fatherhood of God by caring for their families. Men don't have to buy sex. Men can protect their wives and children from HIV and AIDS by being faithful. Men can be loving husbands who protect and provide for their wives and children. Men can pour resources into educating their daughters instead of getting drunk. Men can renounce violence and cherish their wives as equals and partners. They can be servant leaders who put the needs of their families above their own.

To end the orphan crisis we must not only reform orphan care and adoption. We cannot simply solve poverty and injustice. If we want to end the orphan crisis, we have to reach the hearts of men – and women.

But here's the good news. We believe in a God who changes things. God's redeeming grace can transform men into husbands and fathers who will protect and provide for women and children. This is as true in suburban America as it is in slums in India or mountains in Argentina or islands in Indonesia.

We all need Jesus. And the Church – where people meet Jesus – has an incredibly important role to play. The Church can call men to be godly husbands and fathers in a way that no government program or development project ever could.

This may be the most important thing we write in this whole book – and the most significant reason why the Church needs to approach the orphan crisis in a whole new way. If we want to end the orphan crisis, we must reach the hearts of fathers.

In making this point, we do not want to minimize the heroic work that women – often widowed or single mothers – are doing to care for children. It's also not to say that women aren't broken sinners who are in need of grace and transformation. We simply want to point out what we believe is a blind spot.

When men embrace their responsibility as husbands and fathers, women and children are far more likely to be safe and loved. And yet no one is talking about calling men to this responsibility: no one in the development world, no one in the orphan care movement. While this is a blind spot, it is also a tremendous opportunity.

The Role of the Church

We cannot solve the orphan crisis without the church.

Rick Warren

Rick Warren, Pastor of Saddleback Church, believes that orphanages are not God's design for children. At the Orphan Summit in 2012, he argued that God's plan to care for orphans is simple: families and churches.[8] Saddleback Church has launched an orphan care ministry to provide for orphans and vulnerable children in Rwanda. The church partners with the Rwandan government and local churches to empower families to care for the orphans in their communities.

So why is the Church – or God's people in every nation – so critical to fighting orphan crisis?

Warren believes that the global Church 'is able to have a unique impact on the world, making a contribution unlike any other organization. The church can promote reconciliation, equip servant leaders, assist the poor, care for the sick, and educate the next generation.'[9]

The global Church is the largest force for good in the world. There are 2.4 billion Christians in the world today. This is bigger than any nation. One in three people in the world go to church. The Church is everywhere. Christians speak more languages than there are represented at the United Nations. For thousands of years, God's people have been feeding the poor, caring for the sick and providing for orphans. The global Church is growing quickly – 60,000 people become new Christians every day.

Christians have the highest motivation to care for orphans: love. We offer mercy to orphans, widows and the poor in response to the grace we have received from God. Furthermore, we have been given 'all authority in heaven and on earth' to go and make disciples.[10] We believe that we have God's power and that He calls us to do something about the suffering in the world. If God puts a burden on our hearts, He calls us to do something about it – it is that simple.

God's people know the end of the story. Warren describes what will happen when Jesus returns to usher in the Eternal Kingdom

---

8   Warren, Rick and Kay Warren. 'Orphan Summit 2012'. Christian Alliance for Orphans, 2012. Main Session.

9   Kaywarren.com. 'The Peace Plan'. N.p. N.d. Web. 26 June 2014.

10   Matthew 28:18.

of God: 'We win. God's plan is inevitable. One day there will be no orphans.'[11]

We wholeheartedly agree with Rick Warren's perspective. We recognize the crucial role the global Church is already playing in caring for the poor. If you drive around cities in Africa, you will see countless NGO offices – but in many villages the only institution caring for the poor is the local church. As God's people, we have an incredibly important role to play.

The call to protect and provide for the vulnerable is not limited to the American or European church. This calling is not constrained by material wealth. There are profound needs across much of the developing world. There is material poverty, and there is also spiritual poverty. But we aren't the answer – and our money isn't the answer. God calls His people everywhere, including Christians in every nation of the world, to protect and provide for the vulnerable.

Families that reflect God's heart

If we want to end the orphan crisis, we must go deeper than addressing the circumstances that make people vulnerable to poverty or injustice. We must deal with the sin that destroys families. The pain and suffering at the root of the orphan crisis ultimately come down to one thing: brokenness. Poverty and injustice are a symptom of this deeper problem. The world is not as God intended it to be.

And yet, the gospel gives us everything we need to address the brokenness at the root of the orphan crisis. We were dead in our sin, but God has made us alive in Christ. We were slaves to sin, but we have been forgiven and set free. We were fatherless, but God has adopted us into His family. We were poor, but God has made us heirs of His Kingdom.

The gospel also gives us everything we need to address the poverty and injustice at the root of the orphan crisis. We've learned that poverty is about broken relationships with God, ourselves, one another, and creation. We have also learned that justice is ultimately about the presence of peace – or *shalom*. *Shalom* is about healing, reconciliation and restoration. Translated literally, the Hebrew word means wholeness or completeness. It describes the goodness of God's Kingdom, which is filled with righteousness, justice, love and truth.[12]

---

11   Warren, Rick and Kay Warren. 'Orphan Summit 2012'. Christian Alliance for Orphans, 2012. Main Session.

12   Psalm 89:14

If we want to end the orphan crisis, we need to make disciples. Discipleship is about inviting people to experience the goodness of God's kingdom.

Discipleship is about planting churches that are full of people who worship Jesus and who live like He is their King. Disciples live differently in response to what God has done in their lives. We who are the adopted children of God have the opportunity to welcome people into God's family. This is the most important role of the Church, God's people living in every country.

Discipleship is also about helping people experience the gospel, which has the power to transform families. Through God's word, we learn how to deal radically with sin – both the sin we have committed and the sin that has been committed against us. As we have been forgiven, we are able to forgive. The Holy Spirit gives the power to change, setting us free from addictions. God's love heals our hearts from the wounds of abuse. God's word shows us our identity as image bearers: we are children of God with a gift to share. Ultimately the gospel is the power of God to reconcile relationships. The gospel has the power to deal with the sin that destroys families.

The Story of Sojourn Church

We seek to be a church plant that plants other churches as we make disciples that make disciples. We will continue to grow, people will meet Jesus and be changed by the gospel. Men at Sojourn will grow knowing how to love their wives and their kids, and will lead others to do the same. Women will know that their body belongs to Jesus. Kampala will not be left unchanged because the gospel is powerful.

Dan Morris, Pastor of Sojourn Church in Kampala, Uganda

Uganda is a beautiful but complicated country. In recent years, the country has been devastated by political unrest, conflict, and the HIV and AIDS epidemic. The worst poverty in Uganda is in rural villages, where roughly 8 million men, women and children live on less than $1.25 a day.[13]

Many people move from rural areas to the city in the hope of finding a better future. Conflict has displaced hundreds of

---

13   Ruralpovertyportal.org. 'Rural Poverty in Uganda'. IFAD, 2012. Web. 24 June 2014.

thousands of families, many of whom have fled to urban areas.[14] High poverty levels force families to send children into the city to look for work. An estimated 2.7 million children in Uganda work, often as domestic labor.[15] Over the last thirty years, the urban population in Uganda has grown from 800,000 to 5 million.[16]

If you have ever sat in a traffic jam in Kampala, you know that the development of the city's infrastructure lags far behind the growth of the population. An estimated 40 per cent of the people in Kampala live in urban slums. Most of the slums are in wetland areas that lack adequate sanitation facilities and are vulnerable to flooding in the rainy season.

Wabigalo is one of the slums in urban Kampala, Uganda. The name means 'many bad hands.' It is a bad neighborhood, known for thieves, thugs, and prostitutes.

Six years ago, Dan and Loring Morris moved into Wabigalo. Four years ago they planted a church – Sojourn Church – right in the heart of Wabigalo. Dan and Loring wanted to live out the gospel in a way that their neighbors would have a chance to see Jesus. They believe that the gospel can change Wabigalo – that Jesus can bring redemption into the slums.

Dan and Loring are passionate about incarnational ministry. 'We must incarnate to translate,' Dan says, realizing that it's only through moving into the neighborhood that he has been able to see its good and its bad. 'We cannot live outside Wabigalo and make the same impact.'

Soon after moving into Wabigalo, Dan realized that poverty is a culture, not a condition. Though he lives in a slum surrounded by need, he has come to see that the biggest problem in his community is not a lack of resources.

When Dan planted Sojourn Church, he asked Christians *what is the biggest obstacle to the gospel in Uganda?*

'Every time people will say money,' Dan paused, 'but this is a false gospel. This view is rubbish.'

So what is the biggest problem in Wabigalo? Dan believes there is a crisis of broken families.

Traditionally in African villages, extended families and communities would care for orphans and vulnerable children. In urban Uganda, however, this traditional system is breaking

---

14   Mulumba, Deborah and Olema, Wendo Mlahagwa. 'Policy Analysis Report: Mapping Migration in Uganda'. Makere University Kampala, 2009. Print.

15   ibid.

16   '2012 Statistical Abstract'. Uganda Bureau of Statistics, 2012. Print.

down. 'You will find community in the village, but not so much in Kampala,' Dan explains, 'while we have a picture of African families taking care of kids, on the ground it's not good.' In Dan's words:

> The root of the orphan crisis is far deeper than just men being irresponsible. It is also women using sex for resources: sleeping with one man to get clothing, another for shoes, another for rent, another for her hair. Men treat sex as an appetite to be filled, and they are not above giving some compensation. Uganda has the highest teen pregnancy rate in Africa, and more than half of the population is teenagers.

The divorce rate in Uganda is about 4 per cent, but this is misleading because few people in Uganda get married. Men and women live together until the other party is no longer useful and then move on. Dan describes the cycle which leaves families broken and children vulnerable to being abandoned:

> What happens when a mother needs rent? She will sleep with a man and he will pay the rent. She will have another child, and then they will move in together. After a while, the new boyfriend doesn't want the children and will not pay school fees. The children will be sent back to the village to live with an auntie. The extended family will care for the kids, but as soon as the kids become a burden, they are gone. Kids end up neglected. Or they end up in institutions. Orphanages are seen as free boarding school, almost like a great opportunity. The same is true with adoption.

Dan sees this behavior both in and out of the church. In Ugandan culture, it is acceptable for men to have multiple partners:

> Purity is a word used by westerners. Being married to one person without 'side dishes' is American culture, not African. Many Ugandans believe that a man can't be expected to be with only one woman. These and many more are justifications people will give here for promiscuity, even in the church.

While there are many churches in Kampala, Dan points out that many are full of 'false teachers' who talk about Jesus, but who have not been changed by Jesus. They continue to accept promiscuity as a part of the culture, rather than using the Gospel to challenge the culture.

'We believe the gospel changes everything,' Dan says, explaining his approach. 'We have no programs for this. We have the gospel, and it is doing exactly what it does here in Wabigalo.'

Change comes from the Gospel

Dan is emphatic that ministry needs to come out of the local church. He describes a cycle where American churches or ministries come in with resources and ideas, but soon become frustrated by the pace of change. Without local ownership, ministries fail to make a lasting difference. As soon as the missionaries leave, the ministry is gone because it didn't come from within the community.

As a church planter and pastor, Dan believes it is his job to ask questions. When Sojourn was planted, Dan gathered his church together to ask how God was calling them to respond to the needs in Wabigalo. Dan remembers that at first the church said, 'We are the poor and needy, we need people to come minister to us.' Dan encouraged his people to believe that 'We have the gospel, the Holy Spirit. We have everything we need to be the church He's called us to be.'

Although this concept was new, over time the congregation began to see that God was calling them to meet the needs in Wabigalo. The people of Sojourn know the needs of their community. Six months into the church plant, Dan asked, 'What can we do to serve and love our community, to show them Christ?' This time it was 'like a light turned on. The church had lots of ideas – all in response to the gospel.'

The church came up with the idea of serving their community by cleaning up the ditches that run between homes. Few homes in Wabigalo have toilets or plumbing. There is no trash collection. The ditches are where people leave garbage and excrement. When it rains, the ditches flood and contaminated water flows into people's homes. By cleaning the ditches, the people of Sojourn are able to incarnate the love of Christ to their neighbors. In Dan's words, he's seeing 'slum dwellers serving slum dwellers.'

Sojourn Church partners with Vintage 21, a church based in Raleigh, North Carolina. Vintage 21 sent a mission trip to visit Sojourn. Vintage 21 wanted to launch a ministry to serve kids in an urban community in Raleigh. The church could see that there were profound needs in the neighborhood but did not know where to start or how to engage. The leaders of Sojourn and Vintage 21 recognized many similarities between the rough neighborhoods in Raleigh and Kampala:

> There is the same fatherlessness, the same poverty culture. Girls are growing up without daddies. They have no idea how to be loved by a man like a father.

The leaders of Vintage 21 recognized that Sojourn was reaching their neighbors in Wabigalo far more effectively than they were reaching neighbors in Raleigh. By moving into the neighborhood and loving the fatherless in their community, Dan and Loring were demonstrating the heart of God the Father. Vintage 21 wanted to learn how Sojourn was living out the gospel in Wabigalo, in order to transform the church in Raleigh, North Carolina.[17]

Fighting Against Fatherlessness

The majority of people who attend Sojourn Church are young men, whom Dan describes as 'Ugandan hipster kids.' Sojourn is reaching young men who wouldn't typically go to church.

To go deeper in the lives of these young men, Sojourn Church started a fight club in 2012. Dan invited a group of new believers – young men who have been saved in the previous year – to train together. The young men practiced martial arts, such as boxing. When Dan would walk around Wabigalo with boxing gloves, he found it opened up doors for conversations.

'It's not just another thing we do, it's not just exercise,' Dan explained. 'It's a gospel thing; it's about Jesus.' Dan used training as a way to teach teamwork, discipline and principles. He wanted to build community, and for the men to become like family: 'This is the church, we're called to love each other.'

Over the last two years, Dan has experimented with everything from kickboxing to soccer to music to try to reach the young men in Wabigalo: 'Our *orphan crisis* strategy is dealing with the *orphan makers.*'

Dan is passionate about calling the young men in Wabigalo to live differently in response to the gospel. He hopes to train the men to fight for the right things – to protect vulnerable women and children, to become positive role models to kids who are fatherless, and to glorify Jesus in their community.

Four or five children are abandoned every week in neighborhoods surrounding Wabigalo. Dan dreams of the day that the people of Sojourn will 'be in a position to foster those kids, to trace their families.' But little by little, the gospel is bearing fruit in Wabigalo.

While there are many orphaned and abandoned children in Wabigalo, Dan recognizes that this is a symptom of a deeper

---

17   Morris, Dan. 'Interview with Dan Morris, Pastor of Sojourn: Uganda'. Personal Interview. 24 September 2012. Updated 14 September 2014.

problem: 'People don't know, love and worship Jesus.' Dan believes that church planting and discipleship are at the heart of ending the orphan crisis. Sojourn Church is empowering men and women to be faithful, responsible parents who care for their own children and who foster or adopt orphans in their community.

The people of Sojourn Church are getting involved in mercy ministry in their community, visiting families who are desperately poor. In 2012, two young men who were leaders in the church moved in together to foster a six-year-old boy. The boy's mother was an alcoholic who would bring men home and have sex in front of the child. These young men have removed the little boy from this harmful situation. 'These guys are teaching other believers in their community,' Dan explains. 'They are disciples making disciples. They get the gospel.'

By 2014, the people of Sojourn Church were caring for a growing number of orphaned and abandoned children:

> We currently have six kids who are being cared for, loved and brought up by church members not out of compulsion or because of aid, but entirely in response to the gospel. These are families who live in the slum who are raising orphaned children.

Dan believes Ugandan Christians could be the answer to the Ugandan orphan crisis:

> If the churches responded to the Gospel to care for orphans, there would be no orphan crisis in Uganda. Until the local church in Uganda and around the world is wrecked by the gospel, there will always be an orphan crisis. We need the gospel, not aid or orphanages. It is the gospel that calls people to respond. We need Jesus.

So where do we go from here?

The time is ripe for a revolution in the Christian adoption and orphan care movement. Thousands of Christian families and churches are responding to the orphan crisis with tremendous passion, courage and love. We want these responses to be combined with an understanding that most of the world's orphans are living in vulnerable families. Caring for orphans in families should be our primary response to the orphan crisis. From the beginning to the end, the Bible calls God's people to protect and provide for orphans and widows.

Throughout this book, we've seen that good intentions are not enough. We hope this book will give you the tools to think critically about the orphan and widow crisis and how best to respond. We hope this book has helped you to understand the issues at the root of the orphan crisis and challenged you to make a lasting difference.

One thing that is clear to us at the end of this book is how little we can accomplish without Jesus and the Church – without God and His people.

Many of the discussions we have had about adoption with people all over the world come down to the same issues. Caring for children is hard. It requires sacrificial love. Caring for children who are not our own biological children can be even more difficult. Churches have a critically important role to play in supporting the families who are called to adopt children from hard places.

Making a difference in the orphan crisis requires God's people all over the world to study His Word and live out His heart. Our vision is to see a global movement of local churches restoring broken families and caring for orphans in their communities.

Are you ready to join us on this journey? We believe the Christian adoption and orphan care movement should adhere to five principles.

Empower Families
Instead of sponsoring orphans in institutions, we must empower families to stay together or to care for the orphans in their community. Likewise, we must restore broken families.

Strengthen Churches
We must stop building orphanages and start planting churches. Let's stop visiting orphans and start partnering with local believers, equipping them to care for orphans in their communities.

Encourage Adoption
We must encourage indigenous adoption and find homes for the world's waiting children. If we are called to adopt, we must adopt responsibly. We must reform adoption to end the cycle of corruption and to hold adoption agencies accountable.

Alleviate poverty
To work towards the end of the orphan crisis, we must provide vulnerable families a path out of poverty.

Fight injustice

We must fight injustice, protecting children from trafficking and protecting the rights of vulnerable families.

Change Hearts

We who believe in Jesus need to take the call to make disciples seriously. It's only through the transforming work of Jesus Christ that we will see true redemption in our homes, churches, communities, and the world.

QUESTIONS FOR DISCUSSION AND REFLECTION

1. Describe your journey as it relates to adoption and orphan care. What have you learned from your personal experience?

2. Do you agree that much of the suffering in the world is caused by men who fail to protect and provide for their families? Why or why not?

3. Describe the connection between poverty, injustice and broken families at the root of the orphan crisis.

4. What is the unique role of the Gospel in ending the orphan crisis?

5. How has this book challenged, encouraged or equipped you? What are your next steps in orphan care or adoption?

Also available from Christian Focus...

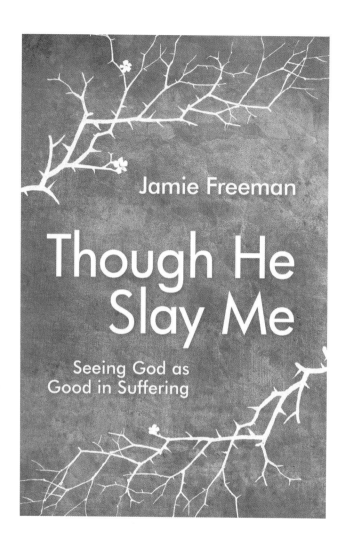

Jamie Freeman

Though He Slay Me

Seeing God as Good in Suffering

ISBN 978-1-78191-427-4

Though He Slay Me
JAMIE FREEMAN

Can you believe that the pain you feel could be the most loving way for God to show you His goodness? Jamie Freeman brings to this book a deeply personal insight into how God uses trials and adversity to promote His own goodness.

No one escapes suffering in this life. Suffering is such a difficult subject to address. It's a topic that has the potential to stir our deepest emotions and remind us of past memories we had hoped to forever forget.

To be able to say that his affliction 'was an act of the grace of God' tells you a lot about Jamie and this book. You won't agree with everything he says, but he's earned the right for you to hear him say it.

Sam Storms
Lead Pastor
Bridgeway Church, Oklahoma City, Oklahoma

...His personal story is riveting, inspiring, challenging, and completely countercultural. This message will not be welcomed in some quarters, but it's right at home with the bloody cross of Jesus.

Hershael W. York
The Southern Baptist Theological Seminary, Louisville, Kentucky

Read this book and grow in grace. Meet Jamie and see that grace embodied in his walking and talking.

Mark R. Talbot
Associate Professor of Philosophy, Wheaton College, Wheaton, Illinois

Jamie Freeman was born with cerebral palsy and not expected to walk or talk. However, God had a wonderful plan for Jamie's life and used his trials with CP to make him into a trophy of grace. Now married with three sons, Jamie is active in preaching the gospel and resides in Arkansas.

THE ENVY
of Eve

FINDING CONTENTMENT IN
A COVETOUS WORLD

MELISSA B. KRUGER

ISBN 978-1-84550-775-6

The Envy of Eve
Melissa B. Kruger

What's truly at the heart of our desires? This book guides readers to understand how desires grow into covetousness and what happens when this sin takes power in our hearts. Covetousness chokes out the fruit of the Spirit in our lives, allowing discontentment to bloom. The key to overcoming is to get to the root of our problem: unbelief – a mistrust of God's sovereignty and goodness. An ideal resource for deeper study or group discussion.

I commend this fine, new book...with a prayer that we all read and follow her Biblical counsel to fully understand the condition we are in and flee quickly to the One who truly satisfies our deepest longings and our true desires.

Michael Milton
President, D. James Kennedy Institute, Charlotte, North Carolina

In an age and culture where we all tend to have an over-developed sense of entitlement, this book makes a brilliant diagnosis that goes right to the heart of the problem.

Ann Benton
Author and family conference speaker, Guildford, England

With I've-been-there understanding and been-in-the-Word insight, Melissa helps us to look beneath the surface of our discontent, exposing our covetous hearts to the healing light of God's Word.

Nancy Guthrie
Author of *Seeing Jesus in the Old Testament* Bible Study Series

Melissa Kruger serves as Women's Ministry Coordinator at Uptown Church in Charlotte, North Carolina. Her husband, Michael J. Kruger, is the president of Reformed Theological Seminary in Charlotte, North Carolina.

Christian Focus Publications

Our mission statement –

STAYING FAITHFUL
In dependence upon God we seek to impact the world through literature faithful to His infallible Word, the Bible. Our aim is to ensure that the Lord Jesus Christ is presented as the only hope to obtain forgiveness of sin, live a useful life and look forward to heaven with Him.

Our books are published in four imprints:

CHRISTIAN FOCUS

Popular works including biographies, commentaries, basic doctrine and Christian living.

CHRISTIAN HERITAGE

Books representing some of the best material from the rich heritage of the church.

MENTOR

Books written at a level suitable for Bible College and seminary students, pastors, and other serious readers. The imprint includes commentaries, doctrinal studies, examination of current issues and church history.

CF4•K

Children's books for quality Bible teaching and for all age groups: Sunday school curriculum, puzzle and activity books; personal and family devotional titles, biographies and inspirational stories – because you are never too young to know Jesus!

Christian Focus Publications Ltd,
Geanies House, Fearn, Ross-shire,
IV20 1TW, Scotland, United Kingdom.
www.christianfocus.com